From Pe

In Our Time

Signed-

269-Vulgate
P.266 — P.271

In Our Time

Rediscovering America—1940-1990s

RICHARD C. PHALEN

Diamond Communications, Inc.
South Bend, Indiana

1993

IN OUR TIME

Manufactured in the United States of America

Diamond Communications, Inc.
Post Office Box 88
South Bend, Indiana 46624-0088
(219) 299-9278
FAX (219) 299-9296

Library of Congress Cataloging-in-Publication Data

Phalen, Richard C., 1937-
In our time : rediscovering America, 1940-1990s / Richard C. Phalen.
p. cm.
ISBN 0-912083-64-6 : $25.00
1. United States --History--1933-1945. 2. United States-
-History--1945- I. Title
E806.049 1993
973.9--dc20 93-10742

CIP
AC

CONTENTS

Introduction		ix

I. FDR and Pearl Harbor

Frank Freidel	*FDR*	3
John Toland	*Pearl Harbor*	10
Edward Hanify	*The Ordeal of Admiral Husband E. Kimmel*	16

II. The World at War

Forrest Pogue	*World War II*	27
Roger C. (Bill) Terry	*The Tuskegee Airmen*	34
Edwin Hoyt	*World War II*	42

III. Years of Turbulence and Courage

Robert Ferrell	*Harry S. Truman*	51
Carl Erskine	*Jackie Robinson Breaking theColor Barrier in Major League Baseball*	57
John Edward Wilz	*The Korean War*	64
Athan Theoharis	*Joe McCarthy*	79
Ann Sperber	*Edward R. Murrow*	86
Elmer Bernstein	*Hollywood in the '50s and the "Blacklist"*	94

IV. Unforgettable...

Dan Peterson	*The 1950s*	101
Bobby Thomson	*"The Shot Heard Round the World"*	107
Stephen Ambrose	*The Eisenhower Presidency*	112
Art Donovan	*Pro Football in the '50s and Early '60s*	118
Dick Clark	*American Bandstand and the Early Days of Rock and Roll*	122

V. "The Road Taken and The Road Not Taken Make All the Difference"

James Meredith	*Race*	127
Clarence Page	*The Civil Rights Movement*	132
Dino Brugioni	*The Cuban Missile Crisis*	138
Governor John Connolly	*November 22, 1963*	145
Michael Barone	*Lyndon Johnson*	151
George Herring	*The Vietnam War*	160
David Halberstam	*The 1960s and Vietnam*	169
Mike Royko	*The 1968 Democratic Convention*	177
George Mueller	*He Put Us on the Moon*	182

Continued on next page

Contents

continued from previous page

VI. Bent and Broken Dreams

Joan Hoff	*Richard Nixon*	191
Stanley Kutler	*Watergate*	202
Robert A. Maheu	*Howard Hughes in Nevada*	208

VII. Change

Adam Ulam	*The Fall of Communism*	213
John Blum	*The Cold War and the Break-up of Communism*	220
Joan Hoff	*The Women's Movement*	227
Dr. Mervyn Silverman	*AIDS*	238
Lou Cannon	*The Reagan Presidency*	243

VIII. Reflections

Jonathan Winters	*Television and the Times*	255
Jack Woods	*The American Dream Come True*	260
Roger Kahn	*Sportswriting*	266
Tim Pletcher	*The Persian Gulf War*	277
Robert Schmuhl	*The Changing of the Guard*	284

To Tina, the very best history of all.

ACKNOWLEDGMENTS

John Wilz went far beyond the call of duty. His interest and suggestions are deeply appreciated. Stephen Ambrose also gave important recommendations that were of great help. Betty Jones whose help, interest, and encouragement is greatly valued. To all the participants for their cooperation, knowledge, and enthusiasm. And to Alice Vazquez, who as usual, never failed me.

INTRODUCTION

This book is an oral history of America from the 1940s to the present. The intent is to present an overview and background to a very important time in our history. Some are personal accounts and reminiscences. Others are a commentary by those who have devoted years of study and research to their particular field of interest.

The last 50 years represents the most turbulent time in our history. There has been no turning back as we exited a crippling depression and segued to World War II. We fought additional wars, witnessed political assassinations, recessions, domestic unrest, and developed a deep concern about the conduct of our government.

But we survived. The economy expanded and people's lives improved. We proceeded from one problem to another, solving some, bungling others. In the process we became the richest and most powerful nation on earth.

This book will examine many of the successes, failures, and problems of this critical period. You will feel proud, distressed, happy, and sad.

Unfortunately, many of our leaders have had a poor sense of history. Not only ours, but of other nations. A better grasp of history might have prevented our involvement in Vietnam. Conversely, Harry Truman's sense of history helped guide him through the perilous period following World War II.

It is important to remember that we are a nation of strong and resourceful people. We possess an underlying character that has seen us through many storms and will see us through many more.

Keep the faith.

Of a power leading from its strength and pride,
Of young ambition eager to be tried,
Firm in our free beliefs without dismay,
In any game the nations want to play.

—Robert Frost

I

FDR and Pearl Harbor

Frank Freidel

FDR

Professor Emeritus Harvard. Author of several books on FDR and considered one of the leading experts on Roosevelt. He thinks Roosevelt was too intent on balancing the budget and therefore did not put enough money into his various New Deal programs to make them truly effective.

He feels the country was coming out of the depression when World War II began and that the war accelerated better times.

He strongly believes FDR knew nothing of Pearl Harbor in advance and that he conducted the war in great fashion.

Professor Freidel considers FDR one of our greatest presidents, whose lasting contributions to America are the United Nations and his New Deal programs that have brought some basic levels of security to the people.

I was in college during the New Deal years and naturally was intensely interested in FDR and was, to a considerable extent, influenced by the New Deal. For example, when study programs came along, first through the Civil Works Administration and later through the NYA, I got on them and helped get me through college.

Later, as a historian, I became exceedingly interested in FDR's background, particularly at the close of World War I. That grew and grew into four volumes covering Roosevelt from his birth through July of 1933. Then I decided that I was running too long and switched to writing a one-volume biography of him called *Franklin D. Roosevelt, Rendezvous With Destiny,* which came out in 1991. I've also written a number of articles and a brief book on Franklin D. Roosevelt.

How has the country benefitted from the New Deal?

The country benefitted a great deal from the New Deal because it set us off in quite a different tack. Some ultra-conservatives would like to bring us back to a world without social security and so forth. The kind of a world that existed when the New Deal came into effect. There was no social security. There were no national relief programs until a very few were forced upon Herbert Hoover. There was no general security, and these things were essential underpinnings.

Wall Street fought tooth and nail against the Securities Exchange Act to regulate the stock market, which, of course, today Wall Street looks upon as being a mainstay. We were underregulated. At times since, we've probably been overregulated, but there was very little security for the average person. Roosevelt brought a great deal of that about, enough so that various people look upon the New Deal as one of the big changing points in American history.

What were some of his mistakes?

He made a number of mistakes. Primarily, he really wanted to balance the budget. The federal debt was relatively minor at that point, so there was ample borrowing power. He didn't, as Keynesians' later felt should have been done, and as a great many other people later felt should have been done, turn to massive pump priming. It seemed somewhat massive at the time to be sure, about as much as a year's expenditure by the federal government, which is to say about $3-4 billion. That simply wasn't sufficient. I think that if he had engaged in heavier funding of his early programs, they would have worked more quickly. As it was, we were seriously pulling out of the depression before the start of war orders for World War II. We would have recovered without World War II, but we wouldn't have recovered as rapidly.

You believe that his programs were starting to bear fruit?

They were starting to bear fruit. I would make this cautionary remark: this was a time that we didn't have an extremely heavy federal debt, when pump priming was a program which would work. The WPA, for example, was never fully funded, and programs like that could have been. This does not mean that we could do the same sort of a thing in later generations and get away with it because we have a situation today with enormous federal debt.

Many have accused him of "flying by the seat of his pants." That things were not thought out.

Well, he did "fly by the seat of his pants" a considerable amount, but it was the same way with Theodore Roosevelt. He liked to think and think and think about a program, then put it into effect as if it was something that had just come to his mind. So there was rather less spontaneity and a good deal more deliberation than one would think. It served his purpose politically to be rather vague at first because he, in that way, managed to win a coalition behind him in putting into effect his programs that he simply wouldn't have had if he had detailed in advance, bit by bit, what he wanted to do with his program. Actually, when he became president, he had a pretty clear-cut program, but one that didn't include the NRA at first. When the business men wanted a program like the NRA, he was ready to accept it and make it one of the key factors in his program.

You think he definitely had the "big picture" in mind?

He had "a big picture" in mind—not completely—but he was able to pick up various parts of other people's big picture. The NRA, for example. The Tennessee Valley Authority, which was the dream of George Norris, to see federal power development as the yardstick by which to measure the cost of private power. He was certainly the leader and a very effective one.

Someone said that FDR had "a first-class personality and a second-class intellect." Do you agree with that?

That, of course, was the remark of Mr. Justice Holmes, and someone pointed out very aptly recently in writing about Holmes, that Holmes would have considered himself as having a second-class intellect. I think Roosevelt had one of the greatest political intellects that anybody has had in American history. As a theoretician, certainly he would lag rather far behind. As a politician, a man ready to rally an electoral coalition every four years behind him and to rally Congress to enact his programs. He was in front of the general public, but not miles and miles in front of them.

FDR polarized the nation like no other president. You either loved or hated him.

We were getting rather polarized on John F. Kennedy before his death. But certainly no one polarized the nation the way in which Roosevelt did.

Why?

He was a very challenging man and because he was breaking with the old order, most of his old class. Even to this day, those of them who are alive say unpleasant things about him. They felt he betrayed his class. He betrayed the values by which they lived and the kind of values which called for a very small government and for a tax structure which would benefit the rich.

Do you believe Roosevelt knew beforehand that the Japanese were going to attack Pearl Harbor? John Toland believes he knew and this was his way of getting us into World War II.

I have thought a good deal about this, and I would say absolutely, unreservedly, no. Absolutely, impossibly, no. Toland is quite wrong on that. The last thing that Roosevelt wanted to do was to see a part of his beloved Navy destroyed. He wanted to use that Navy, and he expected in the end that Navy would probably be used against Japan. But meanwhile, it was going to be used against Hitler.

He actually was trying to avoid war as long as possible with Japan. He'd reached the point where he thought Japan was going to strike, since he had considerable intelligence that the Japanese were moving to the south. He had every reason to believe that the Japanese were aiming toward the Philippines and Indonesia and, above all, toward Singapore. The great concern in his mind and those of his advisors, including his secretary of war, several days before Pearl Harbor, was what would happen if the Japanese were to bypass the Philippines and not attack the Philippines. Should the United States then declare war upon Japan? And that was not unreasonable thinking.

On top of that, all the evidence, contrary to what Toland says, is that the Japanese fleet that was moving toward Pearl Harbor did not break silence...very disciplined fleet.

How would you rank him as a wartime president?

I think he was a very great wartime president. He realized that the prime threat was from Hitler and Nazi Germany. It was a very serious threat indeed, and he managed to rally America, to become the arsenal for democracy. He gambled several ways in a quite spectacular and a dangerous fashion. He decided that Britain would be able to withstand the attacks from Hitler and was ready to ship all possible supplies and aid to Britain. Then after Russia had been attacked in June 1941, he decided that aid should be extended to Russia.

He made the personal decision to begin work on what became an atomic bomb about the time of Pearl Harbor.

He became head of the great wartime coalition. Our objectives and those of our great allies, the British and the Russians, were of course very divergent in many ways. What Roosevelt did was to manage to work with Churchill, although Churchill was primarily fighting to preserve the British Empire and Roosevelt was working primarily to try to destroy the old colonialism and to bring about self-determination for what had been previously colonial people. He and Churchill were ready to work together as much as they could to get Stalin to relate to them in a fashion which could mean a peaceable United Nations.

Should FDR have run for re-election in 1944? He was very ill at that time.

He was very ill at that time and that's perhaps the toughest question you've asked me. This is a guess. I could be wrong. I think primarily he was so determined to get a great world peace-keeping organization, the United Nations, under way that he thought back again and again to Wilson. Wilson's stroke, the way Wilson had failed to get the kind of peace that he wanted, to get the United States into a League of Nations and was afraid that if he didn't run, and the Republicans came into power, that the war would have been fought in vain. He was ready, despite his ill health, to go ahead in hopes that he would obtain a United Nations.

Was he outmaneuvered at Yalta?

I'd say, as firmly as concerning Pearl Harbor, that the stories about Roosevelt having given away great amounts of Eastern Europe aren't true. He was not outmaneuvered. He was not in good shape, but he was firmly in command at Yalta. I was able to talk to Admiral Leahy, his chief of staff, and various others who had been at Yalta with him. He was in command at Yalta. The dominant figure there, even if he wasn't in good health. He gave the Soviet Union nothing that the Soviet Union either did not have, or was in a position to get. And in return was getting what seemed to be very important still; firmer Russian assurances than he had before that Russia would come into the war against Japan.

You feel that under the prevailing circumstances, he did about as well as he could with Stalin at Yalta?

He did as well as he could because the alternatives would be to go to war against the Soviet Union. Nobody wanted to do that. He was worried how far the Russians were going to get to the West; he hoped very much that it would not be as far as Italy. He had no expectation that it would be possible to keep them out of central Europe.

It really was a fait accompli. They were there.

Fait accompli. The fact is that he obtained a promise from Stalin that there would be free, democratic elections in the liberated areas. There, of course, were not. No sooner was the Yalta Agreement agreed to and no sooner had Roosevelt returned home, than Stalin began violating, or at least interpreting it in ways totally contrary to the understanding at Yalta.

In recent years his character has been attacked. The girlfriends, pitting people against one another, a pettiness that he seemed to have.

Well, concerning the girlfriends, he had a great political relationship and was a loving man toward Eleanor Roosevelt, but he and she had long since passed the romantic stage, and she had her interests elsewhere and so did he.

His relationship with Lucy Mercer was a rather charming, victorian one. I think Jonathan Daniels, who knew Roosevelt quite well, summed it up that way long ago. At the end of his life, he was seeing something of her because it gave a great deal of comfort to him. But as to whether or not it was a physical relationship, I just don't really know. I don't think anybody really knows. He was pretty discreet on that.

Now, at pitting people against each other. That, of course, was a joyous way in which he enjoyed operating. It can be argued this was a great way to get people to work hard and to come up with new ideas, to be innovative, to achieve things. It was also a magnificent way to create chaos. On occasions it was on the plus side. Other occasions, it certainly was a negative.

What is his most enduring contribution to America?

If he were alive, I know perfectly well he would say his most enduring contribution was to bring the United States into a world security system, the United Nations. But ranking along with that, as I said at the beginning, is the fact that he modernized the United States. This government has developed in the last half century, or more, in keeping with the great changes that the New Deal brought about. They were not ones which redistributed wealth. They were not revolutionary. They were evolutionary. They brought us some basic levels of security, and no people are ready now to give that up.

What was his greatest fault?

Well, his greatest fault was that he didn't really go ahead and build as effective a security structure as he might have. In terms of the world pattern, I don't think that any longer is of any great consequence since the Soviet Union has disappeared.

As for the New Deal itself, the great problem was it didn't go far enough. It just wasn't sufficiently funded. It didn't go far enough insofar as money is concerned. Too much of it was temporary. That can be blamed on Roosevelt, but it also can be blamed upon the very effective conservative opposition against him, especially in Congress.

How would you rank him as a president?

I'd rank him as one of our greatest presidents. It's customary among historians now to rank President Lincoln first, Washington second, and Roosevelt third. I think that that is a game that is not very useful simply because these men were so different. They were presidents at such totally different eras. Certainly Roosevelt is among one of our greater presidents.

JOHN TOLAND

PEARL HARBOR

Author of Infamy —Pearl Harbor and Its Aftermath, *he spent considerable time and energy investigating the Pearl Harbor attack. This noted writer and historian believes there was a cover-up regarding Pearl Harbor which "makes Watergate look like a picnic."*

Who in our government was responsible for the surprise attack on Pearl Harbor by the Japanese?

Primarily Franklin Roosevelt and others, but I'd rather stick to him. I think a very small group was acquainted with the facts.

Who was in that group?

Well, I'm sure General Marshall (Chief of Staff General George C. Marshall).

I can't say definitely Roosevelt knew. However, I think the primary information that was coming into Naval Intelligence occurred about the 2nd of December. That is based on my interviews with Captain Ranneft, the Dutch Naval attache. He told me that he had gone to Naval Intelligence Headquarters to see Admiral Wilkinson (Chief, Intelligence Division, Office of Naval Intelligence). Wilkinson informed him that two Japanese carriers apparently seemed to have been located, and they seemed to be heading to the east. These were undoubtedly from the Kido Butai (Japanese striking force), and we had lost track of them about Thanksgiving time, when they went up north.

This was very spotty information, but it was enough to give Wilkinson the idea that this could be the Japanese carrier force. Now, I've been asked a number of times by people who don't believe this, "How come a Dutchman would be allowed into Naval Headquarters?" The answer is that, previously, Captain Ranneft had been asked by our Navy to get hold of the secret plans of the Bofors anti-aircraft gun. He had risked his reputation to get this material to the U. S. Navy and, of course, this was one of the reasons that we won at Midway and other battles. Because of this, he was persona grata. Later he was given the highest award we can give any foreigner by Admiral Nimitz. That explains why he's at Naval Intelligence Headquarters.

On December 6 he again came to Wilkinson's headquarters. He told me that he asked Wilkinson, "Where are those two wandering Japanese carriers?" Wilkinson nodded to one of his men who went up to a map and pointed some three to four hundred miles from Pearl Harbor. And this man said, "They are here, sir." Ranneft told me he was so excited, he immediately reported this to his ambassador, who was in Washington. He also told me that he had put it in his official war diary. I said I had to have facts and evidence and not just his word. He told me that much of his diary had been destroyed in a fire in Houston, but he had sent the remnants to Holland. He told me to get in contact with them. I did and a week later I got all of December 1941. The events of December 6 had been saved.

Now, a number of people said, "Well, yes, they could believe that this happened and that Wilkinson knew. However, that doesn't prove that Roosevelt knew." But this is where common sense comes in. Can you imagine that Admiral Wilkinson, who was a very rigid man, would dare not to pass on such important information to the commander in chief of the Army and Navy? We don't have any, as they say, smoking guns. But, my goodness, it is impossible for me to imagine that this information should be coming into the head of the U. S. Navy Intelligence in the presence of a number of people and not go on up to Roosevelt.

There was other information that I had indicating that others knew about the approaching Japanese carriers. On December 2, the man that I called Seaman "Z," tracked them down. It started on the 2nd. He was pretty sure their destination was Pearl Harbor. On the 3rd it was more obvious and on the 4th of December, he said he was sure they were heading for Pearl Harbor. On the 6th the Japanese were located just about where Navy Intelligence told Ranneft—some three to four hundred miles from Pearl Harbor. That night Seaman "Z" and his immediate boss and several others had a little party because they knew the next day the Americans would wipe out the Japanese force. And, of course, they were shocked the information never got through. But they were told never to pass on this information, otherwise they could be prosecuted.

I was accused of inventing Seaman "Z," but he had asked me after about a month of working with him and getting his picture that he was getting married and his wife-to-be was very nervous about this. "Do you mind not using my name?" I said, "All right, I'll call you Seaman 'Z.'"

I said, "Do you mind if I use your picture?" He said, "Absolutely not." I believe he wanted to be found. And he was several years later. His name is Robert Ogg. He lives in California.

I have all of Ogg's story on tape. Ogg is a very impetuous guy, and he made several slips of the tongue when he was later interviewed at length by a Navy official. I believe they were trying to tear him down. But there he was, and his story stands, and the people who claimed I invented him now will have to find new reasons for not believing there was a Seaman "Z."

Were Admiral Kimmel, who was commander in chief of the Pacific Fleet, and Walter Short, who was the Army commander in Hawaii, made scapegoats? Were they not given all the available intelligence?

Well, there was much intelligence they were not given. They had first been getting information from the Purple Code (Japanese Code). That was the code that went directly to capitals. This went to Washington. It was the diplomatic code. And as the year wore on, Marshall became very squeamish about secrecy leaks. So they stopped sending information about the Purple Code without telling Kimmel and Short. They didn't know, of course, when the final message was received in Washington. The main part came on the night of December 6 and the last couple of paragraphs on the morning of December 7.

But even more important was the information that Washington had been getting on the Consular Code. This was a code that did not go to Washington, instead it went to places like Honolulu. In this code, the most glaring mistake was in not passing on what is known as the "Bomb Plot" in which the sole Japanese spy, they could only afford one spy, was told to fly above Pearl Harbor pretending to be just a visitor, and he was to observe everything. Then he was to go down on the ground and find out at the mouth of Pearl Harbor the depth and so forth. He got all that information, and he sent it describing the position of all the ships. Among intelligence people it was known as the "Bomb Plot."

You see, Safford (the Navy's foremost cryptanalyst and head of OP-20-G Security Intelligence Communications) and others in Washington thought that information had been sent to Pearl Harbor. It never was. At the Navy Court of Inquiry starting in June 1944, the lawyers defending Kimmel kept insisting on bringing forth secret messages that had been withheld but were turned down. The lawyers finally made it obvious they were going to the press if this material was not admitted. So, the next morning all that information was dropped on the desk of the three admirals who were trying the case. When they saw it, they were furious. They were irate because it showed that this information would have warned Kimmel that there was going to be an attack. They were so angry that, in their final report, they put the blame for being caught short at Pearl Harbor, not on Kimmel, but on Stark (Chief of Naval Operations Admiral Harold R. "Betty" Stark) in Washington. This information was passed on to the Army inquiry going on just a few hundred yards away. They brought over Captain Safford, who presented this material. The Army report also put the blame on Marshall—not General Short. None of this information was released to the public because it was declared too sensitive. This was just before the election of Roosevelt. Only after the election was it released.

Why weren't Short and Kimmel made aware of this activity from December 1 forward? What was going on? It's inconceivable!

It's inconceivable, but I don't think it was a plot. I think Marshall was convinced that there were many leaks in intelligence, and he was trying to cover them up. He did not believe that this information need go to Hawaii. Starting December 5 and 6th, when the information came that there were two Japanese carriers wandering eastward, was when I believe Roosevelt made his big mistake. He decided to take a calculated risk and let the Japanese carriers come in, and he had been assured by Marshall that Oahu was the strongest fortress in the world. That no Japanese air or sea attacks could cause much damage. I can only assume that he did this because our intelligence from all sources indicated that Japanese capabilities were very low. Their ships were not too good. Their planes were not good, and their pilots all wore glasses, and they weren't very good. So, he must have figured he was not taking a chance.

Also, you must remember, Roosevelt was only told there were two carriers coming. However, there were *six* carriers, and, of course, they did not want to send any of this information to Pearl Harbor because, if they had told Kimmel and Short, somebody might have overheard and then the Japanese would have found out and turned back. Now, if they turned back, then Roosevelt would not have what he wished. One bomb dropped and then war. And then he could get into the war with Hitler through the back door because Hitler had refused to fight on previous things that Roosevelt had done, such as sending shiploads of armaments to both the Soviet Union and England, which was an act of war in itself. But Hitler did not want to fight the United States. Germany had lost the First World War when America joined the Allies in 1918.

Admiral Samuel Eliot Morison, author of the 15-volume History of United States Naval Operations in World War II, *said that, "one can search military history in vain for an operation more fatal to the aggressor. On a tactical level, the Pearl Harbor attack was wrongly concentrated on ships rather than port installations and oil tanks. On a strategic level, it was idiotic." What he was saying is that if they had bombed the oil depots, there's no oil, the ships can't get out. Then they could have put a cordon of submarines right outside the islands and picked off the tankers as they came in from California, and this would have been very effective, as opposed to just going after the battleships. What's your opinion?*

Well, I think there's much truth in what Morison said. Admiral Kusaka, the de facto planner of Pearl Harbor, was also the de facto commander of the operation. He told me that the greatest mistake he made was refusing to allow Genda (Commander Minoru Genda in charge of naval air operations for the Pearl Harbor attack) to go back, which would have taken out the oil tanks. Probably even more important was the fact that they should have gone back to hit the submarine pens, since subs turned out to be a great factor in American victory. So that was true, what the admiral said.

You're saying that Pearl Harbor was not a conspiracy.

Not at all, it was a goof-up. Safford was the key man, he was the top man in Navy Intelligence. At first he thought that Kimmel had screwed up. Then he discovered that Kimmel had not received the messages that he thought had been sent to Pearl Harbor. Safford was so angry he went to the civilian lawyer who was defending Kimmel and told how he had taken for granted that these messages had been sent to Kimmel. And now Kimmel was being made the goat.

When he started looking for his material, he found that most of it had been destroyed and this made him angry. What they did, they promoted him, put him in a little office, and tried to get rid of him. But being the man he was, he devised a scheme based on something that his friend, Friedman, who had broken the Purple Code, had devised to make a code very difficult to break. Safford married this system to his own findings and figured how to devise *the* unbreakable code. But when he informed his superiors of his success, he was ordered to discontinue his experiment. He was to turn in all his papers on the devise and work on another project. Instead, Safford continued his work and succeeded in finishing the code. In the next four months almost two million gross tons of U.S. shipping were sunk at the cost of only 50 U-boats. Still Safford's system was not used. Finally in 1943, when General Marshall learned that a British troop ship, containing some 1,900 Americans, was sunk because the Germans had broken the code, he became boiling mad. Safford revealed to Friedman that he had already devised the unbreakable code, and in December 1943 it was finally put into use. And the effectiveness of the German wolfpack submarines was terminated. We lost unnecessarily thousands of tons of shipping and many men, yet, I had never read anything else about this astounding incident until it was revealed to me by one of Safford's closest friends. Poor Safford was savaged during the congressional hearings on Pearl Harbor. His life was ruined. But when Eisenhower learned of Safford's accomplishment, he awarded him $100,000.

The refusal of the top Naval officers to let Safford complete his famous devise was not a plot. This was, I believe, another case of Naval bureaucracy. As one officer told me, "They just had their heads in their asses as usual."

Pearl Harbor is definitely one of the major cover-ups in American history, isn't it?

Yep. Oh, this makes Watergate look like a picnic.

EDWARD B. HANIFY

THE ORDEAL OF ADMIRAL HUSBAND E. KIMMEL

Edward Hanify was one of the lawyers who defended Admiral Kimmel at his court martial nearly 50 years ago. Kimmel was the commander in chief, United States Pacific Fleet, stationed at Pearl Harbor on December 7, 1941.

According to Hanify, the verdict of the court martial was rendered in October 1944, but not made available at that time because he believes the judgment might have resulted in Roosevelt's impeachment. Kimmel, along with General Walter C. Short, the Army commanding general, Hawaiian Department, were both exonerated.

Hanify believes the government's action to blame the surprise attack on Kimmel and Short was disgraceful.

How did you get involved in the Pearl Harbor investigation?

I was a lieutenant (jg) U.S.N.R. and was assigned by the Navy Department in March of 1944 as one of Admiral Kimmel's defense staff because it was expected that he would have the court martial, which through the years he had been very anxious to have. Kimmel had retained Charles B. Rugg of the Boston firm of Ropes, Gray, Best, Coolidge and Rugg as his civilian counsel in early 1944. Before Naval service I had been an associate assisting Rugg at Ropes, Gray. At Rugg's suggestion, Kimmel requested the Navy Department to assign me as one of his counsel. We were going to have an opportunity to face court martial charges which Kimmel hoped would be brought so that he would have a chance to state his case before the public. Kimmel had waived the two-year statute of limitations which otherwise would have barred court martial proceedings. He wanted a court martial in order to have an opportunity to refute the charges of the Roberts Commission. The Roberts Commission was appointed by President Roosevelt to investigate the Pearl Harbor disaster. It was headed by Associate Justice Roberts of the Supreme Court and the two Navy representatives,

Admiral Standley and Admiral Reeves and the Army representatives General McNarney and General McCoy.

They were hard on both Kimmel and Short. They placed the blame for Pearl Harbor on them.

Well, they were not only "hard," but they were thoroughly intellectually dishonest. They nearly succeeded in burying the truth forever. One of their members, Admiral Standley, later repudiated their report. They effectively, I think, probably prevented historians for years from getting at the root causes of Pearl Harbor.

In what respect?

They failed to take testimony under oath from the chief of staff of the Army and the chief of Naval Operations...indeed from anybody familiar with what was going on in Washington prior to the attack. And, as a consequence, by the time other investigations were commenced years later, the individuals who should have been thoroughly examined by the commission claimed loss of memory and couldn't recall what they were doing, and when they were doing it. So the Roberts Commission, in the opinion of Admiral J.O. Richardson (Kimmel's predecessor), published the most dishonest document ever printed by the United States Printing Office. And in my judgment, that is correct. It was a total "white wash" of the administration. The Navy Department and the Army asked no one but Admiral Kimmel and General Short to waive the barrier of the statute of limitations. They were anxious to have Kimmel and Short interred in history under the cloud of the Roberts Commission with the real responsibility for the disaster never having been determined. The only reason there was an investigation by the Navy was because Rugg, with Admiral Kimmel's approval, caused legislation to be introduced in May 1944. I drew the legislation in longhand under his instructions and delivered it to the chairman of the Senate Naval Affairs Committee, who gave it to Representative Dewey Short for introduction in the House and Senate. And that legislation *ordered* an investigation. Kimmel was forced, as a result of the lassitude and inertia of the Navy Department and the War Department, to take aggressive steps to cause this investigation, and, if that hadn't happened, you wouldn't have any reliable material on Pearl Harbor.

So the Navy did not want this hearing.

The Navy did not want the hearing.

And you were one of his lawyers.

Yes. Rugg was the chief attorney and he was a civilian. He carried all the burden both of the preparation for the Navy Court of Inquiry, as well as initiating as far as he could, the later Congressional Investigation of Pearl Harbor through contacts with certain members of the Congress. In addition to Rugg, there was Captain Robert A. Lavender (USN), who was a loyal friend of Kimmel's and an excellent lawyer, and we were also assisted by Admiral Harry Yarnell and his aide, Commander Chambliss. Yarnell followed the matter very carefully, but he did not take any speaking role in the proceedings. After long hearings in Washington, Lavender and I went out to Pearl Harbor by ourselves because Rugg was a civilian, and I don't believe they let civilians into the war zone at that time. The court took testimony out there. So, I actually heard the testimony of practically every significant witness. However by 1944, people like Admiral Stark, chief of Naval Operations, were able to say repetitively in answer to questions as to "Where were you Saturday night, December 6th? Where were you Sunday morning, December 7? What did you know?"; "I cannot recall. I don't remember." And Stark went so far as to forget that the president called him up the night before Pearl Harbor. He couldn't even remember that.

The Navy Court of Inquiry was the only proceeding which gave all interested parties "due process." Kimmel was permitted to participate by counsel. Admiral Stark, who was chief of Naval Operations, was also permitted to participate by counsel as well as Admiral Claude Bloch, who was commander of the 14th Naval District and the Naval Defense officer at Pearl Harbor. The court also took testimony from General Marshall. The Navy Court convened in July of '44 and filed its report in October of '44 which cleared Kimmel of any charge of dereliction of duty. The court found that his dispositions were sound and appropriate in the light of the information given, and that he had effectively collaborated with the Army's General Short to the extent that their duties coincided in preparation for the defense of Pearl Harbor and the Hawaiian area. The court also found that Kimmel had been deprived of the vital information he had a right to expect. Secretary of the Navy Forrestal suppressed the court's report.

Did they submerge that because Roosevelt was running for re-election?

Well, I assume so. I think Roosevelt was the supreme architect of the whole suppression of the real facts about Pearl Harbor.

Why?

Because Roosevelt had entangled himself by way of secret commitments at the Atlantic Conference to come to the assistance of Great Britain in the Far East, and he had told the Japanese when he came back from the Atlantic Conference, pursuant to his agreement with Mr. Churchill, that any move which they made which brought them down into the Kra Peninsula, Thailand, and threatened the British lifeline would probably involve war with the United States. He didn't say that in so many words, but it was a plain inference of what he said to the Japanese ambassador. The Japanese were thus on notice that they were making their moves in late 1941 at the peril of war with the United States. However, this commitment was unknown to the American people and was not revealed as part of the Atlantic Conference. The result was that when the Japanese started to move down from Indo-China in November and December of 1941, the president was confronted with a dilemma as to how he could extricate himself from the problem of keeping his secret commitments. The only way of extricating himself from the problem was to avoid having the United States commit the first overt act and making very sure that the Japanese committed the first overt act. The suppression of vital information from Kimmel and Short in Hawaii was due to these circumstances, in my judgment.

Frank Knox, secretary of the Navy, made a report to the president. He went out to Hawaii before the Roberts Commission to investigate the disaster and its causes. He went out there about the 15th of December 1941, and he asked all the officers in key positions in the Army and Navy, "Did you get the warning message we sent Saturday night?" And they all said they had not. Despite that, in his report to the president, he said in substance that, while the Army and Navy in Hawaii had a general war warning on the 27th of November 1941, a special war warning sent on the night of December 6 was not received. That warning doubtless would have warned of war the next day in the light of the available intercepted intelligence. This part of Secretary Knox's report to the president was suppressed and concealed, and we didn't discover his description of the "warning" until 1944. Now, had that report been published when it was submitted, Congress would have asked Secretary Knox on the witness stand doubtless in an investigation, "Why did you say that? What kind of a message did you think was sent December the 6th to warn these people? If there was such a message, what happened to it? If it was prepared, who suppressed it?" If it turned out that there was such a message composed in Washington and it was suppressed and the suppression came directly or indirectly by order of the president of the United States, you might well have had a demand for impeachment proceedings. And God knows what would have happened to the future of the war effort. So it was a very perilous situation.

Who sent the message?

It was never sent. Knox clearly believed such a message was sent by the chief of staff of the Army on December the 6th, warning Hawaii of the outbreak of war the next day.

That would be Marshall...

Yes, he was chief of staff of the Army. No one has ever found out what happened to the message Knox described. The Roberts Commission had Knox's report and never followed up on this issue. Knox had deceased when the Navy Court convened in the summer of 1944.

No one knows who supposedly sent it?

No. Nobody even knows who prepared or tried to send it. As I have said, the Roberts Commission had Knox's report. They didn't ask anybody connected with the top brass in the Navy, or the Army, what they were doing Saturday night. What kind of a message was Knox talking about? They eschewed any substantial inquiry into behavior of key officials in Washington. They just presumed that they were out there to get a basis for holding Kimmel and Short responsible and make them the scapegoats. And they did this on the basis of the totally false accusation that they did not meet and talk about their so called "war warnings," which was contrary to the evidence that they had before them, and would have been contrary to other evidence which was available if they had taken it. So, it was a "white wash" job of Washington. A piece of colossal dishonesty.

There are two types of historians who have been involved in the study of Pearl Harbor. There are the non-ideological historians trying to find facts. Then there are those who I call the "Palace Guard Historians," who start off on the basis that we had to get into the war. Reasonable people did believe that Hitler was a menace to Western civilization and had to be destroyed. Holding the thesis that it was necessary to destroy Hitler, these historians will not face any subterfuge, or any chicanery in the process by which the nation entered World

War II. They proceed with a bias which has completely obfuscated much conventional history and I think has probably made the truth about Pearl Harbor more and more difficult to come by, except for the non-ideological historian, who faces the facts, however unpleasant. John Toland is a non-ideological historian who confronted and expressed the truth to the extent it is now possible to find the facts.

You feel he's correct?

Oh, absolutely. I can claim some insight into the facts. I am one of the few living persons who heard live testimony from key witnesses. In the intervening half century in my practice in the courtroom, the evasion, the pretended amnesia of the authorities in Washington have never been equalled in my experience.

Explain the role of Captain Laurance Safford in the hearing.

Safford anticipated that he would be a key witness in a prospective court marshall against Kimmel. And inasmuch as the statute of limitations was about to expire— the two-year statute in December of '43 and Congress had renewed it for another six months—there was an expectation by Safford in early 1944 that he would soon be a key witness. Safford, of course, was a party to, and in charge of, the critical business of intercepting the Japanese diplomatic messages, as well as certain other messages prior to Pearl Harbor. He also believed that the so-called "Winds Message," which was in substance the execute of the Japanese war plan, had been received on the 4th of December. For some years after Pearl Harbor, he believed that Kimmel had been duly warned in the light of all this information. Safford, on the basis of that information, expected that war would break out on the 7th, and he expected Pearl Harbor would be a likely target. However, to his great amazement he discovered that the material which he thought Kimmel had, and the warnings which he thought had been sent out to him, had not been sent out. And so he went to see Kimmel in February of '44 and revealed to Kimmel the existence of the "Purple Intercepts" (Japanese Code), which was a highly secret matter.

As a consequence of that visit, Kimmel's counsel were privy to information which was of the most secret, highly classified character from late February of '44. We were anxious, of course, to do nothing that would expose Safford to the problems of punitive disciplinary action. However, Safford had the duty and opportunity as a witness to put that material on the record in a proceeding which Admiral Hart was then authorized to conduct for the purpose of preserving testimony. Safford did that and laid the material all out on the record before Admiral Hart. Therefore, when the Navy Court of Inquiry commenced, we were able to get access to Admiral Hart's record and find that material without prejudice to Safford's position. Thereafter, we spent at least three weeks in futile demands to get access to the intercepts so we could put them on the record of the Navy Court. We were constantly turned down by the secretary of the Navy. Finally, fearful that Kimmel might issue a public statement not revealing the intercepts but indicating that the Navy Court was being deprived of vital information, and, as a consequence of his repeated requests, the secretary of the Navy permitted Kimmel's counsel to get access to the secret files and to introduce those crucial intercepts into the record.

Meanwhile, the Army Board of Investigation has been conducting its hearings, pursuant to the same Act of Congress. That investigation was proceeding with everybody from the Army ordered by Marshall never to mention the "Magic" (Japanese decrypted messages). Finally, Kimmel and I went before the Army Board of Investigation, and Kimmel told them about the existence of the "Magic." They'd been sitting for almost eight weeks in an attempt to find out who was responsible for Pearl Harbor in enforced ignorance of the critical evidence. As a consequence of Kimmel's appearance, they had to reopen their hearings and find that Marshall himself was guilty of a failure to adequately warn General Short in Hawaii. That report was also suppressed.

Both Short and Kimmel were exonerated. But in the minds of most Americans, they were still guilty, weren't they?

Yes. That's a consequence of the Roberts Report, and the suppression of the findings of the Navy Court and the Army Board.

So it began with the Roberts Report and anything after that didn't matter because Kimmel and Short were crucified in 1941.

That is, in substance, what happened. However, I think as time has gone on, there has been increasing evidence of a general public consciousness that the Roberts Report was a sham, and there is a growing feeling that

Kimmel and Short were scapegoats. I've described it as the "anatomy of a scapegoating process." The "anatomy of a cover-up."

What did Kimmel do then?

Kimmel continued an earnest effort to see that history was accurate so far as he was concerned and that the Navy Court of Inquiry findings which cleared him were brought to the attention of the American public. Historians were permitted access to his files. Some historians have enormous confidence in their own views. Thus there is a book called *The Verdict of History*, a title which shows you how dogmatic some of these characters can be in deciding that their version of events is the "verdict of history." I could point out the grossest inaccuracies in some of these "historical books." Moreover, certain historians have a phrase they use to describe anyone who disagrees with them. He or she is a "revisionist." The inference is that the "Palace Guard" have written the verdict. It can not be "revised."

Did Roosevelt know the Japanese were coming?

Well, I think he knew that war was going to break out and that Japan was going to make an attack on the United States on December 7. Whether or not he had knowledge of the force of the actual attack on Pearl Harbor in advance or its potential for destruction is a question that is difficult to answer in the absence of critical records in the White House. William Casey, who was later head of the CIA, and in key intelligence operations in World War II, wrote a book called *The Secret War Against Hitler*. Casey there makes a very plain statement that we learned in advance from Great Britain that the Japanese were moving toward Hawaii.

The British version, in a recent book by James Rusbridger and Eric Nave, is that Churchill knew in advance that the Japanese fleet was moving toward Hawaii because of certain intercepts of their (Japanese) naval code. The British had broken the naval code. It is claimed we did not until some time later. But in any event, Rusbridger's theory is that Churchill knew of the attack on Pearl Harbor in advance and didn't tell Roosevelt. I believe Churchill's archives are still secret in England. If Churchill did not tell Roosevelt, it would have been a very cruel and indecent act of ingratitude—unless he felt Roosevelt had abundant evidence of the forthcoming attacks.

This doesn't inspire confidence in your government, does it?

No, it does not. It does not, when honorable officers of the armed forces are made "scapegoats" for the manipulation of politicians in power, and certain historians try to perpetuate the injustice.

How do you sum it up?

Well, I would sum it up by saying that the initial charges in the Roberts Commission Report that Kimmel and Short had failed to confer about their respective warnings was contrary to the evidence before the commission. The accusation also rests on a failure to appreciate the fact that they weren't "opposite numbers." Kimmel's responsibilities under war plans were entirely different from local responsibilities for defense. However, Admiral Bloch, who was the commandant of the 14th Naval District, was really the opposite number of General Short, and Kimmel kept Short advised of all the messages he had. Naturally, there were certain Navy far-reaching operations in the Pacific as to which Short had no function whatever. And making them appear to be opposite numbers, the Roberts Report confused their functions. It also distorted the real intent and meaning of the so-called warning sent to Kimmel, which did not suggest an attack on Pearl Harbor, although the intercepts made it plainly a target carefully plotted by Japan. As the Navy Court found, Kimmel and Short collaborated to the extent reasonable and feasible with respect to preparations at Pearl Harbor. Critical information necessary for their proper use of scant resources was denied them.

II

The World at War

Forrest Pogue

WORLD WAR II

A combat historian during World War II, he landed at Cherbourg on D-Day, plus two. Ike hired him to write the history of the Supreme Command. It took six years to complete The Supreme Command.

The George C. Marshall Institute authorized him to write the general's biography, which now encompasses four volumes.

He is one of America's preeminent historians.

What degree of responsibility, if any, can be attributed to the United States relative to the war with Japan and Germany? Did we provoke it in any way?

Two or three books came out about 20-25 years ago that had as their thesis that we had indeed the chief responsibility for starting the war. To protect our interest in the Far East, we had laid down the rule that we would not view with approval expansion in the Pacific that threatened the resources of the Dutch East Indies, or threatened the French in Indo-china. Anytime that you lay down that kind of statement, you're responsible for the consequences that flow from them. But the question is whether a superior power can make general suggestions about the type of world they want to live in. You have to be very careful how much you lay out as your part of the world. Laying out spheres of influence, you are in a sense bringing on problems.

Once we drew a line to protect the powers whose resources were the envy of the Japanese, and said we won't stand idly by and see you move into those areas, we advertised the fact that you're going to have to hit us first, or you're going to have to come into conflict with us. So if you say that we forced the war, that's the basis on which we have to say it.

The Japanese, from our standpoint, did not have to take over things that belonged to other powers that we said indirectly threatened us.

When did we make that statement to Japan?

This was a statement that Roosevelt, through Stimson (Henry L.

Stimson, secretary of war), issued fairly early in '41 and, as a result, we began to feel that we had better strengthen the situation in the Pacific, in the Philippines particularly. At this point Marshall and Stark began to build up the defenses in the Pacific. Some time in the fall, those two sent word to Hull (Cordell Hull, secretary of state), that they wanted us to not be involved in any kind of shooting war until at least February of '42 because it would take that long to get the Philippines and some of the islands in the Pacific in a position to defend themselves. Roosevelt was sending more and more belligerent messages to the Japanese about staying out of this point, or that point. We forced them to attack us in a sense that they felt that they had to have the resources they were closing in on in the Dutch East Indies.

They had to have these resources or they would go under in a fight with us. In one sense, we set the stage for the Japanese to attack us by setting certain conditions which they had to observe, or face the possibility that we might shoot a few shots across their bow. The result was that we said we don't want you going any further south, nor any further towards Indochina, at the peril of action on our part. They decided to take the risk knowing that it might lead to action. They decided that the way to settle that situation and be able to take over the Dutch East Indies, and to go into French Indochina, was to strike the entire fleet, because that was the only thing that prevented them from moving.

Now they knew the British had built up a tremendous force in Singapore to protect the British interests there. And that was important. You first had to take out the power of the American fleet, and the great part of that striking force had been sent to Pearl Harbor. Yamamoto had begun to prepare the Japanese fleet to make a surprise attack there. Technically, one could argue that we, by drawing the lines, had in a sense forced the Japanese to attack us. But this is a pretty incredible claim to say that if we said, "You're gonna have to stop that," and they said, "Well, we're going ahead and do it anyway," that we somehow started the war.

Do you think Roosevelt knew we were going to be attacked at Pearl Harbor?

I don't think so, but then I just don't believe all the conspiracies charged against the Borgias'. I don't believe most people are that clever, and I don't think that you can hide evidence this kind of conspiracy. They never really found convincing evidence that Roosevelt did that. I think that Roosevelt, certainly as a well-informed man with considerable intelligence sources, was aware the Japanese were into all sorts of things. But I don't believe for a moment that he knew the fleet was on its way to attack Pearl Harbor and let it happen on the theory that's the way to unite the United States. This gets farfetched.

FDR went to considerable lengths to assist England. Hitler turned the "other cheek."

He had no alternative up to a certain point. He needed time to prepare. He didn't want to bring on a general world conflict. But he was quite prepared, if allowed to grab one little power after another, until he could move up to a good size power, which was Great Britain. He was prepared to take control of a part of Latin American, part of the Caribbean. Now, I'm not a believer that had we not acted on Day One, or Day Two, or Day Three, that he could have in six months time taken over a good part of the Atlantic. I don't think the thing worked that way. I do feel that if you intended to stop him short of war, that you had at some point to say, "Now you're moving into an area which we have claimed a special right." Technically speaking, under positions which Britain itself favored, we had no control over the hemisphere. But we had set forth in the Monroe Doctrine, in John Quincy Adams' time, that we had not attempted to take over control of South America, and therefore we would not look with favor on other powers doing it.

The European powers began to argue from early days that unfortunately we had not kept the first part of that bargain. We did meddle in Mexico and the Caribbean whether we claim we didn't or not.

He was quite willing, through deals with Spain or Italy, to push their claims and make use of any special rights they gave him in their territories toward moving into greater control in the Mediterranean and through Spain into Latin areas. He was quite prepared to push that but to stay out of going to war. He would prefer not to have general war, but was quite prepared to continue that business he started with Czechoslovakia and Poland.

Hitler was surprised when Japan attacked Pearl Harbor, wasn't he?

I don't believe they told him. I think he would have argued against it because he had certain requirements in case they did get involved to come to help them. And it worked both ways. One of the arguments is that the main reason Roosevelt pushed Japan into the war was so that we'd get the war with Germany that he wanted. Now there was no question in the world that Roosevelt did want to clip Hitler's wings. He felt that Hitler was making threats to our special interests in the Caribbean and in the whole of Latin America. Some of those powers were more Fascist, more pro-Italian than pro-German. There again is a question of how far do our interests dominate the politics of Latin America.

What was the turning point in the Pacific War for the United States?

Midway certainly marked the point at which the Japanese had to stop these sudden extensions of their power by surprise and preemptive strikes. I remember this very well as a teacher in International Relations. Every week I had to put up new maps showing the Japanese taking a greater and greater area to illustrate the extreme aggression. It showed a lot of the world being gobbled up in a big way.

Now the first thing that challenged that, and really brought that expansion to a halt, was the victory at Midway. It inflicted losses on Japanese aircraft that they could ill-afford, and it revived a lot of our self-confidence.

What do you think was the turning point in the European Theater?

The survival of Stalingrad and the survival of Leningrad are reversals for the Germans. The victory at Alamein, or before that, the actual British stopping the [German] drive on Cairo. These were things that marked an end to the apparent easy conquests of the German army.

You can pick any number of things in Russia to say that, after this point, the war didn't go Hitler's way.

How do you evaluate our military leadership during the war?

Marshall, building on the experience he got in World War I, was the chief planner of the Meuse-Argonne offensive, which helped us win our part of the war and contribute to the victory in France.

Marshall built on that background and his knowledge of the Army. As the assistant commandant for instruction at the infantry school for five years, he trained 169 generals, future generals, people like Bradley and Stilwell. Marshall had influence on setting a stamp of requirements for people who would take part in the war.

Marshall was able to convince Congress that we could no longer get along with a force that had barely sufficed in the 1920s. He began fairly early in his tenure as chief of staff of the Army to ask Congress to begin to make modest increases in the Army's structure and in the buildup of the Air Force. He did not take personal responsibility for pushing the Selective Service, but he encouraged various civilian groups to do it. He gave every assistance possible to the Selective Service Act, and I think if that had not been put into effect in 1940 that we would have been in a very bad situation.

What do you think would have happened if Selective Service had not been passed?

Well, we certainly would not have had a force of any size. We would have had to attempt some kind of diplomatic arrangement, or an alliance with whatever power that we could ally with to bring some slowdown to the German and Japanese expansion. Roosevelt had already taken the lead with a buildup earlier of the Navy.

Without the manpower, obviously the war would have been prolonged.

It certainly would have been prolonged. Whether or not the Germans and the Japanese would have been able to run roughshod for a number of years, I don't know. We had no means for two or three years to say to anybody, "You stop here." The best we could do was extend credit. Britain did practically all it could do with our help of certain unneutral acts in the North Atlantic. They had a hell of a time staying in as it was.

How do you evaluate Roosevelt as a wartime president?

He had more strength there than as a peacetime president. It's hard to know if the war had stayed away from our shores whether he could have taken us out (of the depression) with the policies he was pursuing. We fairly quickly, with our military expenditures, got out of the economic doldrums. Certainly, he would not have been re-elected a third and a fourth time if it had not been for the war. It was a tremendous political thing to happen, and as popular as many of his acts were, those last two elections showed him dropping even though he was still getting extraordinary backing.

Do you think circumstances would have materially changed if Henry Wallace had stayed on as vice president in 1944?

Well, certainly if Wallace had become president at the time of

Roosevelt's death and continued the policics that he later pursued, we would have had a less active foreign policy than we did. I think that Wallace as president would have been forced by events to take some of the actions that he disapproved of under Truman.

Do you think Wallace would have agreed to dropping the atom bomb on Hiroshima and Nagasaki?

I very much doubt it. I don't mean that he was a pacifist per se, but he was not an activist in the sense of vigorous or aggressive foreign policy, which Truman more or less showed almost from the beginning. In part, I guess, because of his background as an artillery captain in the first war. This always marked his thinking— "Don't tread on me."

But I think that no matter what your principles are, if you become president of the United States, the various pressures build up, you're bound to change somewhat toward a more aggressive policy than Wallace might have been inclined to do. His hope was that by means of international cooperation you build a new type of international environment that would be much better for the world than an aggressive policy that would almost insure some sort of confrontation between us and the Soviet Union or some other budding world power.

FDR was not in favor of the bomb, nor was General Marshall. They had reservations. Truman didn't have any reservations.

Marshall and Roosevelt were not terribly happy in developing a bomb that involved a great lot of money. The thing that sold both of them was that we were in a race to beat the Germans to it. The whole driving force behind the development of the bomb in the U. S. military, and in Roosevelt's mind, was that the Germans were already bent in that direction. We're getting this background from non-Mussolini supporters in Italy. We were getting this information from people like Niels Bohr, other scientists, and other people interested in scientific development. Normally Marshall would not have pursued the notion of spending the tremendous amount of money that was involved at the expense of conventional arms. I don't think he would have pursued it, but if the enemy is using every means of destruction that he can get, Lord knows what he'll do if he has a free hand.

One reason that Marshall got in it at all was that Roosevelt decided that he had to make preparation; looked about to see which part of the military was in a position to shift present appropriations to a different field with a minimum attention of the public. Keep in mind that the Army had billions of dollars being appropriated and not absolutely specified. Then billions were specified for certain purposes; they were allowed to shift—I believe it was up to 20 percent—from item to some other item. This did not require a debate in Congress. Marshall had this power to shift.

A lot of the money was handled through the Army and a great part of the early planning was done without a thing being discussed with Congress. Fairly early on some of the leaders of Congress were made aware of it, that is, the leaders of both parties, in both houses, the Speaker of the House and, of course, the vice president. But, by and large, it was tremendous the degree to which the bulk of the political hierarchy was left in the dark about the whole thing.

Will we ever be as united as we were during World War II?

The thing that made it possible for us to work together in the war is we were scared not to. I don't think it's 'cause we loved a lot of the powers that we were allied with. Certainly we didn't love Russia. The only thing that made Churchill willing to go along with Stalin was the fact that he felt if he and Stalin both didn't put pressure at the same time on Hitler, Hitler could pick one, or the other off, as he saw fit. So, it was that joint fear that made them cooperate and the same thing applied to us.

ROGER C. (BILL) TERRY

THE TUSKEGEE AIRMEN

The Army Air Corps initiated an all black pilots unit during World War II. The first class of pilots graduated in March 1942.

They trained at the Tuskegee Army Air Corps Flying School in Tuskegee, Alabama. By the end of the war, nearly 1,000 had graduated and approximately 450 fighter pilots saw action in Europe and North Africa. The bomber pilots were not sent overseas.

Roger C. (Bill) Terry was trained as a bomber pilot. He was also one of the "Freeman Field Three," court martialed in 1945 for entering a "Whites Only" Officers' Club.

Terry is now president of the Los Angeles Chapter of the Tuskegee Airmen. They speak at schools and to civic groups and encourage young people to stay in school and better themselves. They also fund educational programs and award scholarships for the underprivileged.

You enlisted in the Army Air Corps in February '42. Where did they send you?

They swore us in and three days later called and asked why didn't I tell them I was colored. They didn't ask me. There was no place for race on the form. So they told me to go home and wait. I waited around until I got a letter saying I was too big to be a fighter pilot—I was 6'2½" and 175 lbs. They had a limit of 5'9" and 160 lbs. or something. I sat around for two or three months, and then I got a call from Civilian Pilot Training stating if I would come to Tuskegee they would train me to be an instructor.

I went down to Tuskegee in the middle of 1942 and entered Civilian Pilot Training to become an instructor. Incidentally, that's where I met Chappy James (later an Air Force general). He was also in that program because he was a big guy, too.

About a year later, they decided in their wisdom to have a medium bombardment group. It would be eligible for larger fellows, and we were taken into the Army. They were going to send us overseas as enlisted men, and we got in touch with somebody in Washington, D.C. After a month or so of wrangling, we were sent into the program. A year later I graduated as a second lieutenant.

Whose idea was it to have an all black squadron?

The Army. The Army in 1925 or '26 had a study and came to the conclusion that Negroes were not capable mentally, physically to be combat pilots. That was the official stand that the government and the Army had until about 1940-41. But pressure from the newspapers, black newspapers and from other representatives that we had contact with in Congress, pressure was brought to enlist the talents of Negro Americans and to teach them to fly.

We had a special relationship with Mrs. Roosevelt. She went down to Tuskegee for a visit, and while she was there she heard that there were Negroes flying, and she went out to Moton Field where the primary flyers were taught. She went for a ride and said, "Well, they seem like they can fly all right to me." Two or three weeks later the program was set up—separate but equal.

It is our feeling that they set it up, separate but equal, down in Alabama number one, because they had a CPT program there. A CAA program. But secondarily, it was out of the way, and they felt it was doomed to failure. So if it failed, nobody would know and if it succeeded, nobody would know. They built an airfield. They engaged a firm of builders and architects to build the field. They hacked out an area in the piney woods and built a field. The head architect on that was a black guy, which was unprecedented. But they built a nice training field. The primary and the post-flight activities would go on at Tuskegee Institute. They set aside Sage Hall for the cadets. And flying would be at Moton Field, and it was taught there by Negro instructors. That was your primary training. They were civilians.

We had very good instructors. We became pilots and we were well trained, and these pilots were dedicated to the proposition that they would turn out the best product that they could. And they were interested in the outcome of it. They weren't just there doing a job. They were black, but they had a white command. It was a civilian operation with the military over it.

You graduated as a bomber pilot.

That's correct. All of those military instructors were white. We had some very good instructors. Some of them were not. Some of them thought that we weren't qualified to fly.

The black instructors were just for...

Primary...

The white instructors were for what?

They were for basic and advanced. For transition. They were military.

Were you treated fairly by the white military?

Hell, we didn't have anything to do with them. They directed you. Your instructor was white. You never socialized with them. You didn't have anything to say with them outside of whatever was done militarily. They didn't associate with you and you didn't associate with them. You saw them on the field and that was your contact. When they went to town, I guess they went to their part of town. I was not accustomed to that having been born and raised in California.

Explain the problem you had at Seymour, Indiana.

We were preparing for overseas. They were moving us to Seymour, Indiana, to Freeman Field, because it was a bigger installation. Before we went they sent a cadre up there. This cadre noticed how they were laying things out. It looked like they were segregating. There was an executive order that there would be no segregation on any military installation. We got up there and found that certain places were off limits to Negro personnel. They had it in their minds that all people who were not white were trainees. All whites that got there the day before were supervisory personnel. And you've got doctors, lawyers, returned veterans from the fighting over in Italy...they were all trainees. In other words, a way of discriminating. And they had taken the enlisted men's club away from the enlisted men and put a sign on it, "Officers' Club No. 2."

Everybody that was black was a trainee. We were sick and tired of the official way of staffing. They would staff the different squadrons, and they would have a white fellow in charge. And they would come in and get a promotion, and they would move on, and then another white fellow would come in as first lieutenant, and he would get a captaincy. And our people just stood in rank. Chappy James was a first lieutenant eight or nine years. He didn't get to be a captain until they integrated.

And he eventually became a...

...four-star general. While we were flying together, he was a first lieutenant. So we determined that we would test this particular thing because if we're going overseas— it was before the surrender of Japan —we're going to be called on to do whatever was necessary. Some of the guys were coming back from overseas and meeting this same damn thing that they'd left.

We decided to test it by sending officers down there three at a time to seek admission into the club and see what they would do. That was Officers' Club No. 1. They were told they were under arrest, and they would return to their quarters. We went three by three, three by three...they arrested them. But when they saw that they were going to keep coming, they closed down the officers' clubs.

Now, when I went in there, this guy tells me, "Get the hell out of the way. You're not coming in here. We just don't let your kind in." So I brushed on by him and, of course, I was placed under arrest, too. They closed down the clubs, and we still had a pool of guys who were going to go down there. When they opened it up the next day, we were sending guys down there—when I say "we" I mean the conjunctive "we." They closed the club again and decided they would give this order. This order was written out...that I read and I understand that I'm to use only this, that, and the other. They were given a direct order to sign this order, which they refused to do. And when they refused to do that, 101 officers were placed under arrest. We had told the enlisted men not to get involved in this because they could do anything they wanted with enlisted men. They had to court martial and use the proper procedures in dealing with officers.

So, by their policy, they did something that the Japanese and the Germans couldn't do. They put a whole squadron, a whole group, of airplanes out of commission. And these were ready for overseas. The Japanese hadn't surrendered as yet.

When we first went into Freeman Field, Roosevelt was still alive. We went in there on April the 5th. We had a secret weapon. One of our officers, his mother was the chief housekeeper at the White House, and she was on familiar terms with Mrs. Roosevelt, whom we counted as a friend. He went to the White House to talk to his mother, to have his mother talk to Mrs. Roosevelt. Mrs.Roosevelt would talk to her husband, and then we would get out of it. That was the thinking. But Mrs. Roosevelt wasn't there. She was at Hyde Park, and so Forbes' mother went up to Hyde Park and told her. But in the meantime, Franklin had gone down to Warm Springs. And before we could get to Mrs. Roosevelt, to talk to Mr. Roosevelt, he died. Then we were in a vacuum. Harry Truman was an unknown quantity at that time. We didn't know what he was going to do. He was a southerner as far as I was concerned. But he turned out to be one of the better presidents.

We're fighting to free people throughout the world. We're fighting against segregation and discrimination. We're fighting against the Aryan hordes who see the Aryans as the dominant race and other people to be put away like the Jews, etc. To be put away and shunted aside. Fighting against the Japanese. They shunned all these people. And we're fighting against this tyranny, this type of separateness, and yet here we are in this country and we're segregated. Nobody else is segregated, except one battalion of Japanese, which I think was terrible, too.

So, in that context, we decided this was a good time to see what kind of life there would be after this war and during the war. What kind of life you would come back to, if you came back. Was it going to be free? Was it going to be the same thing—separate but equal, but separate never meant equal. That's why we all stuck together, and they court martialed —what they call a summary court martial— these 101 guys who would not sign this order. And we had some very good guys who have reached some prominence in their lives. Like Coleman Young was the mayor of Detroit—he was a second lieutenant. He was one of the recipients of one of those 101 letters. We had a lot of guys—Bill Coleman, who was the secretary of transportation. We had a lot of guys—guys that are doctors, lawyers, Indian chiefs, in their life since then, who were essentially fighting just for the American way of life. We felt that the battle line was here as well as overseas.

What finally happened?

Finally, they tried three of us. The first two were acquitted. Then they tried me. I, of course, called my parents and told them. My mother said she was not going to wait until they convicted me, or shot me, or something like that, and then try to see what they could do. So she got in touch with friends that we had like A. Philip Randolph—the most powerful black, who was a childhood friend of my mother's. She got in touch with Vito Mark Antonio. Then another brother that was in the Merchant Marine. We got in touch with Harry Bridges. We got in touch with the NAACP. She hired lawyers. And for just a middle class family, that cost $14,000-15,000. That was a hell of a lot of money in the '40s, to assure that I got a fair trial.

Did you?

If there was such a thing as a fair trial, we wouldn't have had a trial because the order not to enter was illegal. And that was our defense. They convicted me of jostling them. Jostling—without touching. It's one shade this side of assault. In his official capacity he could tell me to stay the hell out. But I was 22 or 23 at the time and another guy telling me you can't go in someplace when you believe you have the right because you are a lieutenant, too. And you are a flyer. And if they tell you that you can't do this in your own country, what the hell are they going to tell you when you get someplace else?

What happened?

Well, I stayed in arrestive quarters for 94 days. And then I was tried and they convicted me of "jostling." Now I'm black and I'm a "Jonah." You know, a pariah. What the hell. The white folks are mad. They're mad because number one, one of their own is taken out of command—Colonel Selway was in command of it. He was taken out of his command, and the white command was shipped away, and they brought Ben Davis back from overseas. He got his first command where a Negro had command of any installation in the United States or any other place.

To show you how ingrained the segregation and discrimination was, when they brought him back into Godman Field, Kentucky, Air Corps supply was staffed by civilians. And these civilians—most of them were white—they refused to work for him. They said they wouldn't work for a nigger. So, Ben Davis, having guts and having training—he didn't evade the issue. He got a couple of companies of WACS. Black WACS from Des Moines and brought them in. Brought them in and staffed Air Corps supply. Then the civilians, knowing that their jobs are gone, now they want their jobs. But it's too damn late now.

You were fined $150?

$150. But see that wasn't it. That put an end to any career I might have wanted with the Air Force.

It ended your career?

Yeah. I couldn't get a ride. You know, I couldn't get on a crew. Then a very good friend of mine, he took me in. He gave me a ride. In one word, they didn't know where to ship me. They were going to ship me back to Tuskegee. There were only a few places that you could ship a black flyer. And nobody, you know, all these other guys—these captains, were head of these other squadrons, black captains— they didn't want a pariah in their unit, because they thought maybe the "Great White Father" would be mad at them. They didn't want the onus of saying, "What you did is all right with us."

Where did you finish your service?

Well, I went back to Godman Field, and I finally got a ride as a co-pilot. The pilot on that ship was a friend of mine. He was from Los Angeles—George Matthews. George and I had known each other for years, and he said he would take me on as a co-pilot if CI would take me in the squadron. CI took me into the squadron. Then the war ended. The war with Japan ended August the 14th. We were preparing to go overseas at that time. We were combat ready. We were going to go over to the Far East. And I think it was General Kenney over there, he didn't want us. MacArthur said, "We'll take anybody we can. We need 'em." But this guy in the Air Force, he didn't want us. And, of course, Hap Arnold was anti-Negro. He didn't want us. But we were going to go and then they dropped the atom bomb about the 5th of August and I think they capitulated on the 14th. After that, it was just a question if you had enough points, you could go home. Well, I didn't have enough points, but had made enough minus points with the administration that they allowed me to leave in October.

So they wanted you out.

And I got out. I got out and went to law school.

What are you doing now?

I'm retired.

You are the president of the Los Angeles Chapter of the Tuskegee Airmen.

This is a non-profit corporation of veterans of the Tuskegee experience, and we have 38 chapters throughout the United States. We saw over a period of 30 years that nobody had put into the history books the fact that we were there and that we had a part in that. A lot of people didn't know, a lot of black people didn't know, that there were black flyers. So we decided that we should pass this information on to our children and our children's children to let them know that you could do these things.

So we formed the Tuskegee Airmen. We get together once a year, and we started a scholarship fund. Our friend, Chappy James—Chappy was a personal friend of a lot of us here in Los Angeles—and he was going to come to the convention we had here in '74. A week before he had a heart attack and died. So, a bunch of us thought we should do something in his honor. We decided we would have a small scholarship, and we were going to call it "The Chappy James Scholarship." But his family thought that they should run it. It was just a small thing, so we named it "The Tuskegee Airmen's Scholarship." We give 30 scholarships a year for $1,500 a piece. It's $45,000. We're going to expand to give more. We go around to high schools, grammar schools, and colleges and give talks. Motivational talks. We are engaged in a tutorial program when we are welcomed by the school authorities, in tutoring students in the inner cities, regardless of race, creed or gender. We tutor them for the SAT courses. It appears to us a lot of these educational authorities really don't give a damn about what happens to these kids in the inner city. They've written them off. So we tutor them in math. We have a lot of people who have—since they've left the Air Force—become aeronautical engineers. They have become teachers, etc. And we can use that expertise in helping them get over the hump to take the SAT course.

We try to guide them into places where there are available scholarships like the Air Force ROTC. They have scholarships for $16,000, $22,000 a year. A lot of these kids don't know about it. They don't know about the Air Force Academy, that they have a prep school before the Air Force Academy. We bring that message to them. We're just not big enough to try to save a whole damn generation of inner city kids—black, white, green, blue, brown—that are suffering from the moral decline of the leadership that feels that these kids are expendable.

Edwin Hoyt

WORLD WAR II

Military historian who has written many books on World War II. He feels MacArthur could be small and spiteful as well as brilliant; some Italians were better soldiers than given credit; the GI was a quick learner and a very good soldier and America would produce as fine a fighting man today, as back then.

He discusses our pre-war Army, Patton, Montgomery, using the Atom Bomb on Japan, and much more.

What was the regular Army like before World War II? You read From Here To Eternity *and it was pretty brutal.*

Well, it was a composite. First, you had the professional soldiers; the professional, trained soldiers from West Point, the military academy graduates. They were well educated, or let's say trained, in their profession, and they were officers and gentlemen. Then you had the rank and file enlisted men, who ranged from people who might well have been in jail if they hadn't been in the Army, to the noncommissioned officers, who had the same kind of professional attitude toward the service that the officers did.

I think that *From Here to Eternity* gives a pretty good view of the brutality and cruelty that existed in the services. The Army was very harsh, and men were paid very little money, and it was a place for people that didn't have much else to do.

From 1918 to the start of World War II, we were able to keep people like Eisenhower, Marshall, MacArthur, Bradley, Patton, and Arnold in the service. It's incredible.

They were dedicated people and many of them came from military families. They were used to this kind of deprivation. Not all did. For example, Jimmy Doolittle was a flyer in World War I. He got out of the service at the end of the war and went into stunt flying and into commercial aviation. He came back into the service again about 1940.

What was the condition of our armed services at the start of the war?

I don't think it was very well trained. I can remember as a boy I went from time to time, my father was a newspaper man, with him to maneuvers at Fort Vancouver, which is not far from Portland, Oregon, where I grew up. I remember seeing soldiers in the field and airplanes coming and dropping sandbags on them. The problem was they didn't have any money, so they couldn't fire very much artillery. Just like the Navy. They didn't have any money, so they couldn't fire warheads, except dummy warheads with their torpedoes in the submarines. They had a limited amount of money to spend for firing practice. So, consequently, our peacetime Army was not very well trained. It was pretty much of a ragtag, bobtail operation.

Did this encourage the Germans and Japanese in thinking they could defeat us?

I don't think that's quite true because nobody was more surprised than the Japanese when, after Pearl Harbor, they opened up their campaign and what ease they won against the white man.

Midway was the turning point of the war in the Pacific.

I think Midway was the turning point in the sea war in the Pacific. Of course, there were two different wars. There are other turning points, too, for example; Stalingrad was the turning point of the war in Russia, and the first battle of El Alamein was the turning point of the war in Africa.

We were embarrassed at the Kasserine Pass, Tunisia, when we landed in Africa.

The Battle of Kasserine Pass is very important. The 1st Division—Infantry Division—was as highly trained as we had, but actually, in maneuvers in North Carolina, two years to a year and a half before, they had not had the material to work with. For example, they had sticks that they used as machine guns, and they had socks full of dirt that they threw at tanks, and when they hit a tank, they said, "You're dead."

When they got up against the Germans, they came up against the Afrika Korps at Kasserine Pass. The Afrika Korps had better equipment, and they had the support of the Luftwaffe.

At Kasserine Pass the Americans broke and ran, and the only thing that stopped the Germans was the American artillery. The artillery was the best trained part of the American Army at that point and the toughest part of the American Army. And so proved to be all the way through. The Japanese, too, said the same thing about Marine artillery in the Pacific. They had the greatest respect for the American artillery.

Was the GI a good soldier? Was he a quick learner?

They were very good learners and they were very good soldiers. The divisions in North Africa—among them were the 1st and the 9th Infantry—this was their first battle. They were green and they broke and ran in the beginning, but by the end of the Tunisian Campaign, they were tough, trained soldiers, and after that they were extremely effective in Sicily, and they were extremely effective in the invasion of Europe. They learned very quickly. The Germans were quite surprised how fast they learned. So were the British.

When we went into North Africa, the British used to call the Americans "Our Italians." Meaning that they were unskilled and unable to fight. That lasted just about 30 days, and after the Battle of Kasserine Pass, the Americans knuckled down and began to fight very hard.

How much friction did we have with the British through the war? It was considerable at the beginning. Did that subside as we proved ourselves?

Not too much. Patton, for example, used to say when he was waiting in England for the invasion, "There's nothing will keep us from winning the war, if we could only drive the British into the sea." So, the feeling about Americans and Britains persisted and still persists a great deal. The British took the position that the Americans were not good fighters and didn't know anything about it, and they'd been in the war since 1939. They said to the Americans, "You become our arsenal. Give us everything to fight with and we'll win the battles for you." It was a little cocky of them.

Who was our best field commander in Europe?

I think Bradley, by far.

Who was our worst?

I'd say Fredendall (in charge at Kasserine). But he didn't last very long. The bad ones didn't last very long, you know. They had one battle, and, if they lost that, they were shipped out real quick.

One of the American complaints was that the British would not attack unless they had numerical superiority.

That was Montgomery primarily. There were other British commanders who were not like that. Auchinleck was not like that. He was the man who won the first Battle of El Alamein and set up the Battle of Alam El Halfa, which was fought by Montgomery, but to Auchinleck's specifications and was won. He reorganized the British armor.

The British went into World War II very badly trained. They had a very bad army. They had no experience and almost all of the strength of their army was from people who had been in the Indian army, where they did a lot of fighting in that part of the world. But there were British commanders in North Africa, and elsewhere, who were eager to move. Montgomery is the one who gave the British the reputation of only moving when you had absolute superiority—3 to 1 or something.

Was the German soldier as good as portrayed and the Italian soldier as bad as portrayed?

The German soldier was every good as portrayed. They were highly trained. The German military machine was a strong military machine in World War I and the officer corps continued. The German soldier was probably the best trained, and the best disciplined soldier in Europe.

As far as the Italians are concerned, they were good and they were bad. Some of the Italian units that fought under Rommel were extremely good, and he gave them great praise. But some of the Italian units were badly trained, and the badly trained soldier is one who's going to break and run because he doesn't know what to do. That's what happened to the Italians. Their equipment was terrible. Mussolini did not spend enough time and money on his arsenal, and they didn't spend enough time and money in the training of their men.

The Italians were always four or five years behind in the modernization of their equipment.

Yes, they were. I don't think it's because the Italian soldier is innately any worse than the Greek soldier or the Romanian soldier or whatever. I think it's a question of training and experience.

Was the GI who fought in the Pacific any different than the GI who fought in Europe?

I don't think so. I think the American GI's were effective to the same degree. They had to have the training. The first American soldiers in battle were in New Guinea. The 32nd Infantry Division, which was a National Guard division; they did not perform very well. General Harding, their commander, was relieved by MacArthur, improperly so, I think. MacArthur was very adamant that these people had disgraced "him," and he badmouthed the division, and he badmouthed his own soldiers. What was wrong with them was that they weren't trained. The Australians helped them and taught them a lot of things about fighting in the jungle.

What about MacArthur? How would you sum him up?

Well, I'm very ambivalent about MacArthur. I think he did a very bad job in the New Guinea campaign. I think he was very mean and unkind to his own people. He was a great egotist, but I think that he also had great moments of brilliance.

In the Korea War, his Inchon landing was an absolutely brilliant strategy. But then, MacArthur never knew when to stop. He had many strong views, and he wanted to go on and fight the Communists to the end and destroy the North Korean government and maybe take on the Chinese Communists and possibly the Russians as well.

In the Pacific, his strategy of island hopping was very successful.

Island hopping—you mean bypassing certain islands. MacArthur has taken credit for it and other people have too. You'll find in the history of the Joint Chiefs of Staff that that strategy was evolved in the meetings of the Joint Chiefs of Staff. It did save lives, and it put a lot of Japanese into the gardening business.

Should we have dropped the atom bomb on Hiroshima and Nagasaki?

Well, you can justify it from the standpoint of saving lives. I would like to have seen Truman make an offer to demonstrate the atomic bomb to some Japanese high officials before they dropped [it]. They could have dropped one to show them what would happen. I don't think it would have made much difference because the Japanese generals after the first bomb, and even after the second one said, "We can live with the bomb." It was the emperor who finally forced them to surrender.

We had some tough people, particularly those pilots who flew those "Buffalos" at the Battle of Midway, knowing they weren't going to come back. Do you think we have that type of person in the United States today?

Oh, I think the Air Force and Naval pilots and people like that are extremely dedicated and extremely skillful. Americans have one great characteristic. They rise to the occasion. I think adversity always brings out the best in Americans.

III

Years of Turbulence and Courage

ROBERT FERRELL

HARRY S. TRUMAN

Robert Ferrell has written seven books on Harry S. Truman. He believes we might have had a different world if F.D.R. had kept Henry Wallace as vice president in 1944. Instead, Roosevelt decided to go with Truman.

When Truman left office in 1953, he had a very low approval rating. In a relatively short period, historians and the general public have revised their opinion of him—upward.

Well, I met the man in 1957. I liked him but had no idea that I would be spending so much time with him. I've now done seven books on him.

Started out with a piece of good luck back in 1978. I went to a library in December of '78 and suddenly stumbled on his private papers. I didn't realize they were as good as they were. The result was the book that Harper published called, *Off The Record.* They sold 100,000 copies. So I liked that.

FDR thought of himself and the presidency as one. Truman thought he was a temporary visitor.

Yes, that's true. In that respect, you can compare Truman with Calvin Coolidge, who had exactly the same view of the presidency. The presidency was an office he happened to fill, he was the president only in name, there was somebody else named Calvin Coolidge, and the two things were not the same. Truman looked at it that way—very much that way.

Would you say that Truman was president under the most trying circumstances in the 20th century?

Oh, sure. I think there's no question about that. There were other trying circumstances. World War I was a very sudden occasion, and it lasted only a year and a half. The possible disruptions that could come out of World War II were much, much larger than in 1918-20. Truman, by and large, handled those things very well.

The one big surprise, of course, was the Korean War. In some respects I don't blame Truman for it, one can blame the military. It was something that they didn't plan. They wanted out of there, and at the same time they wanted in there, and you couldn't be two ways.

What do you think was the most important decision he made? And what he handled the best?

I suppose it was the problem toward Europe. That's 1947-49, beginning of the Marshall Plan, the Berlin Airlift, then ending with NATO. This involved turning American foreign policy from where it had been really since 1775 or '76. It had always been a policy of the new world, and the old world, and the two didn't join. This suddenly became different.

Truman could be very partisan. The politician from Kansas City would come out at inappropriate times. Did this hurt him?

Sure. But there you can compare him with Roosevelt. Roosevelt had the aura of Harvard. If Truman's father had not lost practically all of the family money, this was in the speculation of 1900-01, Truman could have gone to college. It would have put a sheen on him, and he would have been more presentable. There were times when he was gauche.

Roosevelt had all sorts of finesse. Roosevelt could make a quip. He knew how to make a speech. But behind all of that is the need for the proper policy. Roosevelt was not always correct in that regard. In fact, Roosevelt sometimes just held back on decisions. I'm not sure where leadership was. There was never any question about that with Truman.

Truman was quite a different man. What he needed was perhaps...I say this advisably because college educations don't always provide this result...but he needed a little more shine on his speeches, his private remarks sometimes. There was a fair amount of profanity in private. Although Roosevelt was capable of that too.

What was his biggest mistake?

I think it was the Korean War. If they'd kept a battalion up there, just one, that might have been enough to prevent trouble. MacArthur, then Acheson, [said] that we would not defend Korea. This was read, I'm certain. Furthermore, of course, we had some nuclear problems at that time which were also read. There was a great deal of spying. Some of it awfully good on the part of the Soviets. The British spy Maclean is the big problem here. The Soviets knew a great deal about our nuclear situation, and we opened ourselves to trouble there.

That was Acheson's speech you refer to...not defending Korea.

Yes, the January 1950 speech. But MacArthur had said the same thing a year before. It was on the record to a British reporter. So, the Chinese, the North Koreans, the Russians knew about this.

What should he have done?

Dean Rusk said this, it's not original with me. But if there had been just a battalion of American troops up at the 38th parallel, just a trip wire. Some evidence that we were not going to leave. Instead, there was all the evidence the opponents seemed to need that we were going to leave.

We had very few troops in Korea at that time...

We had none. We had a 500-man, so-called "use-mug" force—U. S. Military Systems Group. But these were not fighting troops.

After he fired MacArthur in April '51, Truman's approval rating fell to 23 percent. Was that the lowest it ever went?

That's the lowest it went. Nixon's, on the eve of his resignation was 24 percent. Whatever those approval ratings mean.

I was an adult at that time, and I highly approved of getting rid of MacArthur. I remember that occasion very well indeed. I was a graduate student at that time; none of my friends favored MacArthur. But there was much unwitting public sentiment.

Of course, this was a sign of the man's steel. He just wasn't going to have this.

Of whom did he have the greatest respect?

He thought the sun rose and set on Marshall.

Dean Acheson was his secretary of state. Comparing them, they were poles apart. Acheson—urbane, eastern establishment. Truman—down-to-earth, midwestern. What was their relationship like?

It was a very easy one. It was the same relationship he had with Marshall. Marshall, incidentally, breathed a sigh of relief when Roosevelt passed from the scene because he could deal with Truman. He could deal only with difficulty with Roosevelt.

Why is that? Roosevelt would play games?

Oh, yeah. Sure. Roosevelt was inviting Marshall up to Hyde Park, and Marshall never went up until it was safe, which was April 14, 1945.

Acheson...there was a directness about him which some people translated to arrogance. I suppose it was some arrogance. What he was able to do was go from A to B, and that's a strange and uneasy route for most people. Truman could do that, too. In fact, Truman had trained himself from his first public office back in the '20s to do that, and they just delighted in each other that way.

The perception of Truman during that time was that he was not very bright.

Oh, sure. He had this public reputation which came out of some of those almost outrageous speeches. Yet, the man was extremely bright. That's evident in his letters and in these little essays that he frequently wrote; his diary entries which sometimes are written with a little too much verve. Nonetheless, the clarity is there.

Truman after his presidency went from "goat" to "hero" in a relatively short period of time.

Well, that I think has a fairly clear explanation. It's the people who succeeded him. Eisenhower was, of course, much better than most of us realized at the time. I've got an Eisenhower book coming out shortly, it's on presidential health. I claim there were seven cover-ups, beginning in 1893 with Grover Cleveland. They covered-up Ike's health, too.

Eisenhower was really pretty good. His basic problem was that physically, he was not in good shape. He lived out his second term by the grace of God. But following him, of course, you had Kennedy. The public realized that Johnson was a bit of a maneuverer. I don't think Johnson was as bad as people thought. I actually think he was better than Kennedy. But then you had Nixon and that's when Truman's reputation began to rise. Nixon was just impossible. This was called by, I think, *TIME* or *LIFE* "Trumania." It was in 1969-70-71.

Actually, though, Truman lived until December 26, 1972. By that time he was out of it. He had an accident in his house in 1965. He stumbled when he was walking into a bathroom and hit his head on a sink and was knocked unconscious. Had to go to the hospital. I won't say he didn't recover, but after that there was just a whole series of physical problems.

He wrote very few letters. The signatures we see in the late '60s are probably not his. But, even though he was not making very many public statements, and those were dubious, his reputation suddenly went through the stratosphere.

How would Truman fare if he ran for office today? Television plays such a big part.

Well, it's a different time, of course. One can speculate on television. I think you could argue it's had a good deal to do with the recent Soviet revolution. But that's something else.

He might not look too good on TV. I'm not sure. The television of his time was very primitive. But you know the phrase about "what you saw is what you got." That was the case with Truman. People came to see that. It's not Bill Clinton. That is something people want very much.

His daughter writes in one of her books, and I think it's true, he began to get tired. And that's a danger in the presidency. Of course, that's taken some of the presidents. Roosevelt being a case. I think he got tired, and that combined with Korea, hurt him.

Walter Cronkite thinks...I don't talk to these people very often but I did talk to him once, and he was pushing me on this point, and I refused to go with it. Cronkite thinks that he took on a big head. At one point Cronkite had a television program, showed the refurbished White House. This was in 1952. Truman, with his somewhat characteristic lack of flair, would point out rooms—he'd say, "Now, that's my study." Cronkite told me this. Then he'd say, "That's my bedroom." This got to Cronkite, who I think fundamentally didn't like him.

I don't think that was true, though. Truman was a humble fellow.

How would you rate him as a president?

Well, Steve Neil, then of the *Chicago Trib*, had a rating, it was I think 1983, and Steve's result was about No. 8. I would put him a little higher.

Would you say that Truman was the man we needed at that time? That if we had gone with Dewey, we'd have a different world today?

I'm not sure about Dewey. The great confusion might have been in 1944-45, if Henry Wallace had received a second term as vice president. Wallace was not a secure man. He was a rather admirable, nice fellow, but shy, not a good mixer, and a terrible politician.

Wallace was considered fairly radical—close to being a socialist.

Well, I'm not sure I would say that. He certainly was willing to be patient with the Soviets longer than Truman would have and that might have been a danger.

So you think the problem was not so much with Dewey being elected...

...but that Wallace might have continued...

...as vice president. He would have taken over when Roosevelt died.

Yeah. In this book that I have, one of my points at looking at presidential illnesses is who succeeds. This was a very real problem in 1944. Wallace wanted the vice presidential nomination, his second one. He wanted it so badly he could taste it and the reason was obvious. He knew Roosevelt wasn't going to make it. In fact, all the leaders of the Democratic Party knew that. That's why they put Truman in. That I think was a danger that given Roosevelt's insouciance and his feeling that he was going to live forever, he might not have cared if Wallace had pushed just a little bit harder. Wallace pushed very hard. They went to the length of counterfeiting tickets on the floor, and they packed the galleries—the Wallace supporters. I think Henry must have known about this. He was not quite as virtuous or simpleminded as sometimes people drew him. But it didn't work.

One of the Chicago people, I think the mayor of Chicago, looked this mob over. He knew they were all for Wallace, and he pronounced the hall overcrowded. He said it was a fire hazard and he adjourned the meeting.

Carl Erskine

JACKIE ROBINSON BREAKING THE COLOR BARRIER IN MAJOR LEAGUE BASEBALL

On April 15, 1947, Jackie Robinson became the first black to play in the major leagues. Many times being first makes things easier—this was not one of those times.

Carl Erskine came up to the Brooklyn Dodgers in 1948. He proceeded to become one of the top pitchers in baseball.

He played with Jackie from 1948 through the 1956 season when Robinson retired. They were friends.

You came up to the Dodgers in 1948. Jackie Robinson's first year was 1947. He befriended you as a rookie.

Jackie introduced himself to me earlier that year of 1948 while I was on the Ft. Worth roster; Ft. Worth Cats was a AA farm team of the Dodgers. The big club came through and played there in the spring. It was just my second year in baseball, and I was scheduled to pitch three innings against the big club. That was a thrill beyond words at the time, and I pitched three innings. When the game was over, Robinson came over to our dugout and looked me up. I didn't know Jackie. I didn't know anybody on the big club. He came over and said, "Young man, I just want to tell ya, you're not going to be down here very long. I hit against you today, and, just mark my words, you're going to be with us before long."

Well, by July of that year the Dodgers did call me up. I'd won 15 at Ft. Worth and they needed pitching. Robinson came over to my locker, just as I walked in the clubhouse in Pittsburgh, stuck out his hand, the first one to do that, and said, "I was right. I told you you'd be here." That set the stage for a strong friendship, as well as being teammates for the next nine years.

We were good friends, and we were together off the field some. Pee Wee Reese, Ralph Branca, Clem Labine, and others were genuinely respectful of Jackie and considered him to be a class person, and I'm sure they consider him to this day a close friend. Jackie and I had a special relationship because he thought I went out of my way on a couple occasions, which truthfully I did not, and told him so.

There was an area in Ebbetts Field that was fenced off in which the families, or close friends who were authorized, could wait protected from the push of the crowd. We'd open that gate and go through to get to our cars or whatever. I came out one day and Rachel, Jackie's wife, and their young son, who was at that time probably six or eight years old, little Jackie Jr., were standing outside, and as I came out I went over to Rachel and spoke to her and talked to young Jackie and stood there for a few minutes and then went on my way. The next day, Jackie came to my locker and said, "Carl, I want to thank you for that yesterday." I said, "What's that?' "Well," he said, "Gee, right out there in front of all those fans and you went over and spent some time with Rachel and Jackie." I said, "Jackie, you can't thank me for that. I didn't do anything unusual. Just seemed natural to me, and your family's a beautiful family." But he thought that was an extension of myself that was intended to help him. I hope it did help him. But I said, "You compliment me on a good pitch or a well-pitched inning or something, but I can't take credit for that."

Were the Dodgers behind him from the beginning?

You know, Mr. Rickey [Branch Rickey, the general manager of the Dodgers who signed Robinson] was a very smart and sensitive man in reading people. Mr. Rickey always called this try with Jackie an experiment, which said he wasn't sure that it would work. The players had a feeling of respect. As soon as Jackie got to the big leagues, and they saw what kind of ability this guy had, and he was winning ball games for us with his bat, his glove, and, of course, his running ability, I think they quickly respected Jackie and understood he was big league calibre. That, in itself, took the color out of the picture, more or less.

Now, there was always kidding and there was always...if you had a big nose or a funny walk, a long neck—you got the business. Not only from the fans but from your teammates. But, in a sense, that is total acceptance when you can do that. So Jackie fit in, in the early years. I think the first two or three years, we weren't holding our breath, but it was like we were awestruck ourselves to be in the big leagues. We were all young and we were all battling for our jobs. I don't think we had as much concern for Jackie sometimes as we did, you know, "Am I going to make it this year?"

The crowds in some ballparks were segregated in those days. That is hard to imagine today. But certainly in the South as we came through we were always segregated. And the black fans were totally, of course, for Jackie. And the white fans, sometimes you wondered if the score meant anything. If Jackie made a good play, the blacks would cheer and if he happened to make an error or get thrown out at a base, whites would just erupt. It was that kind of atmosphere. But on our bench and in our clubhouse, I didn't see any, or hear any remarks that would be seriously opposed to Jackie's being there.

There were teams and individuals that were hard on him at the beginning. In particular, Ben Chapman, the manager of the Philadelphia Phillies.

Chapman made some strong statements. There was an exchange in the paper between he and Jackie. But you know, you've got to put it in perspective because the guys got on me. I wasn't too controversial. But when you're in the big leagues, and when you're under the umbrella of baseball where rhubarbs and gettin' on players and riding players was common, you had to discount some of what happened. It wasn't 'cause Jackie was black. It was 'cause he was a rookie. He was a star. And, he stood out as being unusual. Something different about this guy. When Frank Howard came in the league, he was a little unusual. He was so big, and I don't know if they got on him like they did Jackie. But, I mean, anything peculiar about a player or anything you could manufacture something out of, you get on him.

We came through the South and on more than one occasion coming north, and maybe it happened during the season in the early years—Jackie would get threatening letters sent to the ballpark. "If you take the field, you're going to be shot."

I remember them reading one of those in the clubhouse in Atlanta one day. We always stopped and played two or three days in Atlanta on the way north. In the early years, they wouldn't let the blacks even buy a ticket. They sat on the levee behind the right-field fence and watched the game. They could not get into the ballpark. The Klan picketed the hotel one occasion, and they, of course, wrote threatening letters.

Burt Shotton [Dodger manager] in about '49 read a threatening letter to Jackie, "if you take the field you're going to be shot." It got quiet in the clubhouse and everybody was pretty sober. Finally, Gene Hermanski says, "Hey, Skip, I've got an idea. If all of us wore No. 42, they wouldn't know who to shoot at." Well, that broke up everybody, and we go out on the field, and I remember warming up along the sidelines waiting for batting practice to start, and Pee Wee is saying to Jackie, "Hey, Jackie, do you mind getting over a little farther? I mean, after all, it might bounce offa you and hit me." That was the mood of the players. Yeah, this is serious. But, I think it said Jackie's total acceptance here.

There were times when Jackie would slide and the tag would be more of a swing than a simple tag. You know Jackie was a real man. Let's face it. You couldn't fool with Jackie. I mean, he had a real build on him.

I always felt that Reese was the perfect guy to play shortstop with Jackie because he had great respect in the league. But nobody talks about the guy on the other side of Jackie—Gil Hodges—who had extreme respect in the league. I think Gil Hodges in his temperament and his respect among fans and players kept an atmosphere defused that saved some problems for Jackie.

Gil was a great peacemaker. If there was a confrontation at second base involving Jackie, Gil was right there and he more or less broke it up quickly. I don't think you have any recorded incidents in which Jackie was in a fistfight. But there were plenty of times that it was provoked. I know that Mr. Rickey had an agreement with Jackie that for two years he would turn the other cheek and not make any motion of retaliation, even an expression. He was to get up, dust himself off, and not make any indication that he wanted to retaliate.

There was an air of caution around Jackie. There were a few people totally against the idea. There were a few people totally in favor of the idea. But there was a whole raft of people in the middle who were neutral and wanted to see if this was going to work or not before I take my position.

Was Robinson the best man available to break the "barrier"?

Well, number one, he did it. There could have been others who might have done it in a different way. Campanella certainly was a superstar, and he had a totally different attitude about it than Jackie did. So, I think if Campy could have done it, it would have come out in a different way.

There were some 50 screened black athletes as I remember, that the scouting system of the Dodgers had identified as potential. My understanding is that Mr. Rickey led his scouting staff to believe that he was considering the Brooklyn Brown Dodgers. And that they were scouting for a team to be like the Kansas City Monarchs, a black team to play in the black league. And that when Robinson came in to be interviewed, he thought that's what the interview was about, only to find he'd been selected.

I didn't have any feeling that Willie Mays or somebody else could have done it better. I think Mr. Rickey, if he had a strength beyond a good general manager, a good baseball mind, if he had an intuitive strength, it was reading the character of the people he kept and the people he traded.

I went through the exhibit that Coca-Cola helped to put together with the New York Museum of History; they put together a traveling museum of Jackie Robinson's life. I went to that. It was a black tie affair a few years ago. They assigned a *Sports Illustrated* writer to walk around with me and just get my reaction since I'd played with Jackie.

It was a beautiful experience. They had tapes playing. They had quotes printed on some of these exhibits. They had pictures of Jackie and so on. I came to one and it was a quote by Jackie's mother. I got to thinking about that. He was born, I believe, in Alabama [Georgia] and then moved to the West Coast. The indication was that his mother was a very strong Christian person. She talked to them constantly about the dignity of their life.

Jackie was a college graduate. Most of us had not been to college in baseball in those days. It was rare. It was rare to find a college grad in pro baseball. Pro football had more. But Robinson was an intelligent person.

But when I saw this illustration of his mother I knew Mr. Rickey's convictions as a Christian person. He took a lot of heat for that. People said he was a hypocrite. He wouldn't come to the ballpark on Sunday, but he didn't mind selling out a doubleheader. But I think Rickey tried to apply what his mother had been strong in as he grew up as a farm boy in Ohio.

Suddenly, a light went on. That's why he picked Robinson. The training that Robinson had had by his mother and the instilling in him of the dignity of a human being and the education that Jackie had gotten overrode, in Rickey's mind his militancy and his combativeness, and I think Mr. Rickey said, "Here's a man who'll understand what we're trying to do. He'll have enough self-control to know what he has to contain. And that he is intelligent enough to read what's happening and be able to make it work."

He meant a lot to the Dodgers. You weren't there in '47, but the Dodgers won a pennant in '47, as well as in '49, '52, '53, '55 and '56. Would you have had this success without Robinson?

I doubt it. Although I'll have to tell you that that ball club didn't win by virtue of any one person, as no club can. But Jackie brought a dimension to that talented team that maybe had only been there in part in previous years. Jackie brought an intensity to win. The Dodgers had won on occasion, but they never had a sustained, to my knowledge at least, a sustained decade until the "Robinson Decade." You just clicked off the years that the pennants were won in the late '40s and '50s, and what you didn't say was that we got beat on the last day in '51 and the last day in '50. We could have won eight or nine pennants in a row.

So, yes, the difference in us being a contender or being a winner could well have been Jackie's intensity. And even when he was past his peak and couldn't play every day, he would save himself for the big games. The big series. He would go on the field against Milwaukee, for instance, when they were contenders; Jackie would tell these guys, "Hey, I'm in there today. I want you to know I'm playing. I rested two days for this series." He would intimidate the opposition in the right way. And that would lift us.

Did he look on himself as a crusader, or a ballplayer, or both?

Yeah, I think both. I think Jackie was a natural athlete. He loved to play. He loved to win. He had all those qualities. But when he was selected to be THE first black, I think Jackie put a mantle on himself. Maybe he didn't put it on himself. It was there. What he did was so critical to what would happen after him that he couldn't afford to fail. And yet, Jackie was human. He didn't hit .600, or he didn't do something nobody else had ever done. But he did qualify to be a major leaguer. A big league ballplayer and a Hall of Famer.

But Jackie's other side of life was never satisfied, and I'm not so sure it was ever really even closely satisfied. He used to take strong exception when people would say to him, "Boy, Jackie, you've made it. You've really done it. You've broke the line. You're here. You're established. You're going to be in the Hall of Fame." He'd take strong exception to that and say, "Wait a minute. That's nothing to what needs to be done. I mean, I haven't even scratched the surface." So, I think he went to his grave with that on his lips. "Don't tell me how I made it."

You know, history is big. Jackie's part was big, but considering, it was just a small piece of the whole picture. I told Jackie, "Jackie, you know you've helped your race tremendously. But you helped my race a lot more." I believe that. He opened a new understanding and a new sensitivity that I think people had, but was buried in the culture of the time, and that's the way it had always been done, and the extremists in the racial picture kind of had the upper hand. Well, Jackie, through sports, did what I think is the ideal way to earn a place in the work force, in the sports picture or wherever.

I take exception to some degree to laws that force acceptance where Jackie, when given the chance, proved he belonged. Nobody took exception to that. You never heard anybody say, "Hey, he got to the big leagues on the color of his skin. They had to have a black and he was it." No, he earned it. And everybody respected that. To me, that's the right way to do it, and I'm real proud that baseball was the stage in which that was presented and proven to be the right way to do it.

JOHN EDWARD WILZ

THE KOREAN WAR

The Korean War was an ugly affair. It lasted 37 months, resulting in two million dead. Eighty percent were civilians and 54,000 were Americans.

John Edward Wilz served in Korea and upon his return to the States became a professor of history at Indiana University. He has always maintained his interest in the Korean War and has written about it.

The Korean War began on June 25, 1950. Do you think one of the major reasons we got into this war was that Dean Acheson, in a speech given in January 1950, said that Korea lay beyond the American defensive perimeter? Senator Robert Taft said this invited the North Koreans to invade South Korea.

I'm no great admirer of Senator Taft. But I agree with the gentleman from Ohio, who in the 1940s and early 1950s was styled "Mr. Republican," on this point. Various historical scholars who have carefully examined the origins of the Korean War, notably James I. Matray and Bruce Cumings, have tended to give short shrift to Taft's argument. Indeed, Cumings has categorically rejected it. But I have read most of the pertinent documentary materials on the subject, and really suspect that Acheson's speech of January 12, 1950, did send a signal to the North Koreans and their Soviet patrons that the United States would not move to South Korea's defense in the event of a North Korean invasion of South Korea. Had Achesan sent a different signal—had he merely hinted that the United States might defend South Korea against aggression from the North—I suspect the North Koreans would not have attacked. Until scholars gain access to archival records in Moscow and P'yongyang relating to the Korean War, of course, nobody can be absolutely certain. Still, in his recently published memoirs, Dean Rusk, who was the assistant secretary of state for Far Eastern Affairs in 1950, cited a remark allegedly made by the Soviet diplomat Andrei Vyshinsky, shortly after the onset of the war, that the United States had done everything within its power to tell the Communists that it was not interested in Korea, only to dispatch troops to defend South Korea when the North Koreans launched their invasion.

For my part, I remain persuaded that, in 1949-50, the United States indicated in a variety of ways, not only in Acheson's "defensive perimeter" speech of January 12, 1950, that it would not intervene militarily in the event of a North Korean attack across the 38th parallel. But then, during the day or two following the invasion of June 25, 1950, the Washington government, presided over by Harry Truman, dramatically revised its estimate of Korea's importance to American interests and security, and, as a result of that revision, made a 180-degree turn in policy vis-a-vis Korea.

Frankly, I think the Truman administration's management of policy regarding Korea during the year or two before June 25, 1950, constituted a colossal blunder. For if the administration, as Taft insisted during the two years following June 25, 1950, had made clear that it intended to defend South Korea against aggression from the north, the Korean War—one that claimed more than two million lives, including those of more than 50,000 Americans—would not have come to pass. But was America's stake in a non-communist South Korea greater in late June of 1950 than it had been during the previous year or so? If the answer to that question is yes, then the Washington government might be excused for having failed during that year or so to take a strong stand on behalf of South Korea. I believe the answer to the question is no.

Truman called this a police action and he committed U.S. troops without congressional approval.

Truman apparently reached his decision to order United States forces to move to the defense of South Korea without touching base with congressional leaders. But he met with senior members of Congress, Republicans as well as Democrats, on the morning of June 27, 1950, before announcing the decision. None of the senior members spoke out in opposition to what the president had decided to do. Then, a short time later on that same day, members of the House of Representatives stood and cheered when the Speaker interrupted proceedings in the House chamber to inform them that the president had ordered American forces to enter the combat in Northeast Asia. Alas, Truman didn't ask Congress to declare war against North Korea. And for declining to ask for a declaration of war, he subsequently came under sharp criticism, notably from Senator Taft. But even Taft supported the president's decision to deploy American forces to stay the communist tide in Korea.

Our troops were in very poor shape.

There's no question about that. I received a letter some years ago from a retired colonel who had commanded troops in Japan during the period before the outbreak of the Korean War. The colonel observed that Army units—the same ones that would be dispatched to Korea in the summer of 1950—were understrength. Moreover, he said, many of the troops were misfits. Many were young men who had been on the "lam" from the law or been entangled in family problems back in the United States. The troops deployed in Japan before June 25, 1950, he went on, were poorly trained. Inadequate training resulted in part, he explained, from the fact that there simply wasn't sufficient space in the Japanese countryside, given the requirements of Japanese agriculture, to conduct full-dress military maneuvers.

In the first weeks of the war we were badly beaten. We retreated to what was called the Pusan Perimeter in southeastern Korea.

Yes. United Nations forces, mostly American, took a pounding during the first month of their involvement in the Korean War. They were pushed backward from Osan and then across the Kum River by manifestly superior North Korean forces. Taking heavy casualties, they were driven from Taejon, a town whose name was seared into the consciousness of scores of millions of Americans in July of 1950. At length, in the first days of August, they dug in along the so-called Pusan Perimeter in the southeast corner of the Korean peninsula. Over the next six weeks, until mid-September, they turned back repeated North Korean assaults.

This stalemate continued until MacArthur moved at Inch'on, which was September 15, 1950 and landed the Army and Marines. Inch'on was about 150 miles from the North Korean's rear. By October 1, 1950, we believed the North Korean army was all but destroyed. Was the Inch'on landing MacArthur's finest moment?

I think it was his finest moment in the Korean War. I'm not sure that the Inch'on operation surpassed his campaign for the Admiralty Islands in 1944, perhaps his most brilliant campaign in the Southwest Pacific during World War II. In any event, Inch'on was a high moment for MacArthur. No doubt about that. One of the high moments of his career. Inch'on was a brilliant stroke. In conception, it was reminiscent of the ill-starred Anzio operation in Italy in 1944. The difference between

Inch'on and Anzio was that MacArthur did it right. He marshalled sufficient forces to do the job, whereas at Anzio a similar type of operation had failed largely because American forces were understrength —and were not led by an aggressive commander.

Following the Inch'on operation, of course, UN forces of Tenth Corps drove the North Koreans from Seoul, the transportation hub of southern Korea. As a result, the logistical lifeline of North Korean forces fighting far to the south along the Pusan perimeter was severed. The UN Command's Eighth Army thereupon broke out of the perimeter, and within 10 days of the Inch'on operation the North Korean army had collapsed and was fleeing northward in disarray toward the 38th parallel.

From this point forward, we went north, took the North Korean capital, proceeded toward the Yalu River. But we were receiving bad intelligence at this point. MacArthur said, "There's no problem here."

MacArthur divided his command when he sent his forces to the north of the 38th parallel, a decision that ran counter to time-honored military maxims. Tenth Corps carried the UN offensive on the eastern side of the peninsula, Eighth Army on the western side. I'm not sure that there was an intelligence failure. There was ample evidence that Chinese forces were moving to the vicinity of the Yalu River in Manchuria. And the Chinese premier and foreign minister Zhou En-lai announced on October 3, 1950, that the Beijing government would not stand by if UN forces crossed the 38th parallel and threatened to overrun North Korea. MacArthur and his superiors in Washington, of course, believed that Zhou was bluffing. In any event, MacArthur clearly didn't anticipate that the Chinese would enter the war in Korea. When UN forces first clashed with Chinese units, in the latter part of October of 1950, MacArthur was not alarmed. He didn't believe those units were a harbinger of a full-dress Chinese military intervention in the war.

Allow me to add that various writers and other commentators have placed upon MacArthur virtually the entire burden for the disaster that befell the UN Command when the Chinese threw overpowering forces into the Korean War at the end of November of 1950. Some critics have said categorically that MacArthur was responsible for what proved to be the disastrous decision to send UN forces into North Korea in October 1950. To be sure, MacArthur very much wanted to unleash UN forces against the fleeing North Koreans after those forces had liberated South Korea. But the decision to roll back communism on the Korean peninsula by liberating North Korea from the grasp of Kim Il-sung's regime in P'yongyang was made in Washington. And it was not a decision that leaders in Washington made reluctantly on the urging of MacArthur.

Given the dynamics of domestic politics in the United States at the time, frankly, the decision was probably inevitable. Republicans had been battering the Democratic administration of Harry Truman for several years with the charge that Democrats were, in the language of the day, "soft on communism." The fall of China to Mao Zedong's Communists during Truman's presidential watch the year before, in 1949, had accelerated the battering. Had Truman, in early autumn of 1950, ordered a halt to the UN advance at the 38th parallel, he would have passed up an opportunity to undertake what appeared to most Americans to be an easy and, in view of North Korea's aggression against South Korea the previous June, entirely justifiable campaign against the remnants of the North Korean army to the north of the parallel. As a result, the battering by Republicans of Democrats in general and the Truman administration in particular would unquestionably have soared to new levels of intensity.

The military intervention of the Chinese in the war, of course, turned the UN drive through North Korea toward the Yalu and Tumen Rivers into an unmitigated disaster. And hardly had its dimension become apparent before partisans of President Truman and the Democrats set about to dump all of the blame for the disaster that had befallen the UN Command in northernmost Korea on MacArthur, himself a partisan of the Republican Party. Such dumping, of course, was manifestly unfair to the general.

I'm no partisan of MacArthur. In fact, I would say that, in most matters relating to politics and diplomacy during the years 1945-53, in the time of Truman's presidency, I was, and remain, a partisan of Truman. But in the matter of distributing blame for the disaster that overcame UN forces, mostly American, in the closing weeks of 1950, I think MacArthur has received unfair treatment at the hands of various writers and commentators, not to mention partisans of Harry Truman.

We had an intelligence problem because the Chinese had about 850,000 soldiers in Manchuria, and they already had about 120,000 south of the Yalu River. On November 25, 1950 the Chinese attacked with about 300,000 men.

The Chinese attacked both parts of the separated UN commands. And in the northwestern region of the Korean peninsula, where Army troops of Eighth Army were deployed, the result was nothing less than a rout of UN forces. Vastly outnumbered, some Army units performed poorly—and, to their shame perhaps, introduced the term "bugout" into the language. Now Marine and Army troops of Tenth Corps on the eastern side of the peninsula put up a stiffer fight, and on the east side of the Chosin Reservoir, in the most ferocious combat of the Korean War, Army units were virtually wiped out. In part because of the stand made by those Army units, the Marines were able to fight their way southward from the Chosin Reservoir to the port of Hungnam, whence, in December of 1950, they and various Army and South Korean units were evacuated by sea. Arguably, those six or so weeks after the Chinese let fly their all-out attack, on November 25, 1950, were the darkest that the people of the United States had endured since the fall of Bataan and Corregidor in the Philippines in spring of 1942.

We were outnumbered as much as 3 to 1.

In some areas, or sectors, it was greater than that.

What happened at that point?

At that time, no small number of people back in the United States wanted the Washington government, and, by definition, the UN, to quit the Korean peninsula once and for all. Such people took the position that leaders in Washington, notably President Truman, ought to face up to what prophets of doom and gloom in America perceived to be reality, to wit, that the United States and its allies and friends were beaten in Korea. Accordingly, all American and other UN forces should be withdrawn from the peninsula.

General MacArthur, on the other hand, sought a totally different approach to the Korea problem. He wanted to enlarge the war—wanted to be authorized to order the bombing of what he described as the "privileged sanctuaries" of the Chinese to the north of the Yalu in Manchuria, impose a naval blockade of Chinese ports, unleash United States bombing planes against China's industrial centers, deploy Chinese Nationalist troops of Generalissimo Chiang Kai-shek on Formosa —or Taiwan—in the battle line in Korea.

As for Truman, he had no stomach for the argument that the time had come for America to cut its losses in Korea and leave the peninsula to the Communists. But he had no stomach for MacArthur's appeal that the UN Command be allowed to expand the war either. The president feared that an expansion of the war might cause the conflict in Korea to escalate into World War III. In a word, he was bent on keeping the war confined to the Korean peninsula.

I should add that the Communists, no less than Truman, appeared to be bent on avoiding an expansion of the war beyond the borders and shores of Korea. Accordingly, they never attacked the "privileged sanctuaries" of the UN Command, that is, the bases and port facilities and railways in Japan that supported the UN military effort in Korea. They never attacked a single ship or airplane that was ferrying troops and munitions and other supplies to the UN Command in Korea.

While the argument over what the United States should do with respect to Korea continued, in early January of 1951, UN forces of Eighth Army, after retreating to a point some 40 miles to the south of the 38th parallel, dug in and brought the communist, essentially Chinese, advance to a halt. A few weeks before, on December 23, 1950, Lieutenant General Walton H. Walker, the commander of Eighth Army, had died in a jeep accident, whereupon Lieutenant General Matthew B. Ridgway flew out to the Pacific from Washington and took command of Eighth Army. As for MacArthur, he appeared to be demoralized in the aftermath of the destruction of his dream of liberating all of Korea from the grip of the Communists. In any event, he gave Ridgway virtually a free rein to conduct the war in Korea as Ridgway saw fit.

Well, Ridgway proved to be precisely what the battered UN forces of Eighth Army needed. He restored the army's confidence—also instilled in it a new spirit of aggressiveness. And by the end of January of 1951, Eighth Army had returned to the offensive. Thanks to the renewed fighting spirit of UN infantrymen, the fearsome firepower of all UN forces— air power, artillery, armor—and also thanks to a typhus epidemic that ravaged the Chinese army at this particular point, Eighth Army ground its way northward, and in mid-March reclaimed Seoul. It was the fourth time the South Korean capital, or what remained of it, had changed hands during the previous nine months. Pressing forward beyond Seoul, Eighth Army soon re-established a line roughly in the vicinity of the 38th parallel. The war would remain stalemated more or less on that line for the next two years.

That would be until the Armistice in July1953.

The line underwent some adjustment. Most importantly, the

ferocious combat at Bloody Ridge and Heartbreak Ridge in the rugged east-central sector of the MLR (main line of resistance), in autumn of 1951, was pressed by the UN Command for the purpose of straightening the battle line and gaining some high ground. Neither the UN Command nor its communist counterpart, at that time, appeared to seriously ponder the possibility of trying for a breakthrough of the other's defenses.

A draftee, I arrived in the Punch Bowl area—just to the east of Heartbreak Ridge— as a combat engineer soldier in March of 1952. The MLR in that area moved not a whit during the 14 months that I was in Korea. There was a good deal of shelling back and forth. But, as mentioned, neither side appeared to be thinking of a World War I-style attack aimed at breaking through the lines of its enemy. That was most comforting to GI's in the battle zone, for the number of combat casualties suffered by UN forces during my time in Korea was a fraction compared with those of the first year and a half of the war.

Did the Joint Chiefs of Staff want to recall MacArthur on military grounds in January 1951? By March 1951, Truman wished to negotiate a cease fire. MacArthur took it upon himself to say that he was going to personally negotiate the terms with the enemy. Also, he sent a letter to Joe Martin [Republican leader in the House] regarding the use of Chiang Kai-shek's troops in Korea, and in general an assault on the administration. This was the last straw for Truman.

Although relations between MacArthur and the Joint Chiefs became testy in December of 1950, and remained so through much of January of 1951, largely because of MacArthur's virtual insistence that he be authorized to undertake a dramatic expansion of the war, I know of no evidence that the Chiefs sought MacArthur's recall at that time. Indeed, MacArthur's biographer, D. Clayton James, has observed that General Omar N. Bradley, the chairman of the JCS, only reluctantly supported Truman's order relieving MacArthur of his various commands in April of 1951.

Regarding the relief of MacArthur, on April 11, 1951, I find it surprising that Truman didn't take that action three or so weeks before he did. By the middle of March, UN forces had retaken Seoul, and Truman was anxious to work out a cease-fire with the Communists. Indeed, the president was under heavy pressure by the British and other allies to strive to negotiate an end to the fighting in Korea. And most of his compatriots in the United States had no interest whatever in the prospect of a new UN offensive beyond the 38th parallel for the purpose of rolling back communism in Northeast Asia and achieving thc unification of Korea under a non-communist regime. Accordingly, Truman set about to direct a peace, or, more accurately, cease-fire or armistice, initiative to the North Koreans and Chinese. MacArthur was advised of Truman's intent. Whereupon, on March 24, 1951, MacArthur issued a bombastic public statement that his biographer has described as a challenge to the pride of the People's Republic of China, as well as to the authority of his superiors in Washington. An expansion of the war to the territory of China, which expansion MacArthur manifestly sought, would doom "Red" China to military collapse. Or so proclaimed the general in Tokyo. MacArthur's declaration appeared to undercut Truman's armistice initiative. In any event, the president decided that, in light of the declaration, the initiative would have to be put aside.

Naturally, Truman and other officials in Washington were incensed. And one might expect that Truman, usually portrayed by later-day historians as a non-nonsense type of chief executive, would have fired MacArthur then and there. But he didn't. Not until Congressman Martin made public a letter that MacArthur had recently sent to him did Truman decide to give the Far Eastern commander the sack. In his letter to Martin, MacArthur, in effect, castigated Truman for his determination to halt the advance of Eighth Army in the vicinity of the 38th parallel and to continue to confine the war to the Korean peninsula. He concluded the letter by announcing that "there is no substitute for victory."

Truman got the approval of the Joint Chiefs to fire him, and he was dismissed April 10, 1951. Truman appointed General Matthew Ridgway to take his place as Far East Commander. The Chinese thought Ridgway might be easier to deal with than MacArthur. In July 1953 a truce was signed. Were there any winners?

I doubt that the Communists thought they would find Ridgway easier to deal with than MacArthur. In a word, I doubt that MacArthur's relief had anything to do with the decision by the Communists, in late June or early July of 1951, to enter armistice negotiations with the UN Command. I suspect they agreed to negotiate because they understood that their chance to drive the UN Command from South Korea and unify the Korean peninsula under a communist regime had passed. Eighth Army, after all, had recently, during the second half of April of 1951, broken up a full-dress attempt by Chinese and North Korean forces to return to the offensive in Korea. Communist casualties had totaled something like 70,000 in the combat of April 15-30, 1951, UN casualties about seven thousand. The Communists may also have reckoned that they could turn armistice negotiations to their advantage by resorting to tactics of intransigence and delay. Which, of course, they proceeded to do.

Before responding to the question regarding winners in the Korean War, I should like to address a couple of points regarding the war.

First, it's interesting that President Dwight D. Eisenhower, during his first six months in the White House, in 1953, apparently persuaded the Chinese and North Koreans, and, presumably, their Soviet patrons, to accept an armistice in Korea by threatening to order Eighth Army to return to the offensive—and, more importantly, by hinting that he might order the use of nuclear weapons, presumably against the territory of China, in support of that offensive. It appears, then, that Eisenhower brought the war to a termination on July 27, 1953, by threatening to do what MacArthur had urged the Truman administration to do in early 1951. True, MacArthur had not urged that Truman sanction a nuclear campaign against China. Still, more or less as Eisenhower hinted that he might do in 1953, MacArthur wanted to unleash a massive military-naval assault against China, while pressing the ground combat beyond the 38th parallel for the purpose of unifying Korea under President Syngman Rhee's anti-communist regime in Seoul.

It's interesting that historians and other commentators have often praised Eisenhower for his bellicose approach to the problem of the Korean War, while, at the same time, taking a jaundiced view of MacArthur's approach in 1951. By the same token, it's interesting to weigh the proposition that Truman might have succeeded in bringing the Korean War to a termination before the expiration of his own presidency in January 1953 had he been willing to issue the same kind of threat that Eisenhower quietly issued in February of 1953. One wonders whether Truman ever pondered the question, "What if I had done what Ike did regarding Korea?" Probably he didn't. For Truman wasn't inclined to bother himself with what he once described to an inquiring journalist as "iffy" questions.

Second, I think it's interesting to recall that the Truman administration almost certainly could have secured an armistice in Korea in the spring of 1952 had it been willing to accept an armistice provision that all prisoners of war would be repatriated, against their will if it came to that. Truman and the people of the United States, of course, had learned by spring of 1952 that some 55,000 North Korean and Chinese captives being held in UN prisoner of war compounds didn't want to return to North Korea or "Red" China. The forced return of POW's to what Americans of 1952-53 generally perceived to be the slavery of communism struck most Americans as downright unconscionable. Their president agreed. Accordingly, the Korean War dragged on for another 15 months, during which some nine thousand GI's lost their lives in the ancient Land of the Morning Calm—or, as GI's often referred to it, the Land that God Forgot. Can one in his or her wildest imagination suspect that Americans, during the latter 1960s or early 1970s, would have endorsed a continuation of the war in Vietnam had the forced repatriation of communist POW's been the last remaining obstacle to a cease-fire, or armistice? The willingness of Americans to fight on in Korea in 1952-53 for the sake of 55,000 communist POW's, whatever the disenchantment that most Americans had come to feel regarding the war itself, is powerful testimony, I think, to the depth of the sentiments of Americans with respect to communism and the cold war in 1952-53.

Now, were there any winners in the Korean War? I suppose one ought to address that question, in the first instance, by considering the objectives, or goals, of the combatants. Ostensibly acting on behalf of the United Nations, the United States certainly achieved one of its initial objectives, namely, to rescue South Korea from the clutches of Kim Il-sung and his communist regime in P'yongyang. But then, upon achieving that objective, in early October of 1950, the Washington government fashioned a new objective, namely, to roll back the perimeter of communism in Northeast Asia by smashing across the 38th parallel and bringing about the unification of Korea under the regime of Syngman Rhee. The United States, of course, failed to achieve this latter objective. So, in terms of one of its initial objectives, the United States was a winner in the Korean War. In terms of the objective of driving communism from northern Korea and unifying the peninsula under the Rhee regime, it was a loser—and, conversely, the Communists were winners.

The United States, of course, had another objective when it sent its young men to fight and die in Korea in the summer of 1950. Indeed, this other objective was its overarching objective, or purpose, when it threw itself into what assorted historians and commentators have termed Korea's civil war. It wanted to preserve and perhaps reinforce its credibility with allies, namely, those of the pristine North Atlantic Treaty Organization, and with friends or would-be friends across the world, particularly the Japanese—wanted to preserve and reinforce its credibility as an ally and friend that would rally to their defense in the event the Soviets, or clients of the Soviets, threatened their national survival. In a word, the United States was animated by what one might identify as a psychic objective. It was an objective that, in the international political environment of 1950, appeared absolutely critical in terms of the interests and indeed the security of the United States and the rest of the non-communist world. One must keep in mind that the United States and its allies and many of its friends had no doubt whatever in 1950 that the non-communist world was locked in a struggle to the death, albeit a largely "cold war" (as opposed to "hot war") struggle with the Marxist-Leninist empire of the infamous Stalin. Well, the United States assuredly achieved its credibility objective in Korea; hence, in terms of that objective, it was a winner in the war. The success of NATO was assured, for the time being at any rate, inasmuch as NATO's success depended on the confidence of its European members that the United States would indeed rally to their defense in the event the Soviets or their Warsaw Pact clients went on the warpath. And Japan, its security likewise dependent upon the willingness of the North American superpower to move to its defense, became an unwavering ally of the United States. The American response to communist aggression in Korea, then, dramatically reinforced the celebrated containment policy fashioned by the United States in the latter 1940s. Alas, its success in containing the communist menace at the 38th parallel in Korea was doubtless a factor that prompted subsequent presidential administrations in Washington to commit the United States to the containment of communism at the 17th parallel in Vietnam. The struggle to contain communism in Vietnam, of course, had a different outcome than that to contain communism in Korea.

The Korean War produced other winners. It proved a boon for the so-called military-industrial complex of the United States, for it prompted a dramatic buildup of America's armed forces. The war and the resultant buildup of the armed forces gave new stimulus to the American economy. The outcome? America's economy achieved new levels of prosperity during the 1950s. And, according to the historian Roger V. Dingman, the war in Korea may have provided what Dingman has described as a kick-start for the economy of Japan, one that in 1950 was far from having achieved full recovery from the devastation of World War II. The Korean War prompted the Congress in Washington to enact

Public Law 550, the so-called Korean War GI Bill of Rights, and, as a result, opportunities for further education were opened to great numbers of young Americans. I used to tell students, in my course in United States history since World War II, that if they didn't like the course they should blame their misfortune on Public Law 550, for without that law I never would have been able to earn a Ph.D degree and become a history professor.

Another winner as a consequence of the Korea War, arguably, was the United Nations. As everyone knows, the UN's predecessor, the League of Nations, lost all credibility and influence as an agency of peace during the 1930s when it failed to meet the challenge presented by the aggressions of Japan, Italy, and Germany. To be sure, the UN would not have met the challenge of aggression by North Korea had the United States declined to assume leadership in the struggle to rescue South Korea from Kim Il-sung and his ilk. The UN, in truth, provided little more than a cover for what the United States was bent on doing in the matter of Korea. Still, hundreds of thousands of men of a variety of nations served and died in Korea under the banner of the world organization. Their efforts were directed by what, euphemistically perhaps, was designated the UN Command. Accordingly, the UN gained sufficient prestige from its role in the Korean War, at least in the non-communist world, that it did not suffer the fate of the League of Nations. It certainly did not become the kind of instrument for peace that its founders had envisioned in 1945. But it was given a new lease on life. And now, in the post-cold war era, there is hope that the UN might at last become an effective instrument for thwarting armed aggression and settling international disputes amicably.

Regarding this matter of winners and losers in the Korean War, let me make a final observation. I traveled to Seoul in June of 1990 to participate in a conference commemorating the 40th anniversary of the outbreak of the Korean War. After the conference, I joined a group of American veterans of the war who were visiting South Korea under the auspices of the government of the Republic of Korea. At a concluding ceremony in Seoul's most luxurious hotel, a gentleman from southern Indiana made a little speech on behalf of the visiting American veterans. He remarked that there are few if any memorials or monuments to veterans of the Korean War in the United States—nothing, for example, to compare with the magnificent monument in Washington to the veterans who perished in the war in Vietnam. But, he went on, we

American veterans of the Korean War have our monument. Our monument, he said, is the thriving, pulsating Republic of Korea. His observation struck a chord with me. Our comrades who served and died in Vietnam have been the recipients of numerous memorials and monuments. And it is right and proper that the Vietnam veterans have been so honored. But the country for which those brave men fought, namely, South Vietnam, no longer exists. Rather South Vietnam comprises half of a creaky nation-state that is presided over by a totalitarian and hopelessly inefficient communist regime in Hanoi. The country for which American and other UN soldiers and marines, airmen and seamen fought and died to rescue from the grasp of Kim Il-sung and his henchmen in 1950-53 is surviving and, generally, prospering. South Korea certainly has its problems. Like our own, its political system is manifestly imperfect. Democracy has found it hard to survive, much less to flourish, in the one-time Hermit Kingdom. Some segments of the national society haven't shared fairly in the country's economic miracle. In a word, South Korea hasn't reached the promised land. But, as any American veteran of the war who visits South Korea today will attest, the contrast between the South Korea of 1950-53 and that of the early 1990s boggles the mind. Most notably, South Korea has evolved from a primitive backwater, an absolutely dilapidated and demoralized country, to a veritable economic powerhouse. Communist North Korea, by contrast, remains an economic basket case.

In sum, I would say that the United States was a winner in the Korean War. But bigger winners perhaps, ultimately, were the future generations of South Koreans. The victory, or triumph, whose harvest the post-1953 generations of South Koreans have reaped, was dearly bought. Upward of a million and a half Koreans, above and below the parallel, perished as a result of the war of 1950-53, a truly fearsome toll. Still, one has only to peer to the north of the 38th parallel to catch a glimpse of what South Korea would be like today if South Koreans and Americans—and Britons, Dutchmen, Frenchmen, Greeks, Turks, and brave people of other nations—had not moved to the defense of the Republic of Korea in 1950-53.

In the final analysis, of course, the biggest winners as a result of the determination of the United States and other nations to contain Stalin's North Korean clients at the 38th parallel in 1950 were those hundreds of millions—perhaps billions—of people across the globe who, during the era of the cold war, hoped to stay clear of the embrace of Stalinism. As we all know, the United States and the rest of the non-communist world have emerged victorious in the cold war. What Ronald Reagan rightly identified as the Evil Empire has collapsed—probably, in the long run, to the profound good fortune of its own people. The non-communist world's victory in the cold war, sealed in 1991, may not have come to pass, it seems fair to say, if the United States and its people had failed to stand up to Soviet-communist power by moving to the aid of Greece and Turkey, implementing the Marshall Plan, fashioning NATO, and rallying to the defense of South Korea in the early years of the cold war.

ATHAN THEOHARIS

JOE McCARTHY

The early to mid-'50s was a unique time in American history. Many thought war was imminent with Russia and that Communists had infiltrated our government.

No one played on, or helped to perpetuate this fear, more than Joe McCarthy. He was a major factor in American life for only four years, but 40 years later we still read or hear about him almost daily.

Athan Theoharis is a professor of history at Marquette University and is an authority on McCarthy and the McCarthy era. He is the author of Seeds of Repression—Harry S. Truman and the Origins of McCarthyism.

From the time McCarthy was elected to the Senate in 1946 to early 1950, he was considered one of its most ineffectual members. His Wheeling, West Virginia, speech in February 1950 where he stated there were 205 members of the State Department known to be members of the Communist Party was the incident that gave him national prominence.

The speech came at a very good time in the sense that you had the recent conviction of Alger Hiss on two counts of perjury. What the Hiss Case seems to suggest, given his prominence and respectability, was that there was seemingly very much of a security problem the Truman administration had not confronted. When McCarthy delivers the speech, it was part of Republican/Lincoln Day oratory. It was given to this Republican Women's Club in Wheeling, West Virginia, which shows how insignificant that speaking assignment was and his stature within the Republican Party and Republican Senate. Given his obscurity and lack of identification with Republican leadership, ironically that obscurity was the basis for the reaction to the speech. It was picked up by the wire services three days later. He gives other speeches and then he delivers this speech later in February before the Senate, where he scales down the amount [of alleged Communists in the State Department]. You're right, he was obscure. But that obscurity partially explains why there was this responsiveness to his charges.

Republicans since 1938, and more notably with the control of the Congress, the 80th Congress in '47-48, had been raising the charge of Communists in government. But that meant in the federal bureaucracy. In McCarthy's refinement it was in the State Department which resonated very well in the early 1950s.

There were five Senatorial attempts to investigate McCarthy's charges, and they never found anything. They never found anybody who, in fact, was a Communist?

He didn't uncover a single case of espionage.

He never found a Communist.

Well, some of the individuals so cited might have been members of popular front organizations. In terms of a dues-paying member of the CP, no. But that never was a problem for the senator. He was making these charges of a serious internal security threat. The definition that applied in the '50s was not that you were a "Soviet agent," or even that you were a Communist Party member, but that you had suspect associations. And that was the nature of the evidence that he cites.

But that was irresponsible. He was performing serious character assassination.

Yes, he was. Because the implication that he was conveying [was] this was a serious internal security threat, and these people were engaged in espionage.

Which, in fact, he had no evidence to that effect at all. Early 1951, Gallup ran a poll, and they reported 51 percent of the country supported him. So, he had support. Owen Lattimore was one of the people that he went after. McCarthy said he was the top Soviet agent in the United States.

He made the charge in '50. Lattimore would be investigated again in '51 before the Senate Internal Security Subcommittee. That investigation was part of the committee's investigation of the Institute of Pacific Relations, and the degree of communist influence in the Institute, which was a private research organization. Very well respected. Promoted research in the Far East.

Did they ever find anything on Owen Lattimore?

What they find on Lattimore is that he was left-oriented, and he was the editor of the journals of the IPR. Marxist articles, written by Marxists, or taking a Marxist perspective were published. But there was no evidence uncovered in the 1950s by McCarthy and his Senate supporters of espionage or sabotage.

The Alger Hiss Case was not uncovered by McCarthy, the Rosenberg Case, the Coplon Case or a later case, Rudolf Abel, a Soviet spy. That wasn't uncovered by them. What they were relating was that membership, association, proclivity for potentially disloyal [activity]—that was the thrust. It was accepted as being more sinister. The basic premise, if you were a member of the Party, you were a Soviet agent. Not all Communist Party members were.

Other politicians saw this communist threat as a way to get elected.

Right. Anti-communism was the ticket to fame and fortune. We identified with McCarthy because he was so visible. But he was surely not the most effective proponent of the communist threat.

Who was the most effective?

Far more effective would be Pat McCarren, the senator from Nevada, who chaired the Senate Internal Security Subcommittee. Or, James Eastland, the senator from Mississippi. They were far more effective in the use of anti-communism during the '50s.

As far as getting elected themselves?

No, in terms of national political influence. In terms of legislative influence. McCarren steers through the Internal Security Act of 1950. Immigration legislation in 1952. I mean, if you ask who had long-term impact on national policies, a better case can be made for Pat McCarren than for Joe McCarthy.

McCarthy had no legislative impact. You made reference to this appraisal of his abilities as a senator. He's voted by the Washington Press Corps in 1951 as the worst member of the U. S. Senate. That was an appraisal of his effectiveness as a senator. In terms of lobbying for legislation, introduction of legislation, legislative influence, impact during debate, McCarthy was nowhere to be seen. He made a lot of speeches on the Senate floor and public speeches, but he didn't have much influence.

In January 1954 Gallup published a poll that showed he had a 70 percent approval rating. On March 9, 1954, Edward R. Murrow attacked McCarthy on his television program, "See It Now."

Murrow was considered very courageous because he was direct and confrontational. It coincided with the charges that McCarthy made against the U. S. Army that was the basis for the Army-McCarthy Hearings that spring. McCarthy, in a sense, had lost perspective. By that, I mean perspective in terms of the ability to sustain a belief in his charges. So when he begins to attack Army security procedures at Fort Monmouth and the conduct of the Eisenhower Army secretary, he becomes vulnerable, and the Army-McCarthy Hearings prove to be his undoing.

Roy Cohn and David Schine. Cohn wanted Schine to receive special treatment in the Army.

This attempt to secure preferential treatment for an inductee coincided with McCarthy's investigation of Army security proceedings, and they became linked with those hearings that spring. The basis for the investigation was to penalize the Army for not adhering to these demands for preferential treatment.

The hearing was televised. I think a lot of people just became aware of television and it was a dramatic soap opera. It was good theater because of this confrontation between McCarthy and members of the administration and his charges about laxness in the administration security procedures. And the countercharge that the reason that the committee was pressuring the Army was because it wanted favoritism.

So it made it a personalized story and more interesting. It wasn't complex as, say, 205 or 81 known Communists in the State Department.

Joseph Welch was his antagonist during the hearing. McCarthy was acting like his "Fifth Amendment Communists" that he pursued. In other words, he wouldn't answer questions. It was a bad performance.

McCarthy had access to classified reports. Individuals within the Defense Department and State, Loyalty Review Board, the FBI, and reporters were feeding him information.

To sustain his charges he had to assure them he would not disclose their assistance, so he had to refuse to disclose.

In the case of Welch, he had this very sophisticated attorney who was folksy. He was a far more credible adversary for that reason. The way this drama played out, he was more than McCarthy's match. He could turn a phrase very nicely. Was able, because he was a very sharp attorney, to go for the jugular. Those points where McCarthy was vulnerable, to turn McCarthy around as a "Fifth Amendment Communist," not disclose his sources. McCarthy was taking a position that in order to obtain this information, he had to assure these individuals of confidentiality.

McCarthy attacked a young attorney in Welch's firm by the name of Fred Fisher. McCarthy and Welch had an agreement before the hearing not to mention Fisher. McCarthy "crossed" him and went after Fisher. There is some theater, but Welch was angry and depressed. He proceeded to attack McCarthy in a very effective manner saying, "Let us not assassinate this lad further, Senator. You have done enough. Have you no sense of decency, sir, at long last? Have you no sense of decency?" McCarthy tried again. Welch then said, "Mr. McCarthy, I will not discuss this with you further. You have sat within six feet of me and could have asked me about Fred Fisher. You have brought it out. If there is a God in heaven it will do neither you nor your cause any good. I will not discuss it further. I will not ask Mr. Cohn any more questions. You, Mr. Chairman, may if you will, call the next witness." The audience cheered Welch and McCarthy was finished.

An agreement had been worked out. Fred Fisher was a member of the firm and Welch, knowing McCarthy's tactics and what would be done by the committee, wanted to be assured that none of those who went with him, and he was the counsel for the Army, would have any questionable past. As it turns out, Fisher was a member of the National Lawyers Guild, a left-oriented legal organization when a student in law school. So it was decided that this matter would not be pursued. And essentially what McCarthy did, he broke that bargain.

It was to be a quid pro quo. Welch had agreed not to mention that Cohn had not been in the service.

That was part of the bargain and what he was doing unnecessarily was on TV besmirching the reputation of this individual who could not defend himself. That's what made that such a dramatic event. Beyond the fact that he violated the agreement.

This was a stake in the heart for McCarthy.

Oh, it was. It was a very dramatic event. And Welch played it to the hilt. I think that his expression of outrage was not simply theatrical. He had made the conscious decision to work out this agreement because he didn't want to have Fisher's name besmirched. And all of a sudden here it was. I think he felt outraged. He didn't have to act. That he played it to the extent he did, reflected his realization that this was a point to drive home and to raise doubts about McCarthy and his methods.

McCarthy was finished after that. He was later censured by the full Senate by a vote of 67 to 22.

That was in December of '54. There was a special committee that was established and reported back in September. But the vote on this report recommending the condemnation, the censure on two counts was delayed until December, and partly because McCarthyism was an effective issue for the Republicans, and Nixon was trying to play anti-communist politics, talking about the number of subversives, communist sympathizers during the first two years of the Eisenhower administration.

He died May 2, 1957. Of what did he die?

Cirrhosis of the liver. He really, after December '54, became a rather lonely figure in the Senate. People who rallied around him within the Senate, in his own party, came to consider him a pariah. The charges he made that commanded great attention before were essentially ignored. He tried to raise doubts about the Geneva Summit Conference in '55. Introduces a resolution which is ignored. And then, after '54, the Democrats regain control, and he doesn't have a committee chairmanship, so he doesn't have the base that he did in '53 and '54.

He wielded power from 1950-54—only four years. Hardly a day goes by that you don't hear about McCarthy or McCarthyism. How would you sum him up?

I don't think that the issue he championed was one that was serious for him. I don't think he believed that there was a serious internal security threat; that the Communists infiltrated Washington and shaped and controlled American foreign and national security policy. I don't think he believed that at any time. There was no evidence for that. This was an effective political tactic because it reflected the then very strong concern that the nation confronted an internal security threat.

Do you think he did any good?

No. I think that he did more harm than good. He sort of poisoned the political climate. There was a serious problem that derived from membership, belief, association; had a very chilling effect. The lesson I think people learned in the '50s: you don't join controversial causes, because it can come back to haunt you. So you played safe. And that's unfortunate. You don't think certain ideas, or at least express them publicly, because they might come back to haunt you.

So he added significantly to a degree of paranoia in the country.

Well, not he alone. Oh, he taps into that. There was that mood and he sort of personified it, which is why we call it McCarthyism. It comes from his name, but not that he was the sole practitioner.

ANN SPERBER

EDWARD R. MURROW

Edward R. Murrow was the dominant person in broadcast journalism in the '40s and '50s. His broadcasts from London during the blitz brought the war home to Americans. On March 9, 1954 he publicly attacked Joe McCarthy on his program "See It Now" and became a national hero.

On October 15, 1958, in a speech delivered before the Radio-Television News Directors Association, he attacked the broadcast industry as being complacent, too bottom-line oriented, and generally not caring for the public good. This effectively ended his career in broadcasting.

Ann Sperber wrote a biography on Murrow that took 12 years to complete. It was a finalist for a Pulitzer Prize.

When you think of Edward R. Murrow, you remember his live broadcasts of the war from Britain and his attack on Joseph McCarthy on his television program "See It Now." There was another episode though that occurred in October 1958 at the Blackstone Hotel in Chicago, Illinois, that changed his life forever. But first, he was instrumental in developing a permanent news staff in Europe for CBS Radio during the late '30s. This had never been done before.

It was the concept of linking various capitals. It simply had never been done on 24 or 48 hours notice. It was also a concept in which other people shared: William Paley and Paul White who was, for all intents and purposes, head of the news department and who had preceded Murrow's coming to CBS by several years. White was basically a shoe leather newsman, what they call an "ace reporter." Murrow had the international concept. Murrow was working to have a news staff just for radio. That was almost revolutionary in those days. It seems incredible for us to think a radio station or a network not to have its own reporters. But when Murrow came in, they did not.

March of 1938 you had the first "CBS Roundup" at the time of the Anschluss. You really have to think of how it was in 1935 when Murrow first came to CBS, when the entire news department, which wasn't even called a news department, it was called special events, consisted of something like seven people that included the secretaries. Bob Trout was their announcer. When they needed some kind of news report, they went out and got a newspaper person and paid them $50 or something to do the job. So when you had this "Roundup" in 1938, you had a quantum leap in news reporting and broadcasting.

You had Murrow in Vienna, Schirer in London, Gervasi in Rome. You had Pierre Huss in Berlin. The only people who actually worked for CBS were Murrow and Schirer, and they were not even supposed to be broadcasting.

That was really the beginning of the idea of having a news staff.

What Murrow was campaigning for was—we have to get our own people out there. Every time something happens, we can't go running to some newspaper.

His official title was "European Director." That was the title he had when he was sent to London in 1937, and it had been strictly an executive job. He was to set up broadcasts, maybe say a few words to introduce people and then let a "journalist" take over. "Journalist" meaning print reporter. Or maybe he'd do an interview with the Pope, or Mussolini. But he was essentially an executive. What happened in Vienna (the Anschluss), overnight he became a shoe leather reporter out there on the street getting the story. Giving the story over the air. These three days or so of reporting on the Anschluss in Vienna turned into weeks of reporting, literally, on what looked like the beginning of World War II.

After that he was back in London. H. V. Kaltenborn, who at that time was working for CBS, was in New York as the anchorman. Also, as the person who was expert on Germany, could give interpretations. He was sort of like Walter Cronkite with a historical perspective. Not saying that Cronkite doesn't have one, but Kaltenborn was a specialist in this area. He knew German. He could translate documents, etc.

Murrow came back to New York as he would every now and then, and he sat down with Paul White—probably Bill Paley, too, and a wonderful man who was the one who hired him, who, if anything, is like the grandfather of CBS news: a man named Ed Klauber. He was the one who decided Murrow ought to go to Europe and realized that this guy really had a good news sense.

They knew then and there that war was coming. If it wasn't at the time of Munich, it was nevertheless going to come, and they needed a staff to cover this. This is around Christmas, 1938. They weren't going to be given a whole lot of money to start hiring. Murrow hired Eric Sevareid in France. He hired Mary Marvin Breckinridge, who was probably the first woman to be hired as a network correspondent.

He was out to get good people. They had a few people in place by September 1939, when the Germans invaded Poland.

Murrow was stationed in Britain. He was sent to London in 1937. He remained there for nine years. He didn't go back to the United States until March of 1946.

What was his major contribution during the Battle of Britain?

I would say two things. The more obvious is that he raised American consciousness as to not only the precarious position of the last holdout (Britain) against the German military machine, but also these very powerful images of how war affected civilians. He got people off the idea of a battle field mentality, for want of a better word. Soldiers up against soldiers. By using metaphors he could give Americans an idea of what it was like to have something drop on their homes.

It was very effective.

Very effective, indeed. But the best thing about Murrow is that he did that while remaining an honest reporter. In other words, he was very anti-Nazi, very pro-Ally. However, he never concealed facts in his eagerness for a sympathetic American public. I'll give you one example:

Early in the war, after the fall of France, Winston Churchill said, "The Battle of France is over, the Battle of Britain is about to begin." From June 1940 until the London Blitz that September, the Germans were out to knock out the RAF. That air power, that control of the skies, was what was keeping them from invading Britain. Murrow would go around the south of England, which was the heaviest under attack because that was where the air bases were, and report. I remember one of his broadcasts from that time. Talking about a Luftwaffe attack on either a Navy or an RAF installation. He said, "From what I have seen, I am convinced that the Germans were after military targets." Then he talked about the attack on this installation and, that for security reasons, he was not allowed inside and could not report it. Therefore, he was confining his reports to the collateral civilian damage.

Of course, what he reported on was absolutely heartbreaking. He was talking about these bombs that might have been thrown against a military installation, but were also hitting the small cottages in the areas around. But he was making it very clear, even when it came to Hitler's Luftwaffe, he was being a good reporter. He was being fair. This was terrible devastation, but this was not planned.

This gave America an on-the-spot view of what was happening. We didn't have that in World War I.

The big swing in American sentiment was when the Nazis entered Paris. Those news photos of the Wermacht marching down the Champs de Elysses; that shocked a lot of people. Those pictures of the German troops going under the Arc de Triumph made a great many people say, "Hey, just a minute. This thing has gone a little too far."

March 9, 1954, Murrow attacked Joe McCarthy on his program "See It Now."

What happened was a newsman was stepping into the vacuum as far as McCarthy was concerned, and as far as the mass media were concerned. Murrow had been doing anti-McCarthy programs, but he had not done one on the man himself. He had been doing anti-McCarthy editorials on the radio, but this was a much more difficult thing to do.

They called it "A Report on Senator McCarthy." The heart of that program was his concluding editorial, the so-called "tail piece," when he said, "This is no time for those who oppose Senator McCarthy's methods to keep silent." That was the one and only time on television that you had somebody get up who was not, like Adlai Stevenson, a politician of the Democratic Party. But a person from the outside who could be called nonpartisan, who had tremendous prestige and was regarded as a war hero and was also regarded as a pretty much middle-of-the-road guy. I mean, liberal and so, but certainly no flaming radical and with no ties to the left, getting up and saying, "This man is bad for the country."

Somebody I know compared it to a boil being lanced because it was over the mass media, on commercial television, and by someone with immense credibility. There was a consensus supporting Murrow; it was as though a door had been opened. I went through the letters...there were something like 100,000 letters that came in the next day. Thousands and thousands of phone calls. And the amazing thing was that these letters had peoples names and addresses on them. That was the key. They weren't anonymous. People who were ready, in time of great fear, to step forward because there seemed to be that psychology: if Murrow can get up there, I guess I don't have anything to worry about.

He quoted in that broadcast from Shakespeare's Julius Caesar, *"The fault, dear Brutus, is not in our stars, but in ourselves."*

He said to his staff, no one can terrorize the country unless we are all his accomplices.

This was the beginning of the end for McCarthy, wasn't it?

Oh, absolutely.

The coup de grace occurred that spring at the Army-McCarthy Hearings when Joseph Welch drove the stake in his heart with the Fred Fisher speech.

Exactly.

I'll tell you something. I was a sophomore in college at the time, and I remember the impact of that program. It blew everybody's mind. The air was somehow lighter the next day, the way it is after an electric storm.

Now McCarthy, strangely enough, for some reason his timing was off—this was on Tuesday night—McCarthy didn't reply until Thursday. He let 48 hours go by where the program could do its work.

Interestingly enough, he didn't reply on television. He replied on the Mutual Broadcasting System, on Fulton Lewis, Jr.'s radio program.

This business about "extreme left wing elements..." Murrow, who obviously had been tipped off, came on about half an hour later on CBS Radio with his "Edward R. Murrow With the News," 7:45 P.M., and he made this wonderful rejoinder: "I may be a bleeding heart, but as for extreme left wing—something like that—that is political shorthand. But if the Senator means that I am to the left of his position, and that of Louis XIV, he's correct."

It was all over the place. Friday morning everybody had picked it up. And the idea of Joe McCarthy with his jowls and his 5 o'clock shadow and a great big Louis XIV wig. People were laughing. And the minute I heard that laughter, I thought, "He's had it." The minute people start laughing, the armor is gone.

The Radio-Television News Directors Association had a meeting on October 15, 1958 at the Blackstone Hotel in Chicago, Illinois. Murrow delivered a very damning speech, which he distributed to the higher-ups at CBS just before delivering it.

He began by saying, "This will probably do nobody any good," and everybody laughed. Here is a man who has two weekly television programs. By the way, "See It Now" had been canceled. That had been canceled that spring, and that certainly was one of the things that gave him impetus to write the speech.

But here is a man who is making hundreds of thousands of dollars a year. One of the highest paid men in America, his name on everybody's lips, gets up there and says television was a money-making machine, of decadence, escapism, and insulation from the realities of the world in which we live.

He said, "I can see no reason why the networks have to raise their profits each year less the republic collapse." Now that is a declaration of war. Not only that, he had this duplicated and sent to every radio and TV editor in the country with a release time. And just before he was to give that speech, he had things arranged so that his secretary would deliver it "upstairs." It was almost as though he were deliberately seeking to enrage them.

And it killed him.

Yes.

Why did he do it?

Good question. My feeling is...this is just a private feeling. There was in him a terrible anger and a terrible despair. He was worried about the world—that was always prime with him. In the speech, he talked about the delay of an important policy broadcast of Eisenhower and said that that delay was about the equivalent that it took for an ICBM to go from Russia to the United States...something like that. He was worried about the possibility of war. He felt that the network news departments had *regressed* in informing the public.

Do you know that in October of 1958 there wasn't a single half hour newscast on television?

It was lamentable and his own program ("See It Now"), which was the only one that was really looking into things, had been canceled the previous March. He knew that this was the result of political pressure. When his program was canceled, obviously over his protests, he had pretty much lost out at CBS. He was big on the screen, but within the company, he was no longer a power factor.

They buried him then. During the 1960 convention, CBS had him as a floor reporter.

It certainly wasn't good for his health. Murrow had always been working conventions. He even worked them as an executive back in 1936. But this is 1960, he's 50 years old. A floor reporter is a young person's game, and even then it is exhausting. And here was this man, who had come back early from his sabbatical. He looked like death warmed over. He had a horrible, hacking, cigarette cough. He was tired and they sent him out there to work the floor.

When did he leave CBS?

I believe in January of 1961.

Under what sort of circumstances?

Pretty bad circumstances. It was petering out.

Were he and Paley (chairman of the board of CBS) talking at that point?

They were talking, but it was all sort of on the surface. Paley told me that when Murrow got the invitation from Kennedy to head the USIA, he talked it over with Paley. Interestingly, Paley didn't say, "Oh, don't go. We'll offer you this or we'll offer you that." What Paley said, according to his own account was, "I don't think you should take it. However, if you do decide to take it, I'd have this condition and that condition...and you can have a job with us as long as you want." Well...

He got the point. How long was he with the United States Information Agency?

Roughly three years. He was not confirmed until about March or so of 1961. The FBI was holding up his confirmation. But he did start in January of '61. He resigned in January of '64. However, in late 1962 on his way to India, he stopped to visit their base in Tehran and collapsed and was rushed back to the United States for what was diagnosed as pneumonia, but was already lung cancer. It was only two years that he was really active and the rest of the time he was sort of in and out.

He died April 22, 1965 at the age of 57. What's his legacy?

I would say that of the responsibility of the broadcast news media.

A call to responsibility. You know, his last speech, which they pay very little attention to today, was to an executive's meeting. His last speech as a newsman at CBS. It was a kind of appeal to his colleagues to report the news honestly and fully. I would like to read it to you:

"There can be no real democracy unless the people understand the basic political, social and economic issues upon which their welfare depends. If a deceived or confused public is betrayed into creating, or allowing to be created, an America in which it loses faith, democracy will not survive. If the people finally come to believe, either that they cannot grasp, or that they cannot cope with America's problems, or that those who inform and those who act are inept or maligned or both, then distrust, dissatisfaction, fear and laziness can combine to turn to desperation to that strong man who can take them only to destruction."

ELMER BERNSTEIN

HOLLYWOOD IN THE '50s AND THE "BLACKLIST"

One of the truly great movie composers of all-time. He won an Academy Award for Thoroughly Modern Millie. *He has also written the music for movies such as,* The Magnificent Seven, The Man With the Golden Arm, The Ten Commandments, My Left Foot, *and many more.*

He began his Hollywood career in 1950. In 1955 he was investigated by the House Un-American Activities Committee regarding possible communist affiliation. This resulted in his being "graylisted—working, but not making much money. It took the intervention of Cecil B. DeMille with one of the most powerful men in America to get him "unlisted."

You came to Hollywood in 1950. It was in the last throes of the big studio era. What do you remember of that time?

I first came out here in August of 1950. At the time, the major studio apparatus was still in place. Harry Cohn was the head of Columbia, Jack Warner was the head of Warner Brothers, Louis B. Mayer of MGM, Zanuck was at Fox, and they still had contract players. In fact, after I did my first film for Sidney Buchman, who was then vice president of Columbia Pictures, the first thing Harry Cohn did was to offer me a seven-year contract; they still had those kinds of things. I very wisely turned it down. Wisely, because they were sort of chattel contracts, and I think independence was already in the air by 1950.

The studios were in some ways very comfortable places. They were quite grand. They had wonderful cottages for the stars. Wonderful offices for the people that worked there. They had tremendous backup because they were heavily staffed. Very heavily staffed, so that if you were a composer you had your office. You had a librarian to help you with anything you needed. All the materials. It was in many ways a very comfortable situation.

They were tough guys. Harry Cohn, Mayer, Warner.

All these people were sort of legendary to me. I remember the first time I ever saw Harry Cohn. I was having a meeting with my producer,

Sidney Buchman, who, as I say, was his vice president. I was coming up to the office and this rather large man was backing out of the office. I remember he had a huge red flower in his button hole and a jacket that looked like a horse blanket. He was backing out, absolutely purple with rage, and screaming at the top of his lungs. He said, "You're a thousand percent wrong!" That's the first time I'd heard that kind of mathematics. "You're a thousand percent wrong!" Backed out of the office and I walked in and I said, "Sidney, I presume that was Harry Cohn." He said, "Absolutely!"

I never met Louis B. Mayer, unfortunately. I did meet Jack Warner because I did a picture over there. He was a very, very colorful character. Harry Cohn wanted to entertain the public. Warner went a step further. He wanted to entertain the public, but he had some sense that he had some intellectual responsibility. He did, in fact, develop a studio full of pretty good writers. He did some fairly serious subjects. He was a very colorful character, who couldn't say a single sentence without a few four-letter words. A writer friend of mine told me this story about Warner:

He was at his house, at a party. It was a weekend, daytime, and he had his infant son with him who fell into the pool [and] as children will do sometime they don't fight if they're very young. They kind of sink. They jumped in and grabbed the kid out. Later on he ran into Jack Warner, and he said to him, "Oh, we had the most terrible time back there in the pool. The kid almost drowned." And Warner said to him, "Well, don't worry about it. We're insured."

Why did the big studio era die?

One of the things that hurt the studios was that the pioneer guys like Sam Goldwyn, Harry Cohn, and Jack Warner were just getting old. They'd had their great pioneering days. And quite honestly, I don't think they kept up with what was happening with the advent of television. Instead of realizing what an amazing tool television was going to be, they fought television all the way. Instead of absorbing it at that time into their command. Actually, television would have fit very well with the kind of setup they had there, the kind of assembly-line factory setup.

But in fighting television, they found that they had these vast studios with tremendous overhead. The number of pictures that they were making began to diminish because people began to watch television. They weren't going to the movies that much anymore. I think it was that lack of forward vision, the kind of vision that those people had in the '20s. By the time the '50s came along, they were old. They'd run out of vision.

In the early '50s, the House Un-American Activities Committee was the impetus behind the "blacklisting" in Hollywood. You were caught up in that.

Yes. I was personally caught up in it. I think one of the things that happened to everybody, on every level, was fear. It was a fascinating phenomenon, looking back at it now. At the time, I remember experiencing just the fear. Looking back at it now, it is amazing what fear these people were able to generate. I mean, 1952-53-54-55—we were less than 10 years away from Hitler. We had the Hitler example. We'd had all that. And yet, instead of laughing at them—because mostly they were clowns, you know, they were real clowns. I mean, it seems funny now, if you go back historically, imagining the communist threat the United States would have to worry about. It's a joke. They may have had to worry about the Soviet Union, that's different. But internally, it was a joke. Most of these guys were clowns. What they did do successfully was to instill fear. And that's what you really remember most from that period—fear. The kind of thing if somebody were named, as a Red, did you really want to associate with them? Did you want to be seen in public with them? They did do a very, very good job of that, I must say, and it really worked. But the reason it worked was that they were able to frighten the studio heads.

So it started at the top.

Started at the top. There used to be in every contract in those days, morals clauses. In the '20s, with the Fatty Arbuckle-Virginia Rapp thing, when movies began to get a reputation for being immoral and full of immoral people, they were very worried about public relations. They were very, very public relations-oriented, these studio heads. And they got this Czar, like baseball has. They got Will Hayes to make sure that everything was sanitized. So, the heads were very vulnerable to feelings of where the public was, so to speak. And they were afraid that these Un-American Activities people would convince them (the public) that Hollywood had a communist hue. So the studio heads were frightened into being sort of Mr. Clean.

You were "blacklisted."

I suppose my official status in those days—because there were fine gradations—I suppose I would have been "graylisted" actually, rather than "blacklisted." "Graylisted" was when they weren't sure you were actually a card-carrying member of the Communist Party, which I wasn't, but if they weren't sure, they wouldn't put you on a list where you couldn't work at all. I didn't realize I was being listed at all. But I suddenly realized I wasn't working. I began to get offers from producers like Al Zimbalist, who was making pictures like *Robot Monster* and *Cat Women of the Moon.* Finally I was doing things like *Robot Monster.* I got $800 to compose, orchestrate, and conduct. That was $800 for two months' work.

I don't remember exactly how I found out I was on any kind of list. I believe somebody in the Allied Artists' organization let it slip that I was in trouble. There was a guy called Mike Connelly. He was [with] the *Hollywood Reporter.* He was of Shirley MacLaine fame. He was the one that she crowned with the handbag one time. He carried an item in his column that I had been named, among others. He said, "So far, none of these people has come forward to either confirm or deny."

At the time that this happened, I was working for Cecil B. DeMille. He had engaged me to work on *The Ten Commandments.* DeMille called me into the office when it became public. I was very fond of him. I know he is a very controversial character. But he was so kind and so nice to me. And, semi-arguably, the most interesting person I ever worked for.

Anyway, he called me into the office and said, "Listen, I'm going to ask you a question that I have absolutely no right to ask you. But I'm going to ask it anyway." And he asked me, just straight across, was I a member of the Communist Party. Or, had I ever been a member of the Communist Party. I did not stand on my constitutional right to refuse to answer. I said, "No." Wherewith, he was obviously very, very well connected and took it upon himself not to clear me, because he couldn't do that. No one person could clear you, so to speak. He spoke to people in Washington. The attitude he took was, because I overheard the phone call, that he had spoken to me and in his opinion, he was satisfied that I was not a Communist. Subsequently, I was called before the House Un-American Subcommittee, but I daresay that without DeMille's intervention in this matter, things probably would have gone in a much more difficult manner for me.

I was lucky that by the time I was called there had been the censure of McCarthy, and they were having to be much more careful. This was 1955, and they had to be much, much more careful. They kept asking me whether somebody I knew was a Communist. And I would say the only way I could know if anybody was a Communist was if they told me they were a Communist. So, you see, that was already inadmissible. They wouldn't allow evidence like that because that was third-person testimony. And obviously, if I weren't at a Communist Party meeting, I couldn't identify anybody as a Communist.

I was just lucky, the timing was a bit lucky. Also, I think DeMille's help had a lot to do with it.

Were there many people hurt by the "blacklisting" or was it selective?

I think a lot of people were injured. They were injured in their souls. I believe there were a couple of suicides. Illnesses, people whose lives were never the same. That never recovered their composure or their sense of well-being. Yes, I think there was pretty broad injury to people.

Do you think we'll ever see that again?

Well, it doesn't seem likely, except in one sense. That sort of activity seems to be, unfortunately, part of the dark side of human nature. In that sense, it seems to address itself to something that people like to do. We might see it again. For one thing, there is no communist threat in the world right now. So, I don't know what kind of threat they might get up. But there's enough racial strife around now. There are enough issues which could eventually develop into a situation where one segment of society decided that it wanted to protect itself in that way.

IV

Unforgettable…

DAN PETERSON

THE 1950s

Many people believe the '50s were put on cruise control and was a lack-luster decade. Dan Peterson does not agree. He feels it was a decade of profound importance and a great time to grow up.

Dan Peterson grew up in Evanston, Illinois. After coaching basketball in the United States, he became one of Europe's most successful coaches. He has written numerous books and articles and resides in Milan, Italy.

Growing up in the '50s? Before I can talk about that, I have to set the record straight: the misconception that the '50s were the "silent generation." Silent? More noise happened in those 10 years than any other decade in my lifetime. At the same time, this will establish the context in which we grew up. Two birds with one stone.

Why don't we start with sports? Isn't that a common ground for most people? Well, in the '50s, the face of baseball changed forever: the Braves went from Boston to Milwaukee in 1953, the St. Louis Browns became the Baltimore Orioles in 1954, the A's went from Philadelphia to Kansas City in 1955, the Dodgers and Giants went to L.A. and San Francisco in 1958.

If that's not enough "noise," what about major events? They say Babe Ruth called his home run in 1932, but we have no evidence of that gesture. We *do* have proof, right there on films and videotape, of five of the biggest "happenings" in sports history, moments that lifted those sports into another dimension, even in the case of baseball. Let another decade try to top these:

There was Bobby Thomson's "Shot Heard Round The World" in the 1951 NL Playoff, Willie Mays' "Greatest Catch" in the 1954 World Series, Don Larsen's "Perfect Game" in the 1956 World Series, the Boston Celtics' two overtime, at-the-buzzer win in the seventh game of the 1957 NBA Playoffs, and the Baltimore Colts' 23-17 OT win over the New York Giants in the 1957 NFL final.

I'll run the risk of sounding nostalgic here, but I happen to think the athletes and teams of the '50s were vastly more exciting than the teams of any other decade, high fives and sack dances notwithstanding. Actually, there's a sound reason for this: this was the decade the black athlete emerged to dominate team sports and change forever the way they are played.

Take hockey, though it has no black players. I'd love to see an All-Star team from the '80s and '90s, Wayne Gretzky and all, play a team from the '50s, coached by Toe Blake, with Jacques Plante in goal, Red Kelly and Doug Harvey on defense, and with a front line of Jean Beliveau, "Boom Boom" Geoffrion, and the name that ends all arguments on this subject—Gordie Howe.

Take basketball. I agree that it's virtually impossible to compare teams from one generation and another, and that today's athletes are bigger, faster, and stronger. Sure, it's nonsense to try to say who would have won. As Julius Erving said, "Their highlights are in black and white, ours in color." But, let's put Dr. J. with Kareem, Magic, Larry, and Michael and play a game.

Their opponents are my team of the '50s. Red Auerbach is the coach. The centers are Bill Russell and Wilt Chamberlain. Power forwards: Bob Pettit and Dolph Schayes. Small forwards: Elgin Baylor and Tom Gola. Shooting guards: Oscar Robertson and Bill Sharman. Playmakers: Jerry West and Bob Cousy. I think the '80s gang would have a game on their hands.

Take football. Put together a team of the '80s, with Bill Walsh as the coach, Joe Montana at QB, Walter Payton at RB, Jerry Rice at WR, Lawrence Taylor at LB, and what have you. Yes, they'd be favored against a '50s team, but let's play this game in our dreams. The '50s have Hall of Famers, guys voted best all-time at their sports, players of the ultimate in excitement.

Coach: Paul Brown (No. 1). QBs: Johnny Unitas (No. 1) and Otto Graham. RB: Jim Brown (No. 1), Marion Motley, Lenny Moore. All-purpose: Frank Gifford, Kyle Rote, Doak Walker. OG: Jim Parker. TE: Leon Hart, and I'd like to see some CB today stop him after he takes a five-yard slant-in. WR: Tom Fears, voted the best clutch receiver ever. Yes, the '50s would have offense.

Defense? I'd love to see someone try to turn the corner on DE Doug Atkins or try the middle against DT "Big Daddy" Lipscomb. I'd love to see Joe Montana try to "look away" LBs like Ray Nitschke, Sam Huff, and Joe Schmidt. I'd like to see Jerry Rice run a post against "Night Train" Lane. And I'd love to see them punt to Jack Christensen.

Football changed dramatically in the '50s and those modifications are still the blueprint for football as it's played today: the Eagle Defense, the Flex Defense, the Multiple Offense, the Wing-T Formation, the I-Formation, the Play-Action Pass, the Hurry-Up Huddle, Specialty Teams, the Messenger System, and too many other innovations to list here.

Take baseball. Let's forget, for a moment, that baseball today is a joke, that a guy is a superstar if he hits 40 HRs while striking out 160 times, that guys today can't run the bases, slide, hit the cutoff man, pick up signs, hit behind the runner, cover or back up bases, and all of the things that made baseball a thing of beauty in the '50s.

Let's let the '80s play the '50s. Let Tony LaRussa be the manager of so-called superstars like Darryl Strawberry and Jose Canseco. Let him go to the mound and try to talk sense to Roger Clemens. Here there is no argument: the '50s would sweep the '80s 4-0 in any series. Not only that, I fear the games would be out of hand by the fifth inning, runaway routs.

Manager of the '50s team is Casey Stengel. Catcher: we'll platoon Yogi Berra and Roy Campanella. lb: Stan Musial (four batting titles in the '50s). 2b: Jackie Robinson (four pennants in the '50s), who guarantees the victory. Ss: Luis Apariclo (Ernie Banks sits out). 3b: Eddie Mathews. OF: Hank Aaron, Willie Mays, and Mickey Mantle (Duke Snider can pinch hit).

The pitching staff: Warren Spahn, Whitey Ford, Early Wynn, and Robin Roberts. Long relief: Jim Konstanty or Joe Black. And, should Casey want to close out the ninth by striking out the side, he can come in with "The Big Chief," Allie Reynolds. So, I'm sorry for the '80s in this case, but they couldn't carry the collective jocks of this most exciting team.

Let's take golf. Let's have a sort of Ryder Cup between generations of American golfers. Let's put the '80s and '90s group, with their perfect little "repeating swings,' and very little else, against the competitors we had in the '50s. The '80s wouldn't even tee off against Dr. Cary Middlecoff, "Slammin" Sammy Snead, and the all-timer, Ben Hogan.

What about boxing? What about an Olympics-style dual meet: '50s vs. '80s and '90s? It might be a clean sweep for the '50s! Yes, Muhammad Ali might beat Rocky Marciano, but only if it goes 15. If not, forget it. Most of all, I'd like to see "Sugar Ray" Leonard of the '80s go up against the greatest, pound for pound, of all time: "Sugar Ray" Robinson.

What about sports journalism? Let's forget, for a moment, the great sportswriters of the '50s, like Jimmy Cannon, Stanley Woodward, and Red Smith, because I like today's writers, too. Let's talk about *Sports Illustrated*, which was born in 1954. Sports reporting has never been the same since!

Let's leave sports and go to world events. What about the Korean War? The cold war? The Cuban Revolution? Sputnik, which changed the earth and space forever? Events on TV? Today we have Clarence Thomas in front of the Senate. What a bore. In the '50s, we had the Kefauver hearings on organized crime and the McCarthy hearings on Un-American Activities. Wild!

Did I mention television? Name one thing that has had more of an impact on America than TV! Nothing comes close. Nothing is even on the same *planet*! In 1949, TV was a novelty and few homes had one. By 1959, it dominated the life of every family in the U.S.A., and there were few homes that didn't have at least one TV set, and many had two or three!

Of course, TV in the '50s was so exciting compared to what we have today, that there is almost no point in explaining why. Reruns of the '50s dominate cable TV, while '90s programming is taking the major networks to the poorhouse. Silent? TV made noise in the '50s that is still being heard today!

Programs? "See It Now." "The Honeymooners." "Gunsmoke." "Dragnet." "Victory at Sea." "Playhouse 90." "Your Show of Shows." "Toast of the Town." "The Twilight Zone." "The Colgate Comedy Hour." "Perry Mason." "The Untouchables." "Maverick." "Crusade in Europe." "Captain Kangaroo." "I Love Lucy." "American Bandstand." "The Tonight Show." Can you name me one program today that is remotely comparable to those?

Personalities? Walter Cronkite. Sid Caesar and Imogene Coca. Dean Martin and Jerry Lewis. Jack Benny. Jack Paar. Steve Allen. Dick Clark. Jackie Gleason. Edward R. Murrow. Alfred Hitchcock. Ed Sullivan. And I'll close out with the name that kicks the tail of any person TV would like to propose today: Lucille Ball.

TV was the overall dominator of the '50s, but the vehicle that was predominant to those of us that were young in the '50s was music. To be specific: Rock 'n' Roll. It's so hard to explain this to youngsters today but there was a time, before 1954, when Rock 'n' Roll didn't exist.

Hey, even into the '50s, we were listening to ballads, folks songs, and other stuff like that. You know, like "I'd love to get you on a slow boat to China." That was enough to put you to sleep, understand? Then, the next day, it's "One, two, three O'Clock, four O'Clock rock; Five, six, seven O'Clock, eight O'Clock rock. We're gonna rock..."

How can you describe that to some kid today? You can't. It was like giant hands had grabbed all of us by the lapels and jerked us out of our chairs and thrown us into the air. No one had to *explain* Rock to us. We *understood*, instantly. We'd been waiting for this all our lives. When it came, we needed no encouragement. We were ready.

I can recall the exact moment when I *knew*. It was 1954. It was while I was watching the movie that defined our generation, *The Blackboard Jungle*. It was when Sidney Poitier stepped off the curb and into the street at the end of the film, and the first rim shot of "Rock Around the Clock" sounded. I was on my feet. I'd never felt anything like it.

I'm going to digress for one moment here. I mentioned movies. I'm not sure the '50s were the greatest decade for films, but I'll put our best against any other 10-year span: Marlon Brando, William Holden, and so forth. And, we had the only two cult-myth-legends that have lasted, that dwarf all others: James Dean and Marilyn Monroe. End of discussion!

Coming back to music, the '50s defined our generation and were the opening of a frontier that will never be closed. Names? Giants, every one: Chuck Berry, Eddie Cochran, Fats Domino, Jerry Lee Lewis, Carl Perkins, Bo Diddley, The Big Bopper, Ritchie Valens, Buddy Holly (the last three went down "The Day the Music Died," but they'll never die).

I laugh when I see Michael Jackson compared to Little Richard. Yes, Michael Jackson has made more money and sold more records but I am sorry, it's no contest. Little Richard was the *original*, a vastly superior talent, and he had the greatest road band ever, the mighty Upsetters. What song by Michael Jackson compares with any of the top 10 by Little Richard?

Music today is amplification, technology, lip-synching. Music in the '50s was originality, message, soul, and, most of all, *energy*. Well, no point in going on about this, as I only have to mention one name and any possible doubt on this point just disappears. I'm talking about the King himself, our Main Man of the '50s, a legend today: Elvis Presley.

It's the same with any genre of music. In every instance, I can KO any argument with one name. After that, the conversation is over. Let's take female jazz singers. I mean, anyone want to try to equal the likes of Peggy Lee, Lena Horne, Dinah Washington, or Pearl Bailey? Fine, I'll now bring out my "cleanup hitter," the tops, Ella Fitzgerald.

What about male jazz singers? First of all, Joe Williams blows away anyone in any other generation. But, in case there is a doubt or two, here's the "closer," the "Chairman of the Board" himself: Frank Sinatra. Jazz bands? Do they still have those today? We did in the '50s, and we saw them: Duke Ellington, Earl "Fatha" Hines, and himself, Count Basie.

Want to talk about country music? Let's forget that the Grand Ole Opry was in Ryman Auditorium back then. Let's not even talk about Bob Wills, Hank Thompson, Ernest Tubb, or the great Johnny Horton. Let's just anesthetize any possible resistance with the unchallenged number one of all time of country music: the legendary Hank Williams.

Let's forget sports and entertainment. What about politics? I'm sorry, but I've seen our senators on TV and, their beautiful makeup notwithstanding, I'll stick with the senators of the '50s: Lyndon Johnson, Estes Kefauver, Everett Dirksen, and a slew of others. Presidents? Please! I'll take the man who said, "The Buck Stops Here," Harry S. Truman!

Well, I didn't mean to go on a "nostalgia" trip here. I started out saying that I'd talk about growing up in the '50s. Hey, this *was* growing up in the '50s. Every time you saw a sports event, or a TV show, or read a newspaper, you just knew you were in touch with something great, that those athletes, entertainers, and what have you were the best ever.

The "Silent Generation?" Does that mean we didn't have problems like AIDS, herpes, drugs, and the rest of the troubles of today's society? If so, then I'll take the world the way it was when I was growing up. Were we silent because we didn't protest? Hey, there was nothing to protest about. We were even selling Chevrolets in Tokyo and Berlin!

Well, you can't go back in life. The '50s have come and gone like the Big Bang. And that's what it was: an explosion every day! Ten years of across-the-board greatness. 3,652 days of "happenings" and every one an experience in itself. I enjoyed every one of them. I wouldn't have grown up in any other time.

Bobby Thomson

"The Shot Heard Round the World"

On August 11, 1951, Robin Roberts of the Philadelphia Phillies beat the New York Giants, 4-0, dropping them 13½ games behind the Brooklyn Dodgers. From this point to the end of the National League season, the Giants won 39 out of 47 games. They tied Brooklyn for the pennant and went to a three-game play-off. They split the first two games. Game three saw the Giants down, 4-1, going into the bottom of the ninth.

"Branca throws....there's a long drive! It's going to be, I believe! The Giants win the pennant! The Giants win the pennant! The Giants win the pennant! The Giants win the pennant! Bobby Thomson hits into the lower deck of the left-field stands! The Giants win the pennant! And they're going crazy! They're going crazy! Oh-ho...I don't believe it! I don't believe it! I do not believe it!"—Russ Hodges, October 3, 1951.

Truly, "the stuff that dreams are made of."

On August 11, 1951, the New York Giants were 13½ games out of first place. What was the feeling on the team at that point?

We hadn't given up, certainly. Not with Leo Durocher at the helm. We showed up, put on our suits every day, and went out to play ball. We weren't too happy being that far behind, because at the start of the season we had higher hopes for ourselves. We kept showing up, and, of course, if you played for Durocher, you better be ready to play. There was no quitting.

On August 12, 1951, you started a 16-game winning streak and went on to win 39 of your last 47 games. That is .830 baseball. How were the Dodgers playing during that stretch?

Aside from our tremendous streak, they lost their share of ball games. If they played better than .500, I don't think it was much over that. So, we needed them to lose their share.

When did you tie Brooklyn?

It became tied that last weekend, on a Friday night. We were a half game behind the Dodgers, and they had three games with Philadelphia —Friday, Saturday, and Sunday. We were up in Boston to play Saturday and Sunday. The Dodgers lost to Philadelphia on Friday night. I went to bed that night, and I think my roommate, Whitey Lockman, and I must have felt the pressure because we didn't have the best night's sleep. I remember waking up Saturday morning, and we didn't even look at each other. We came down in the elevator, got in the lobby, and the place was full of people. Finally, I remember our eyes met across the breakfast table and we both burst out laughing. We really didn't feel a thing until we tied. You know, when you're behind, you're under a certain amount of pressure, but the real pressure to me is on the frontrunners.

It was down to two games. They won Saturday, so did we. Then we won our game on Sunday and we were in the clubhouse and the Dodgers were losing. The Dodgers were losing by quite a few runs it seemed to me—around the sixth inning or so. When we got on the train headed for New York late that afternoon, we thought we were the winners. We found out when we got off the train the Dodgers had won. I guess Jackie Robinson had played the game of his life, making a great play to save the game...to keep it tied in the last of the ninth. Then he won it with a home run in extra innings. I'll tell you, the bottom just dropped out for us. At least it did for me. 'Cause I didn't look forward to playing those guys.

The Giants won the first game of the three-game play-off, 3-1.

We were losing 1-0, and I hit a home run with a man on base, something like the fourth inning, and then Monty Irvin hit a home run later, so we won, 3-1. That was against Branca.

Game two, Brooklyn beat you, 10-0.

We moved over to the Polo Grounds and Clem Labine—we just couldn't do anything with him, and I think the closest we came was when I got up to bat with the bases loaded and he struck me out.

Now the third and final game. It's the bottom of the ninth and you are behind, 4-1. Newcombe gave up a single to Dark and then a single to Don Mueller. Lockman doubled, scoring Dark, so the score was now 4-2. Hodges was not playing off the bag as he should have with a three-run lead when Mueller hit the ball. It was a ground single to right.

Dark's base hit was just a groundball right through the middle. You know, just out of the reach of everybody. And Mueller's was the same thing. A groundball to right which Hodges dove for and just missed by less than a foot. He was playing on the bag.

If he had been playing off the bag, it would have been a double play and you wouldn't have gotten to bat.

We would have been dead. That's just the way I felt going into the dugout the end of the ninth inning because Newcombe had looked so good in the eighth inning. And I thought, "Heck, I'm the fifth hitter. I'm dead. I won't even have a chance."

You got up to bat.

When Lockman doubled to left and scored a run, Mueller went into third and hurt his ankle severely and it stopped the game. Mueller's lying on the ground and he's hurt. He's in pain. I'm down there with a bat in my hand and a great concern about him. It took my mind right off the game. Just for a few minutes. It wasn't until they carried Don off the field on a stretcher that I said it's time to go to work again.

I remember when I walked to home plate. I never approached home plate from third before. I must have realized that I was on the spot because I started to talk to myself, "Get up there and give yourself a chance to hit. Do a good job. Wait and watch. Wait and watch." And all the time I'm calling myself a S.O.B. Now, I'd never done that before in my life. First of all, I don't know if the word is "numb," where you're going through the motions. Looking back at it, it seemed to me you just followed your instincts. You're a ballplayer and you know what you have to do. And that's what I did. I just kept telling myself, "Wait and watch. Don't get over anxious. Do a good job, you S.O.B. Give yourself a chance to hit."

As I'm walking back to home plate, all of a sudden I realize Newcombe's not the pitcher. Branca's on the mound. And it didn't phase me one way or another. I just got in the box, waiting and watching him.

Jeez, if he doesn't throw the first pitch right through the middle. I was waiting and watching too damn much. The guys later told me—the guys on the bench—they wanted to kill me for taking a pitch right down the middle. Now, Ralph...his idea, I guess, was to come inside with a fastball and then make me hit a breaking ball away. But he got it inside and it was a bad ball, but it wasn't bad enough for me not to get around on it. I was quick with my hands. I was hitting the ball pretty well. I got a glimpse of it and I jumped on it. It was a fastball inside.

So he threw you two fastballs?

Yeah. The idea is to get ahead of the hitter, and, of course, Branca was brought up by Durocher and that was Durocher's way. Get ahead of the hitter.

Did he have good stuff or couldn't you tell with two pitches?

Oh, I don't know. I think he did, otherwise they wouldn't have brought him in. They felt he had good stuff, and he said he felt good and was throwing well in the bullpen. Heck, it was just one of those things. A lot of times they don't give the hitter credit. The pitcher made a bad pitch or...you take your pick.

What was your feeling when you hit it?

I thought I had a home run. I made good contact, and I saw it take off, and I thought "home run." I've never hit a ball like that in my life before because it started up in the upper deck, but then had tremendous overspin. I obviously got a little bit on top of it. It started to sink and, when I saw it start to sink, I thought, "It's not a home run. It's a base hit." But then it didn't take long for it to disappear because I hit it pretty well. I was halfway down to first base, then that was it.

I was kind of hyperventilating running around the bases. I wasn't running my normal home run trot. I felt like I was prancing around the bases. I've never experienced excitement like that before in my life.

Running around the bases, all I remember is, as I got to third, Durocher kind of reached out for me and I just casually pushed past him. I guess Stanky by that time was coming out and grabbing him.

I remember hitting home plate. All the guys were there waiting for me. I took one last leap—I didn't run across it, just one last jump on it. We're all heading to the locker room, and the next thing I knew Lockman's got me up on his shoulders and we're heading out to center field. And, of course, the people started to crowd around. That went on for a bit and, finally, Whitey thought we'd better forget this stuff and get in the locker room.

After all these years, do you still think about it?

No, not really. I've had more to do than sit around and think about hitting a home run. I've become more aware of it for many reasons. Leroy Neiman did a painting of it, and they sold them through the United Way in conjunction with the New York Mets to raise money for the homeless kids in New York. I walk into my own golf club, and they've got the painting with a beautiful frame sitting there in the lobby of the golf club. So you can't really get away from it.

Many think it is one of the greatest accomplishments in American sports history.

Well, that's awfully nice. It's not up to me to judge. It's for you and everybody else. I'm just amazed that I've had all this attention. But it's only come in the last five or six years, it seems to me. I don't know, everything has gotten so commercial. Of course, the 40th anniversary (of the home run) just amazed me. The attention Ralph and I got.

Do you see Ralph Branca?

We get together once in a while. We've become friends and we've gotten to know each other.

After baseball, I had to get a job and go to work, and bring up my family, and just become an ordinary citizen. Got involved, you know. Always like to think of myself as having been brought up being responsible. I've gotten involved in my community just like any normal human being does. I consider myself lucky to still be remembered for having my day in the sun.

STEPHEN AMBROSE

THE EISENHOWER PRESIDENCY

One of the foremost authorities on President Eisenhower, Stephen Ambrose spent hundreds of hours interviewing and talking with Ike. He has written several books on him.

He believes Eisenhower was one of the great presidents of the 20th century. He states: "I think overall the '50s was the best decade of the 20th century, and I think that having Eisenhower as president had a lot to do with that."

President Eisenhower brought more personal resources to the presidency than any president in the 20th century. Do you think he lived up to his potential?

Yes, I think Eisenhower lived up to his potential. He gave us eight years of peace. Eight years of stability. Eight years of economic advance. Balanced the budget three times. He had two minor recessions. I think overall the '50s was the best decade of the 20th century, and I think that having Eisenhower as president had a lot to do with that.

Ike gave a campaign speech in Milwaukee in the fall of 1952. He deleted praise for George Marshall because Joe McCarthy was attending. McCarthy had attacked Marshall previously. He was criticized for that.

I'm critical of him on that. There is an explanation, but it's not a very good one. Governor Kohler had come down to see him in Chicago and had an advance copy of the text. He said, "Ike, you know Joe is going to be on the platform. You can't really just hurl this..." He didn't mention McCarthy in the paragraph. He did talk about what a great man Marshall was.

Ike agreed to pull the paragraph. But unknown to him, the press already had an advance copy of the speech, so the pull was noticed and widely commented on. He probably was more severely criticized for that than anything else in that campaign, and almost for anything in his political life, and I'm one of the critics.

Kohler told him, "Listen, we lost Wisconsin to Harry Truman in '48.

We could lose in '52." And Eisenhower, once he got into that battle, wanted to win. Once the bug bites these guys that they want to be president, as Mr. Bush said, "I'll do anything." But it was not Ike's best moment. Let me put it more than that. As politicking, it was his worst moment.

Did he want Nixon on the ticket?

Well, not as a person so much. He didn't know Nixon. He had met him only briefly for a handshake a couple of times. He wanted what Nixon represented. Youth, vigor, the West Coast, a Republican of the right wing who was a supporter of the Marshall Plan and of the North Atlantic Treaty Organization. Someone who was at least acceptable to the McCarthy-ites and he was not that far from being a McCarthy-ite himself, thanks to the Alger Hiss business. Nixon brought a lot of strength to the ticket. But there was nothing personal about it. It wasn't that Ike had met Nixon and been impressed by him. Because he hadn't. He wasn't impressed or not impressed—he hadn't met him.

Should Eisenhower have rebuked McCarthy early in his administration? He left McCarthy alone.

Yes, I think it's a place where he did not exercise the kind of vigorous leadership the situation demanded. He read it differently than I do. In the first place, he agreed with some of what McCarthy was saying, if not with his methods. In the second place, McCarthy had a very strong hold on the right wing of the Republican Party, and Eisenhower needed the whole party behind him to get going with his administration and was not looking for a fight within the Republican Party.

There were other political factors at work, and he was convinced that eventually McCarthy would hang himself. And he did want to make an effort to try to get along with McCarthy. That didn't work out, obviously, as McCarthy took off after the Army. And eventually, McCarthy did hang himself. McCarthy brought himself down, and there was precious little that President Eisenhower did to bring that about.

On civil rights, would you describe Ike as correct, but not on the "cutting edge," not a "ground breaker." Regarding Brown vs. The Board of Education *in May 1954, he said, "that's the law. We will enforce it."*

Well, he certainly was not on the "cutting edge." He was very reluctant about desegregation. He feared the consequences in the South.

He feared that public education in the South would be all but abandoned. He thought it was a mistake to put the burden of integration or desegregation on the schools, which are the most vulnerable institutions in our society. Whether things could have worked differently had he taken a vigorous and forthright leadership stance as Lyndon Johnson ultimately did—Kennedy didn't. It was not until Lyndon Johnson that we had a president who was committed to vigorous leadership.

Whether Ike would have done it given who he was and the respect that he had, if things would have turned out any differently, we can't tell. He did not put a great effort into it.

As a Yankee who's lived in the South all my adult life, and who came down here feeling that I was going to participate in a great historic change and play a role in it, I must say it's been the greatest disappointment of my life. Integration has not worked in the South. It hasn't worked in the nation. We're more segregated in many ways today than we were in 1954. And we're more divided racially in many ways.

The city of New Orleans—98 percent of the public schools are black. That's de facto segregation, and now the black leadership in America don't want to integrate at the higher education level. They want their own black colleges and universities.

So, these aren't simple subjects. Anyway, back to your point—no, he did not take a strong role.

Did he tell the North Korean government in 1953 to end the war or he was prepared to use the atom bomb?

No. What he did do was to have Secretary Dulles tell the Indian leader, Nehru, to tell his friends in China that if the Chinese did not agree to a reasonable settlement—that's the key to the thing, that the Americans were offering a reasonable settlement—the United States would not feel constrained in its use of force. Now that could have meant atomic weapons. That could have meant an attempt to drive to the Yalu on the ground. It could have meant stepped up air conventional bombardment. It could have meant all three of those. But he did not make an explicit threat to use atomic weapons.

On the other hand, the Chinese knew that he had atomic weapons. The Chinese knew that seven years earlier he had not hesitated to use every weapon in his arsenal against the Germans. He was, after all, General Eisenhower. But no, there was never an explicit threat.

You mentioned earlier, and I think this is overlooked, that Ike did an excellent job with the economy. The gross national product was 20 percent higher when he left office than when he came to office.

Real wages were very much higher, there was no inflation. Real wages went up faster in the '50s than any other decade of the century.

In fact, inflation averaged only 1.4 percent yearly. As you said, he had a budget surplus three out of eight years and we have had only one surplus since. Why isn't he given credit for the economic growth of the '50s?

He inaugurated the biggest public works project of our time. Actually, two of them. The St. Lawrence Seaway, as well as the Interstate Highway System. I'd like to point out that the Republican Party is the successor to the Whig Party, and Henry Clay's big thing in the Whig Party was internal improvements that the states couldn't do for themselves ought to fall to the federal government. Ike did it beyond anybody else. We built this national highway system in the '50s, and we've ignored it ever since. We use it, and it's been a tremendous benefit, but ignored keeping it up.

The highway system was a great, great thing. It wouldn't be right to say that without Ike we wouldn't have it today. But he did it; he's the one who introduced it. He's the one who put it through and drove it through.

For the rest, you're absolutely right. Why he doesn't get credit for the economic success of the '50s, I don't know.

On foreign policy, he stayed out of Vietnam. The French tried to get him involved. He got us out of Korea. The only foreign policy failure, if you want to call it that, was the Suez crisis in November of '56. Some historians say he should have persuaded the British, French, and Israelis not to attack Egypt. How do you rate the eight years of his foreign policy?

Oh, a triumph. As you say, he kept us out of wars that were unwinnable. I think in Suez he had the right policy. There was no way he could have stopped the British, Israelis, and French. It came as a surprise to him when they moved, and he moved quickly to get them out.

The argument is more the other way. Nixon has said that he (Ike) only regretted that he didn't support the British in Suez. I don't know where Nixon got that idea. Ike never told me that. He said the opposite. He was very proud of that.

He got us through all kinds of crises during the toughest, hottest decade of the cold war without ever having to go to war, and without losing any territory. And, meanwhile, kept the cost of defense down. The expenditures were very heavy, but far below what they had been when he came into office. Of course, he shut down a war and that helped a lot. They were far below what his critics, who were Democrats more than Republicans, wanted to be spending.

Did he suspect that Castro was a Communist?

Not at first. They came to that conclusion, but that was true of almost everybody, and remember Castro was denying that he was a Communist. Castro had a very favorable press in the United States initially—it didn't last very long.

Eisenhower was willing to try to work with Castro. He recognized that there were some Cuban complaints about Batista that were quite legitimate. But after Castro had started executions, and had started driving liberals out of his government and started imposing a dictatorship on Cuba, Eisenhower quickly came to see that he was a Communist.

When he left office, what were his feelings regarding Kennedy? Did he respect Kennedy?

No. He thought Kennedy was too young, too inexperienced, too ruthless, too amoral, and he was very much afraid of Joe Kennedy establishing a dynasty and running the country.

He was really concerned?

Very much so. The men that I interviewed from that generation, without exception, feared and despised Joe Kennedy.

How would you rate Eisenhower as a president?

I think that he was one of the three great presidents of the 20th century. The other two being Democrats—Wilson and Roosevelt. Maybe one of four great. Eisenhower is one of two great Republican presidents—Teddy Roosevelt and Eisenhower.

Do you believe as time passes that history will agree with you?

Oh, I see it happening already, and will continue to happen.

Was he the last man of character we had as president? We've had some sorry things happen.

Yeah, we sure have had. It's remarkable to think the big scandal in the Eisenhower administration was that his chief of staff, Sherman Adams, took a fur coat. That was *the* big scandal. You compare it to the scandals that have come since. But, I don't know, comparisons are odious.

Eisenhower was a great man, and we've not had a great president since.

ART DONOVAN

PRO FOOTBALL IN THE '50s AND EARLY '60s

Art was a defensive left tackle for the Baltimore Colts from 1950 to 1962. He played before television became a big factor in the game. His starting salary was $4,500, and his last year $22,000. He was all-pro and played in what many consider the most exciting football game ever: the 1958 championship between Baltimore and the New York Giants. He is also very funny.

I started with a new team that came from the All-American Conference. The Colts were in the All-American Conference from '46 through '49 and the two leagues merged and I started with Baltimore in '50.

The first morning we went to practice there were about 125 guys on the field. There wasn't enough equipment to go around. So myself and two others guys don't take any equipment and by elimination we made the team.

Then the exhibition games started and we looked pretty good. We looked better than what they had. We made the ball club.

How did they treat rookies back then?

They didn't treat us any different. They were as bad as we were.

We had a coach named Clem Crow, who had to be crazy. He was from Notre Dame. He had coached the Buffalo Bills in the All-American Conference. He came to Baltimore in 1950. I guarantee you, he was somethin' else. WHOOOO! All we did morning and afternoon was scrimmage. We hit all the time we were out on the field.

I made $4,500. Guy named Sisto Laverno, who played both ways, he was paid $4,000. We were embarrassed. He played offense and defense and only made $4,000.

The 1958 championship game between Baltimore and the New York Giants is called by many the most exciting football game ever played. What do you remember of that game?

I remember we should have beat the Giants by four touchdowns. And they still think they should have won. We were a much better football team, and we got behind. On the sidelines, near the end of the game, while we were fighting for our life, I said to Marchaetti, "God damn it, Gino. If we lose this game, this has got to be the worst disgrace that ever happened." We were lucky enough to win. I mean we were lucky.

We had John Unitas, and John Unitas was John Unitas. We were a better football team than the Giants, and here we are just trying to survive.

Today you see pro players spiking balls, doing dances. How would players of your era reacted to this?

They'd say, "What the hell are you doing." You know who started all this "BS" was Big Daddy Lipscombe. We'd be in a pile, or making a tackle, and he'd pick the opposing team player up. I'd say, "Hey, don't pick 'em up if we just knocked 'em down. Let him use his own energy." The coaches didn't say anything. They were afraid of him. From there it really got bad. To me, an old player, it's embarrassing that these guys act like they do. I want to throw up. Period.

Why do the coaches allow it?

I don't know. Maybe they don't have any backbone. Maybe the owners don't have any backbone. Maybe the general manager. I don't know. But they let them do it. Maybe the commissioner ought to step in and say, "Hey—enough is enough." With the dances and all that...it's sickening.

Who was the best ballplayer you ever played against or with?

Unitas. I'd have to say he's the No. 1 football player of all time. He's the best quarterback. He's the guy that was the catalyst of our whole team. We had a great defensive football team, but, you know, we had Unitas. We had Lenny Moore, who's the greatest I've ever seen on any given day. We had Raymond Berry. We only had two ends—Raymond Berry and Jim Mutscheler. We had a great offensive line.

The meanest guy we played against would be Hardy Brown, who played for the '49ers. He was a linebacker. But the wildest and dirtiest I've ever seen was a guy that played with us, right behind me. A guy named Bill Pellington. Oh, he was nuts. He was crazy. He did things no other human being would do.

He just was dirty. He was a dirty football player, and another guy that played for us that was right behind him was a wild man, a guy named Don Joyce. He hit Les Richter from the Rams in the face with his own helmet and near killed him. He near got thrown out of the league on account of it.

Was more of that allowed when you were playing?

They did things that were unbelievable, and the officials let you get away with it. Like you hit a quarterback after he threw the ball, and the official would say, "Well, I'm sorry. Watch it. You're getting pretty close." They let you do a lot of things that you can't get away with now.

Pellington did everything. Anything imaginable, he did. One day he clothes-lined a kid, a young guy in the All-Star Game. A fullback from the University of Houston and the kid swallowed his tongue. He never played again.

There were a lot of funny things. I've seen guys get kicked in the ass by the coaches. I remember one time Pellington told me to move the wrong way, or I thought he did, and I moved, and he kicked me in the ass and knocked me over. During the game! Van Brocklin was the quarterback for the Rams—he pulled back and called a time out. He said, "How the hell can I call a play when you guys don't know what you're doing?"

I remember one time the Bears had a big end, an All-American from Stanford named Bill McColl. He's now a doctor. And everything was Bill McColl. Well, I don't know if he was that good or not, I really don't know. But he's walking off the field, and we holler, "Hey, Doc, we're going to shove the football up your ass the next set of downs." And he looked at us. He was a gentleman. He wasn't an animal like we were.

Do you think sports have changed?

It's changed. It's changed. I don't know for better or worse. Big salaries and all that. Well, hey, bully for them. If a guy offers you a million, you're going to take it, aren't you? The owners if they thought they can get you to play for free, they wouldn't pay you. So I don't blame the ballplayers for getting what they can.

I don't watch every Sunday. I have no interest in Green Bay playing Tampa Bay or the Chargers playing the Seahawks. I don't know those guys. I don't know anybody on the team, so why would I waste my time?

I'll watch Miami on account of Shula; the Bears on account of Ditka; the Redskins because I have a TV show every Sunday. But for me to sit down and waste my God given time of three hours to watch some of these teams—I just wouldn't do it.

I was on a cruise with Don Coreyal, the old coach of the Chargers. I sez, "Hey, Coach, I watched the Chargers when you were coaching." He says, "Oh, good for you." I said, "Not for the Chargers—for you, because I think you're half nuts." He got a big kick out of it. He's strange, but he was a great fella.

Do you think there are too many teams and not enough good players?

I'm sure. Baltimore wants an expansion team. I think the people will support 'em. Look at baseball. The prices to get in and the prices at the concession stands. I don't see how some of these young people can afford to take their families to the games.

I spent five innings last year at a baseball game. Of course, I'm not a regular human being. I spent $55 drinking beer and eating peanuts. I said, "Christ, I'd eat myself out of my wallet if I stayed the whole nine innings."

Weeb Eubanks was your coach.

I'd have to say Weeb Eubanks is the greatest coach that ever coached the game. He took two of the worst teams that ever played football and made them world champions (Baltimore and the New York Jets). He was a teacher, that's what he was. He was a school teacher. A frugal little weasel from Richmond, Indiana. A frugal Quaker. But a hell of a coach. I really loved the guy.

Every time I see him we talk, and I tell him about things he said or did. He says, "Oh, I don't remember that." I said, "God damn, Weeb, you don't remember anything." And he's as sharp as a tack.

A truck ran over him. He was out cutting his grass. Can you imagine the cheap little bastard. Cutting his grass, and a truck ran over him. Broke his leg—all kinds of things. But a hell of a coach.

I don't regret anything. I never look back. I've had a great life along the way. I've had a little heart problem, but hey, I've done it all. If I go today, I'd say, "Hey, I haven't missed anything."

DICK CLARK

AMERICAN BANDSTAND AND THE EARLY DAYS OF ROCK AND ROLL

In 1957, ABC went coast to coast with "American Bandstand" hosted by Dick Clark. The show was a great success and established Dick as the "High Priest of Rock and Roll."

He gave many acts exposure they would not have otherwise had—especially black performers. Dick Clark had more power than anyone in the business during the formative days of Rock and Roll.

When did you sense that Rock 'n' Roll was going to be the monster it turned out to be?

I don't really know. It had to be somewhere prior to 1955, because records by Fats Domino were beginning to be heard. Bill Haley and the Comets were down in Westchester, Pennsylvania, making a lot of noise with "Rockabilly" sounds. "Shake, Rattle and Roll," "We're Going To Rock This Joint"...things like that.

The black artists such as Clyde McPhatter, "Big Joe" Turner, Laverne Baker were not getting airplay on white stations. If they had, would that have hastened the popularity of Rock 'n' Roll?

When the "Bandstand" went on nationally in August 1957, that was no longer a problem. Every kid in the world listened to it, and radio stations began to copy what was played on television. There were no restrictions on that show. White radio—you couldn't get a black record on the air, that's why there were so many covers (whites singing black hits). But the "Bandstand" was one of the first to play black music. Freed (Allen Freed), of course, played it on his radio station in New York and when he was in Cleveland. But this is the first national exposure. So, it really broke after 1957.

Locally, in Philadelphia, when the show was on, there was never any problem playing black-oriented music. That's why it was so popular.

1956 to 1960 was Rock 'n' Roll exploded. Who was the biggest influence in its popularity?

It would be a combination of artists. Probably Fats Domino, Chuck Berry, Elvis Presley, Bill Haley. Those in particular had continuing success.

What was the funniest thing that ever happened on "Bandstand"?

I remember the day it snowed, and there was a transit strike, and a half dozen kids showed up, and we had to fill. That's a very terrifying thing when a show based on audience participation finds itself with virtually no audience. And for a straight man who doesn't tell jokes, that'll strike a little terror into your heart.

We were on two hours and 45 minutes. By the end of the two hours and 45 minutes, people straggled in, and we had a handful. We took the camera outside, we had snowball fights. We just filled the time.

The years 1956, 1957, 1958 were a magical period for Rock 'n' Roll. You turned on the radio and you'd hear something new every day. This followed a period when kids liked what their parents liked. Perry Como, The Hilltoppers, The Four Aces. And then all of a sudden—Rock 'n' Roll.

By then I was "a mature professional" in my 20s, and I was playing records for a livelihood. The problem I had was I couldn't convince management who ran the radio station to allow me to play "kid music." They insisted we play the old music, and then they couldn't understand why the audience wasn't young. It was just against station policy. They called the radio show "The Bandstand," hoping to draw off some of the popularity of the television show. There was a radio show and a television show both of the same name running simultaneously—but the radio show was Perry Como, Eddie Fisher, Don Cornell, Ralph Flannigan, and so forth. It was a frustration.

Eventually, bright people in radio everywhere began to play "kid music," and it was highly black-oriented, and that's when they swept the audience.

1955 and on. There was a disc jockey in every town who found out that if you played "Rhythm 'n' Blues," or "Rockabilly," or anything of that nature, kids would come to you...in great numbers.

Is there one piece of music that you remember more than any other that was a big hit?

I don't recall other than "Rock Around the Clock." Maybe that double-sided Presley record, "Heartbreak Hotel," and the other side.

Do you remember that period?

I remember it vividly. I was very young and impressionable and very naive, and it was the beginning of everything. I have fond memories of it. The biggest problem you have as you get older is not to hang on to the old days and let them go, just become part of your life's scrapbook. I don't think those were the best days of my life. I think they made the most impression on me because I couldn't ever, in my wildest dreams, believe where my life was going to go.

Do you think we'll ever see the likes of that again?

No, I'm afraid not. The audience has become far too sophisticated in its tastes. We've raised four generations now of people who are very particular about that which they want to listen to. You can see it exemplified in radio formats that proliferate yearly. They're going after narrower and narrower slices of audience.

It's really hard to visualize the day when you put on the same stack of records Fats Domino, Pat Boone, Perry Como, a big band record, The Chords, The Hilltoppers, Chuck Berry, and Don Cornell.

V

“The Road Taken and The Road Not Taken Make All the Difference”

James Meredith

RACE

In the fall of 1962, James Meredith, a black Air Force veteran, enrolled at the University of Mississippi. This was not your average matriculation.

It took five attempts. On the last try, with the help of federal marshals and the United States Army, it was accomplished. It cost the lives of two people. Approximately 160 people were injured—28 by sniper fire.

In June 1966, on a march from Memphis to Jackson, Mississippi, he was shot-gunned from ambush. Meredith was hospitalized, but the march was continued by Martin Luther King, Floyd McKissick, Stokely Carmichael, and others. It became known as the "Meredith March."

What were your thoughts when you enrolled at the University of Mississippi in the fall of 1962?

Well, for me it was extremely simple. America's based on the concept of citizenship, which carries rights and responsibilities. The question was, "Am I a citizen or am I not a citizen? If I am a citizen, I'm entitled to everything. If I'm not a citizen, I'm not entitled." So that was the question then and that is the question now.

When I came back to Mississippi in 1960, it wasn't to go to the University of Mississippi. It was to break the system of white supremacy. I was a soldier at war. It was simply a matter of where the enemy is more vulnerable to attack...that you're more likely to succeed.

You felt Ole Miss was the most vulnerable?

Yes. All of the "progress" had been made under the Republicans, under Eisenhower. From the Civil War to 1960, the Republicans had always had what they called the better civil rights plank, so to speak. Kennedy, as a ploy, introduced a stronger civil rights plank for the Democrats than the Republicans had and got it passed. It was strictly a ploy. After the election came out the way it did, I saw the opportunity to either force the Democrats or create serious problems for them politically.

Were you the only black in the South enrolling at a major state university in 1962?

Mississippi was the only state that had not had a black in a higher institution at that time. I was a student of politics and power for a long time. I was extremely aware of the British theory of divide and rule. I mean, my objective was to get the forces fighting against each other.

It is not my contention that it is anyone else's responsibility for my freedom. It's mine. The theory that the so-called civil rights thing operated on was that somebody else was supposed to do the right thing. I have never had any such concept. My condition was both my fault and my responsibility. I'm strictly a believer in organized force. People have to be made to do right and prevented from doing wrong. There's no other way to the end.

What was it like? There were five attempts to get you enrolled.

That was all play. There wasn't nothing serious about none of that.

On the fifth attempt you succeeded, but it got very nasty.

Right. But you see, that's where the misapplication is regarding this whole matter. The thing that's significant was the small number of black casualties. That was the miracle of the University of Mississippi.

You were not afraid? You felt in control?

Oh, of course. I mean, I was in charge practically all the time.

You were there two semesters and a summer session. You graduated in August 1963. Did you make any friends?

That was totally irrelevant to me. It wasn't about friendship. It was about power.

Were you basically by yourself during that time?

Well, whatever that means. I had 33,000 U. S. soldiers and 2,000-3,000 U.S. Marshals. I mean, I couldn't be by myself.

What did you do upon graduating from Ole Miss?

I went to Washington and did the embassy scene. Then went abroad touring through Europe and Africa and then I studied in Africa and then toured the Middle East and returned.

"The Road Taken and the Road Not Taken Make All The Difference"

In June 1966, you took a walk from Memphis, Tennessee, to Jackson, Mississippi. Aubrey James Norvell shot you from the side of the road while you were taking that walk. What was the reason behind that walk?

Basically, it was the finishing touches of the mission to break the system of white supremacy which we'd already done with the University of Mississippi. But two factors were very important. Because of history, neither the blacks in Mississippi, or the whites, which was about a million each, knew how they were supposed to react to the new reality. So the principal objective of that effort was to demonstrate to blacks that they could now exercise their citizenship rights, but more significantly to demonstrate to whites how they should react to them. See, the whites didn't know when a black went to register to vote whether he should go up and shake his hand to congratulate him or go to his pickup truck and get his rifle and shoot him. So, I had to set up a scenario where I could demonstrate what they should do.

You were shot outside Hernando, Mississippi, and taken back to Memphis.

Right.

A number of people then took up the march. Martin Luther King, Floyd McKissick, Stokely Carmichael to name a few.

Right, and they conducted what has become known as the "Meredith March." I never participated in the "Meredith March."

Did it help having these individuals coming in?

It was totally irrelevant, because the game they were in—they were not at war. They were in demonstration and protest. They were in their own thing. As a matter of recognition and honor to me, they named it after me. But it was no relationship basically whatsoever.

Your being shot on the march from Memphis to Jackson had a tremendous impact. People were shocked.

I agree entirely with you. In fact, the "Meredith March" was absolutely the single largest thing that blacks have ever participated in in America. That includes the biggest thing Martin Luther King was ever involved in. It was in my scope of things, not even worthy of serious mention.

Where is America heading in race relations?

Well, I'm not really concerned about that at this time. I'm more concerned that America will not deteriorate and degenerate like Eastern Europe and Russia have done. I'm much less concerned at this time about who's going to be running it, than I am as to whether there be something to run.

If the race problem is not solved, we're going to disintegrate for either one or two reasons. One is just the sheer lack of utilizing our resources. The other is Western civilization is at war with the black male. Either they're going to completely annihilate them or they are going to see that they are near annihilation. They're going to react to that. So, we have a very critical situation at this time, and this is really made more vulnerable by what is happening to other people in the society.

White supremacy has been broken. White supremacy has no significance any longer in America. I mean, that's finished. Middle to lower middle class white women have now been re-enslaved in America. That is going to have consequences beyond what anybody has yet imagined.

Re-enslaved in what respect?

They were the element that replaced the black male. The black male was brought into Western Christian civilization for one reason, and one reason only, and America is the best example of that. For their labor. Beginning in the 1970s, and for the first time since the first black was brought into Western civilization, the black males labor as a policy was not used. They (were) replaced (by) middle aged, middle class white women as that labor replacement.

The majority now of whites in America have no supervision of their children. The marginal, to at least middle class white woman, took care of the family and the home. Now they're no longer doing that. No one is taking care of them because they can't afford to hire anybody. See the upper middle class and rich white women still hire other people to take care of those matters. Now, the blacks still do it themselves. Now they've been devastated, but not near to the extent that the whites in that category have been devastated.

Bear Bryant had a policy that regardless of the game, Bear Bryant would put (just) so many black players on the field at one time. Then he made a decision to put the best team on the field at all times. After he made that decision, every state in the South did the same thing. And within a very short time, particularly in basketball, you would have 10 black players on the floor at one time. Nobody complained. Now, basically, that is my best hope that America will see that same reality and simply go for the best person to solve the problem and do the job.

I'm very optimistic at this point.

CLARENCE PAGE

THE CIVIL RIGHTS MOVEMENT

He believes America is "not a melting pot, we're sort of a 'Mulligan Stew.' We've a lot of different elements in the stew, and they don't melt, but they all contribute to the flavor of the whole, and that's always been America's strength."

He states that Martin Luther King and Malcolm X, although coming from different points of view, were the major forces in the black movement in America. Also, that King at the end of his life was becoming more militant and was cynical about the effort moderates and whites were extending to the movement.

Mr. Page is a Pulitzer Prize winner and is a columnist and member of the Chicago Tribune*'s editorial board. His column is nationally syndicated. He is also an occasional guest panelist on "The McLaughlin Group" and a monthly contributor of essays to the "MacNeil/Lehrer News Hour." He is a frequent guest on ABC's "Nightline" and "Good Morning, America," NBC's "Today" and CNN.*

I suppose there were several turning points in the civil rights movement. The most significant that I personally recall would have been in 1965 after the passage of the Voting Rights Act, the year after the passage of the Civil Rights Act. At that point, there was a sense in the white community that the civil rights struggle was essentially over.

At the same time in the black community, there was a sense that we must move on to other issues, particularly economic justice. Dr. Martin Luther King took his movement into northern cities and ran into resistance from many of the same liberals who had supported the movement in the South because they saw nothing wrong with their own ghettos in the North. He became more and more militant in his final days as he began to run into more resistance on this. He became more cynical about the kind of struggle that moderates and whites were giving to the movement. At the same time, following the death of Malcolm X in '65, was the rise of the black power movement in '66.

"The Road Taken and the Road Not Taken Make All The Difference"

What happened to Malcolm X's movement after he was murdered?

His organization died with him. The Organization for African-American Unity.

About a year later, you had the rise of the black power movement fostered by Stokely Carmichael, who was then taking over the leadership of the Student Nonviolent Coordinating Committee. His philosophy was similar in that they were both militant philosophies not favoring turning the other cheek like Martin Luther King did.

Would you say Lyndon Johnson did more for blacks than any other president?

I'd say that probably is a pretty fair statement.

This has been a steady progression. Roosevelt formed the first Black Aviator Unit in World War II, which might not seem like much now, but was a big, bold step at that time. Largely at the urging of his wife, Eleanor. A. Phillip Randolph was head of the Brotherhood of Sleeping Car Porters, and they threatened to march on Washington if they didn't get labor reform passed (in July 1941). It was passed by Roosevelt at that time.

There has been steady progression, a steady expansion of rights over the years that various presidents have either initiated or actually signed into law, either because they personally wanted to, or because of political expediency, one way or the other.

Where did Eisenhower stand in the civil rights movement?

I wouldn't say he led the fight, but he didn't get in the way of it either.

Little Rock was extremely important, and he definitely stuck his neck out when he federalized federal troops to desegregate that high school.

Eisenhower had lots of friends. We forget that, in 1960, the black community supported Eisenhower, and by 1960 a lot of prominent blacks were supporting Nixon, like Martin Luther King, Sr.

Little Rock opened the eyes of many Americans that race relations in America were in a sorry state.

It was very significant to me. I was about 11 years old at the time, and it was of monumental personal significance to me to see these black youngsters going out and making a difference. Until then, my parents had taught me pretty much not to make waves. I think a lot of young blacks, as well as white kids, were quite deeply influenced by that. "Baby Boomer" generation.

Do you believe Kennedy helped the civil rights movement? Or do you think it was more form than substance?

Well, form has substance. Symbols have substance. He was always wavering between reaching out and helping the civil rights movement and taking a position of official indifference because southern white Democrats were on the verge of bolting the party, which they eventually did after '64. In any case, southern white Democrats didn't support Kennedy in 1960. It was a very close election, you remember. When James Meredith went to the University of Mississippi, Kennedy had to be prodded into supporting him. He called Coretta Scott King when Martin Luther King was in jail.

He was encouraged to do this. He was hesitant to do it. Now, that's a symbolic move, but symbols have important substance in campaigns like this. So, he helped set the stage. Remember, very crucial things were happening during his administration. Like the sit-ins in North Carolina and a lot of other early organizing and voter registration that was going on. So, Kennedy was at a very important point.

After a couple of years it became very obvious that Kennedy supported the civil rights movement, and this helped to give impetus to the civil rights marches and civil rights legislation that Johnson signed, and at the time he signed said, "I've just signed away the southern white vote from the Democrats for the next 50 years"...something of that nature. It was indicative of how obvious it was to Democrats that they were going against the political grain of their own party in taking such a bold position on civil rights.

What was Nixon's contribution to the civil rights movement?

He did several things that didn't seem like much at the time. It seems like a lot now in comparison to Ronald Reagan. It was his executive order in '73 that really initiated what we call "Affirmative Action" today. Very tough...pretty much what we call "quotas" today. Didn't begin with Nixon, but he signed the executive order that pretty much mandated aggressive action to hire women and minorities.

On the issue of economic justice, under the umbrella of civil rights, he promised to get blacks a piece of the action. He pushed black capitalism. These kind of ideas were part of the "New Nixon," as his campaign billed him in '68. He promoted actively during his terms the idea of reaching out and getting black entrepreneurship and black business people into the mainstream and reducing discrimination that would keep them out. So he had a Republican spin on the idea of black empowerment and black progress.

What occurred that was significant from the mid-'70s to 1980?

The only thing that comes to mind right now was that during the Ford administration, they opened up J. Edgar Hoover's files and we began to see some of the extent of what was involved in COINTELPRO, and the government's own efforts, by way of J. Edgar Hoover, to discredit and do worse to black leadership in this country. I'm familiar with that because my boss, Jack Fuller, who is now editor of the *Chicago Tribune*, was deputy to Attorney General Ed Levy under Ford, and part of his job was to declassify a lot of that documentation.

Reagan reinterpreted civil rights to be "civil rights department" of the Justice Department. They tried to have a color-blind philosophy, which meant actually reducing the efforts that were intended to help men and women of minorities. They put a top priority on anything that might be viewed as discrimination against whites and males. So, to say they didn't do anything for civil rights is of course an interpretation. They didn't do anything for black progress in that sense. Or, at least to help. Under Reagan, government no longer became a strong advocate for the empowerment of blacks and for civil rights enforcement. There was a good deal of confusion, in the name of debate, in terms of what the government's role ought to be to help protect minorities and women.

Did Bush carry on this philosophy?

More or less. The difference was that Reagan brought in zealots, like William Bradford Reynolds, who were real ideologues in the sense of being crusaders. There were ideas they believed in and they crusaded to get them across. Bush was not an ideologue, didn't have strong ideas, and didn't put people in high office that had really strong ideas. Jack Kemp in Housing had strong ideas but wasn't given much support for implementing them. That was quite different from Ronald Reagan who gave great support to everybody and their ideas. Then there was his appointment of Clarence Thomas; something that came about through a lot of consultation. Like other aspects of domestic policy, George Bush was not really turned on. He wasn't really excited about civil rights and he pretty much followed his advisers insofar as Supreme Court appointments and civil rights legislation. This is why he would not sign bills that essentially continued the type of civil rights policies that existed under Ronald Reagan. He wouldn't sign them because he kept calling them "quota bills." I'm talking about the 1990 and '91 Civil Rights Acts that were proposed. He finally signed the Civil Rights Act of '91 at a time when David Duke was gaining in popularity, and seemed it was more to distance himself from Duke's image than it was to actually support the bill. In other words, it seemed to be a kind of cynical approach born not necessarily of George Bush's own internal inclinations, as much as his top advisors were advising him in that direction. To use race as a campaign rallying tool to win white support.

The civil rights movement in general, I have to separate from the movement for black empowerment. There's a real difference there. I think the two most important names as far as black progress is concerned in the second half of this century would be Dr. King and Malcolm X. They represented the two sides of what W. E. B DuBois called a hundred years ago our "double consciousness" as Africans in America. They were very important figures as far as representing the two most important polls in the bipolar philosophies of African-Americans and their movement toward more political, social, and economic progress. As far as the civil rights movement itself is concerned, there were many soldiers and many officers in the movement, and Dr. Martin Luther King, of course, is viewed as the most significant, but there were many others too numerous to mention who were crucial.

There is some concern that our immigration laws should be tightened—that the cities cannot support more people.

Americans said the same thing 100 years ago when America's population shifted from being predominantly rural to predominantly urban. For the first time in this country's history, we were no longer a nation of farmers, Jeffersonian farmers. We were suddenly...and a fairly homogenous population...primarily urban, receiving more and more new peoples, new groups into the melting pot. The vast majority of them, you will recall, were from Europe. And yet you had William Jennings Bryan, the great prairie populist, who fostered an anti-immigrant nativist sentiment that made him very popular.

America was changing. The "melting pot" emerged during the days of Teddy Roosevelt, and he liked that idea. It was a great political slogan and he used it to great effect. Arthur Schlesinger writes about this in his book, *The Disuniting of America,* which deals with that very question about do we have too many groups, and people who think we've got too many groups hold up Schlesinger's book as evidence. But if you really read Schlesinger's book, he says just the opposite. He says that we've been a multi-cultural society for a long time, and will continue to be so, and that we need to approach this sensibly and not as zealots on either extreme.

I'm sure you and I both wish we had a nickel for every time we've heard a politician say "special interest groups." That term also emerged during Teddy Roosevelt's era. The whole notion of special interest groups comes from a time in which everybody suddenly became a special interest group because there were so many different groups in America. They were all demanding their rights, including women and various others. It was a very exciting time at the turn of the century.

We're about to come to another turn of the century, and now the 1990 census confirms, for the first time, that the majority of Americans don't live on the farm, or in the cities. They now live in the suburbs. Now the immigrants aren't coming from Europe, they're coming from the Third World. They're coming from Asia. They're coming from Latin America. They're coming from Africa, the Caribbean. But there ain't nothing new about the rhetoric that we've got too many groups, or that we need to do something about immigration.

The new minorities want to be American. There might be a movement toward bilingual education, but essentially most foreign-speaking aliens want to speak English. And they try very hard, especially the younger they are. They want to be part of the mainstream and eat Big Macs, etc.

Those of us who are already here need to welcome new people. Need to make them feel more welcome. Not just people who are arriving new, but also those of us who have been here a long time, historically, like Black Americans, and want to enter the mainstream. This should not be made more difficult because they are black.

This is important for Americans to understand. We're not a melting pot, we're sort of a Mulligan Stew. We've a lot of different elements in the stew, and they don't melt, but they all contribute to the flavor of the whole, and that's always been America's strength.

DINO BRUGIONI

THE CUBAN MISSILE CRISIS

Dino Brugioni is one of America's unsung heros. As a senior official in Reconnaissance and Photo Interpretation with the CIA, he helped discover offensive missiles in Cuba in October 1962. He believes at one point we were 48 hours from nuclear war. At the time, Curtis LeMay, Air Force chief of staff, was asked about Cuba and he responded: "Fry it."

All during the summer of 1962, the Russians began sending more and more military equipment to Cuba. It was under the most careful aerial surveillance. On August 29, 1962, we found surface-to-air missiles. Mr. McCone (CIA director) said, "They're not putting the surface-to-air missiles in to protect the cane cutters, they're putting them in to blind our reconnaissance eye."

The finding of the surface-to-air missiles prompted President Kennedy to give a warning to Khrushchev on September 4. Then we found some cruise missiles. These were coastal defense missiles, and we also found guided missile patrol boats. On September 13, President Kennedy gave his second warning to Khrushchev that the "gravest of issues" would arise if they put in surface-to-surface missiles.

He was continually being reassured by the Russians that nothing would be done in that way. So, we had a watch on Cuba. We had a report from a covert agent that there was an area in Cuba in which Cubans were being moved out and Russians were being moved in and we decided to take a look. A U-2 mission was flown on October 14. It was processed October 15, and we discovered two medium-range ballistic missile sites in Cuba.

When President Kennedy was briefed, he asked that the whole island be covered. A number of U-2 missions were flown, and, in addition to the two medium-range ballistic missile sites, we found four additional ones in various states of construction, and three intermediate-range ballistic missile sites in the initial stage of construction. The president ran his options, that is, his advisors of the Executive Committee of the National Security Council ran options from doing nothing to invading Cuba. The president chose the blockade.

On October 22, he informed the nation that there were offensive missiles in Cuba. Then he instituted low-altitude reconnaissance. These are planes flying at about 500 miles an hour from 250 to 1,000 feet, and they brought back spectacular photographs on which we could identify every piece of military equipment.

This prompted the decision by the president to bring the matter to the United Nations. We prepared all the materials, and, on the afternoon of October 25, Soviet Ambassador Zorin denied that there were missiles in Cuba. The code word was "stick him"—meaning bring out the aerial photography. On the night of October 25, there was an angry confrontation between U.S.-UN Ambassador Adlai Stevenson and Zorin. Zorin claimed he was not in an American courtroom and Stevenson said, "Very well, answer 'yes' or 'no' are there missiles in Cuba? I'm willing to wait 'til hell freezes over for an answer." When the answer wasn't forthcoming, the aerial photos were brought down on the floor of the United Nations.

Public opinion, both United States and the world, swung behind the United States, but the Soviets continued the construction of the missile sites. On October 27, we reported to the president that the six medium-range ballistic missile sites consisting of 24 launch pads were operational. That morning, we received word that one of our U-2's had been shot down over Cuba. They were also firing at the low-altitude airplanes.

They were digging trenches all over the island. The Soviets were attempting to camouflage the missile sites, and, in addition to that, the president received a letter from Khrushchev. The letter, according to Maxwell Taylor and others, was a troubled one. At that time they didn't know whether Khrushchev had been replaced or had his position made less important as premier.

When that information was presented to the president that night by Arthur C. Lundahl, the director of the National Photographic Interpretation Center, and John McCone, the director of the CIA, the president decided that it was time for action. All during this period, there was the largest mobilization of U.S. troops since World War II. Troops from all over the U. S. were being moved to Florida. The 82nd Airborne and the 101st were ready for jumps into Cuba. The 101st was to jump at Mariel and Baracoa and secure the port of Mariel. The 82nd was to jump further inland and secure the San Antonio de Los Banos and Jose Marti airfields. The Marines were to come ashore on the beaches to the east of Havana, and then there would be a pincer movement to isolate Havana. Then they were to race to the missile sites and cut the island in half.

Khrushchev knew that an invasion was eminent. On Saturday evening (27th), Bobby (Kennedy) delivered an ultimatum to Dobrynin (Soviet ambassador to the U.S.) that the missiles had to be removed or the United States was prepared to bomb and invade Cuba. On Sunday morning, the 28th, Khrushchev, in the clear, over Radio Moscow, indicated that he would remove the missiles. This was very unusual because normally all of this type of traffic is carried through diplomatic channels. The president was concerned that the Soviets might be lying again. Again, low-altitude reconnaissance planes roamed over the island and the next day, too, and then we began to see indications that the Soviets were going to remove the missiles.

Now the problem was to count the missiles and make sure that all the missiles were sent back to the Soviet Union. There was very close reconnaissance not only of the sites, but also the roads leading to the ports. And heavy reconnaissance over the ports as the missiles were loaded, and then the missiles were also observed on deck as the ships left Cuba.

The last problem was the Russians had sent IL-28 Beagle jet bombers to Cuba. Negotiations began in earnest at the United Nations between Stevenson, John McCloy, and the Soviet Deputy Foreign Minister Kuznetsov. The Soviets agreed to remove the bombers and then Kennedy indicated the crisis was, in a sense, over.

Much has been made that we had, at that time, 60 Thor missiles in England—intermediate-range ballistic missiles—30 Jupiter intermediate-range ballistic missiles in Italy, and 15 in Turkey. Much has been made that there was a deal struck between Kennedy and Khrushchev. But there was no such deal struck. The reason the missiles were moved out of Turkey was the fact that Polaris submarines had taken up patrol in the Mediterranean. Now the agreement, that was verbal between the United States and Russia, was that President Kennedy would not invade Cuba provided that the missiles were removed from Cuba under UN inspection.

The Russians indicated that Castro was getting hard to handle and so the UN inspection never took place. Since the UN inspection never took place, there's a big question—did the pledge not to invade Cuba still exist?

When you look at the Cuban Missile Crisis, it was a time when we were brought very close to a nuclear conflict. The military had gone from defense condition 3 to 2. At that time, there was some 1,400 Strategic Air Command bombers, many of them loaded with nuclear weapons, flying what was known as the HR Control Line. Flying north to the Arctic and then waiting for an indication either to proceed to bomb Russia or to come back. In addition to the bombers, there was always about 125 intercontinental ballistic missiles on pads. There was also nine Polaris submarines at sea capable of firing 144 Polaris missiles at the Soviet Union. In the event of war, there were 70 Russian cities scheduled for destruction.

Now, it was not only the Russians that would be the ones suffering from a nuclear holocaust. I was quite concerned that if one missile was fired from Cuba, it would be the one that would land on Washington. Of course, I had my family here.

That's a quick wrap-up of the Cuban Missile Crisis as seen from the National Photographic Interpretation Center where I prepared all of the notes for the briefing of the president. Also, I prepared the notes for the four foreign leaders that the president decided should be briefed. Those men were Prime Minister Diefenbaker of Canada, Konrad Adenauer of West Germany, Charles de Gaulle of France, and Harold Macmillan of England. They were briefed before the president's speech to the nation on October 22.

Who were the hawks and who were the doves?

At that particular time, the doves, if you want to look at them as such, were McGeorge Bundy and Rusk. And the hawks were Bobby Kennedy and McCone and, to some extent, McNamara.

Where was JFK?

Well, to me, this is his shining hour, because he looked at all of these things very objectively. His favorite word during the crisis was "prudent." He had taken the first step—the blockade—and then he would be tightening the screws. He always indicated he didn't want to paint Khrushchev into a corner. He always wanted to leave him an alley to get out. It was his diplomacy, because certainly the military were looking upon this as a challenge. Maxwell Taylor told me, "The Soviets had invested millions of dollars in transporting all of this equipment and men to Cuba and you don't do that kind of activity with the idea that it would fail." The military looked upon it as a threat and decided that it had to be met with an equal threat. An equal threat was the possible bombardment of the Soviet Union.

How close did we get?

That night of the 27th, I thought very, very close. Too close for comfort.

Within a day?

Well, I think that basically, Khrushchev had 48 hours, and he only took 12 of the 48 hours to make up his mind to remove the missiles.

Do you think this resulted in Khrushchev being ousted from power two years later?

Yes. The Soviet analysts indicated that this was his unraveling, and two years later he was removed. It was a typical Khrushchev move. It was bold, it was aggressive and poorly planned.

Why was Castro so difficult to deal with? Did he have a death wish?

The Russians just dropped him on his head. Once they saw the U. S. threat they did not, to the best of our knowledge, consult with him and he was furious, and the Soviet ambassador to Cuba couldn't handle him. Then they sent the premier diplomat in the Soviet Union, Anastas Mikoyan, to Cuba. When he got there, Castro was a raving maniac, and Mikoyan, a patient Armenian, said, "You let a good cow bellow for a while before you milk her." And that's what he did.

Finally, when he did meet with Castro, he drew him up short. Castro said that he'd fight alone, and Mikoyan said, "Well, there wouldn't be any Russians. That's exactly what the Kennedy boys want. They would like nothing better than to see you hanging from the highest light pole in Havana." That kind of chilled Castro. Castro knew, of course, that the full military might of the United States was out there at sea. He didn't dare make a foolish move that would bring on the complete destruction of the island.

In fact, Mikoyan's wife died during this, and he didn't go back for the funeral.

And he never forgave Castro. We talked to several Russians. They indicated that he never forgave Castro because this was a wife that he had a lot of love for. He had to send his son home to arrange for her burial, and never forgave Castro for that.

Who on our side was the biggest hawk—LeMay?

Oh, no doubt about it. LeMay had created a bomber force specifically for, as he saw it, to defend the United States, and he was ready to use it. He always referred to Russia as the "Bear," and he saw that we had a tremendous advantage over the Soviet Union. We had a strategic advantage of 7-1. The Russians later admitted that it might have been as high as 14-1.

Didn't LeMay say this is the time to get them if we're ever going to get them?

That's basically it—that if they wanted war, they had picked the wrong battle field and the wrong time.

Who was the biggest dove?

It was Adlai Stevenson. Stevenson, in the meeting on October 19, wanted to negotiate the issues. That prompted a remark by Bobby Kennedy to the effect that Stevenson wanted a Munich. In fact, he said loud enough to hear, "You got to put some starch in the son-of-a-bitch's back or get somebody to replace him."

Do you think this might have been because Stevenson was thinking of running in '64?

Well, the Kennedys never did trust the New York faction. That faction was Adlai Stevenson, Eleanor Roosevelt, Governor Lehman and Averell Harriman. They were the liberals of the Democratic Party, and the Kennedys didn't trust them, and the Kennedys were also leery that Stevenson might try to run again. So they cast a jaundiced eye at this New York liberal wing of the party.

I want to point out that President Eisenhower, in his wisdom, saw the need for reconnaissance systems. During his administration the "Genetrix" Reconnaissance Balloons were created, the U-2, the SR-71, and Satellite Reconnaissance. Concomitant with that, there was an organization created called the National Photographic Interpretation Center. I was on the founding cadre, and we developed the techniques to look at this material, and we did it for one reason and one reason alone—and that was to protect the security of this nation. As I look back, I feel good that we've done a pretty good job of doing just that. We did it under a lot of odds, but once there was a good idea, there were men like Dr. Edwin Land and "Kelly" Johnson who designed the U-2 and the SR-71.

There was also Arthur Lundahl, the director of the National Photographic Interpretation Center. Through our efforts, we maintained the peace over the period. That's the biggest contribution of all.

Do you think the Cuban Missile Crisis was the *turning point in 20th century history?*

No doubt about it. We had talked about going to the "brink." There were statements, "massive retaliations," and the Soviets were saying, "We will bury you." We will do this and we will do that. We got to the point of launching nuclear weapons. We looked around and wondered what stupidity our national leaders had gotten us into.

It was the unsung heroes like yourself that really helped get us through this period.

That's the love of country. I had flown in World War II. I had flown in 66 bombing missions. I'd put my life on the line again and again, and then I realized that we had to stop that kind of thing. War; we should do everything to prevent it and we did.

Governor John Connolly

NOVEMBER 22, 1963

It still hurts.

Did you want to ride with JFK in the motorcade on November 22, 1963? You weren't known as a strong Kennedy man. There were some political problems for him in Texas at that time, and you weren't sure he was going to win the state.

I had no hesitancy at all. The only hesitation I had was early in 1963. President Kennedy told me he wanted to come to Texas and hold five fundraising events. I disagreed with that pretty strongly. I thought it was bad. Basically told him through friends of Vice President Johnson that I thought if he came just for five fundraising events that it would be regarded as just a money rape of Texas since he had not been to Texas since his election. So I stalled frankly for several months until we put together a program that encompassed some nonpolitical events, as well as the proposed fundraising dinner at Austin, Texas, the night of November 22. Once the plans were settled and we agreed, I was enthusiastic about it. Had a large hand in arranging the whole thing. Had personally gotten on the phone to sell tickets to the dinner in Austin. So there was no reluctance on my part when we reached that point.

You appeared in San Antonio and Fort Worth before the parade.

Yes, and also in Houston.

Were you and Ralph Yarborough having a problem? Yarborough was considered a liberal and you were a conservative. In fact, Yarborough didn't want to ride in the motorcade with LBJ.

The problem has been grossly misunderstood. The problem was always between Johnson and Yarborough, not between Yarborough and me. The stories were rampant that Kennedy came to Texas to solve the problems within the party between Yarborough and Johnson or Yarborough and me. Well, he had Johnson and Yarborough both in Washington, he didn't need to come down here to settle the differences between them.

That problem started between them when Price Daniel was elected governor. But it really flared when Kennedy and Johnson were elected to their respective offices, and Johnson got a commitment out of President Kennedy that he would get half of the patronage in Texas.

See, Johnson gave up a Senate seat and John Tower, a Republican, was elected. Well, that meant that all the Democratic patronage under Kennedy would go to Yarborough. Johnson got Kennedy to agree to let him have half of it. This infuriated Yarborough because it was normally senatorial patronage, and that's what really precipitated the feud. I was no part of it. I had nothing whatever to do with it.

You were surprised by the size of the crowd during the motorcade.

They were bigger and more enthusiastic than I thought they would be.

Did you think that there might be a security problem?

Not really. I thought there would be some nasty signs or shouts from the audience along the parade route, or something like that. But I was not in the least concerned about any serious attacks such as occurred.

Do you remember what your last conversation was with JFK? Were you discussing a poll in the Houston Chronicle *that was going to come out the next day? It was going to show you running a little ahead of JFK in Texas.*

That wasn't the last conversation, but that was a conversation we had in the car. We had been in Houston. He had talked to the publisher of the *Chronicle,* who told him about the poll. About how he rated in the poll, and in the car, along the parade route, he asked me about the poll, and he said, "How do you rate in the poll?" And I said, "Well, I think I rate a little bit better than you do, Mr. President." That was the extent of it.

Do you remember the last conversation you had with him before the shooting?

No, we were commenting about the crowds. We didn't talk a great deal. The last conversation was with Nellie (Governor Connolly's wife). As we turned off of Main Street and reached the relative calm just before the turn over on Elm, Nellie turned to the president and said, "Now, Mr. President, you can't say Dallas doesn't love you." And he said, "No, you really can't." That was the last conversation anybody had in the car.

But you know, along the route like that, you don't do an awful lot of talking because your mind and your attention is always on the crowds along the way. You're paying attention to them. You're responding to them, and it's really quite difficult to carry on a conversation, and we didn't carry on a conversation of any substance.

Did you hear the first shot?

Yes, I did.

What was your reaction?

I thought it was a rifle shot. I turned to look over my right shoulder because the sound came from behind me and above me, and I looked to see if I could see anything out of the ordinary. But I clearly thought it was a rifle shot.

You turned right and then you turned left...

Then I turned left to look over my left shoulder because I didn't see anything when I turned to the right. And just as I straightened up, I felt the impact of the bullet that hit me, which was the second bullet. Could not have been the first. I heard the sound of the first bullet. That bullet had already passed us. The second bullet I never heard. I felt it. But I never heard, or was conscious of the sound of it, and then the third shot, I saw the evidence quite clearly. I heard it impact the president's head and then I saw the results of blood and brain tissue all over the interior of the car and all over our clothing.

How many shots do you think were fired?

Only three.

Only three. You were quoted as saying, "My God, they're trying to kill us all." Is that correct?

Yes, I did.

Were you down on the car floor when the shot hit JFK in the head?

No, I wasn't on the floor. We were seated on the jump seats. I was on the jump seat in front of the president. Nellie was on the jump seat in front of Jackie Kennedy. After I was hit with the second shot, Nellie pulled me down, my head down in her lap, and then put her head on top of mine so that in the film you can hardly see either of us in those jump seats. But I was actually seated on the jump seat, just leaning over into her lap.

Your head was in her lap when JFK was fatally hit. Did you know at that time it was a fatal shot?

There was quite a loud, sharp slap—like you slapped your hands together. I was conscious, I was looking forward. I was looking into the back of the front seat. The car was covered in a blue velour material and immediately after that loud slap sound I saw brain tissue as big as the end of my finger and blood all over the interior of the car and all over our clothing. I knew that no one could survive it. I knew it had to be the president because Jackie Kennedy said, "My God, I've got his brains in my hand." So, obviously, it was a fatal shot. He was instantly killed.

At that point, did the driver of the car accelerate?

Yes. The Secret Service agent in the front seat said to the driver, "My God, get the hell out of here."

What were your thoughts on the way to Parkland Hospital? Was anything said?

I was in and out of consciousness and really didn't become conscious again until we braked to a very sudden stop in front of the hospital. At that point, to when they put me on the stretcher, is the first time I really began to feel the pain of the shot.

Your wife Nellie was disturbed because they tried to get over you to get to the president's body.

That's correct. She knew he was dead. The door to the back part of the car was opposite me by the jump seat and his seat, the back seat, was behind me, so it was difficult. They ultimately, I think, lifted him over the side of the car. Didn't even attempt to bring him out through the door. That's what was upsetting her because she felt I was sitting there for an interminable period, and no one was doing anything about it. I was still alive and she knew the president was dead.

If JFK was hit like a lot of people say from the front...

It's not so.

You think he was hit from the back?

Absolutely.

As far as you're concerned you were both hit from behind. You were shot once in the back?

Yes. Shot through the chest. It took out two ribs, I believe No. 5 and No. 6 rib. I was holding my hat in front of me, and it just happened to be at a point where the bullet went through my right wrist and broke all the bones in the wrist and then went into my left leg.

Did the bullet that went through Kennedy go through you?

That's what the Warren Commission thinks. Basically, what the House Investigating Committee thinks. They think probably the first shot missed. The second one went through him and then me.

Do you subscribe to that?

I don't know. All I know is that there were three shots. I never saw him. I don't know whether he was hit with the first or the second bullet through his neck. I do know that he was hit with the third bullet and that's all I can be sure of.

Do you believe the Warren Commission's Report.

Basically, yes.

Do you think there was any conspiracy?

No, I do not. I think anybody who alleges that is doing it for purely commercial purposes.

Would the world have been different if JFK had lived?

It clearly would have been different. How different, I don't know. Kennedy had not been successful in getting his program through the Congress. He was having difficulty. Johnson though, in the aftermath of the assassination, passed not only the Kennedy Program but much more as well. So, if Kennedy had lived, he would have had difficulty continually with the Congress in the furtherance of his legislative program. He would have had a tough race, in my opinion, in 1964.

Against Goldwater. You think that would have been closer than people realize?

I think it would have been a much closer race than it turned out to be, of course.

Do you believe that LBJ was a good president?

Yes, I do. You may not agree with everything he did, but no question he was a good president.

Do you believe the country changed forever with Kennedy's death?

I don't know that they're interrelated, but, yes, this country began to change during his time. If you'll think back, a great many things began to take place. There was a revolution of youth in the country. It was all attributed to Vietnam, and I don't believe that. I think part of it was, but it went far beyond that. There was a revolution against religion, particularly among young people. They cast aside all tenants of faith. The graffiti on the walls of the country—"Is God dead?" There was a reaction against any parental guidance. Young people were casting off all anchors, it seems to me, of the school, of the church, of the family. The age of permissiveness began. The days of marijuana started. The rise of the women's liberation movement flourished. It really began to take off, and we're still in the throes of that.

There was a pervasive change that began in the 1960s. How much of it was directly attributable to Kennedy, I don't know. I think some of it clearly was. He was a symbol to the young people. He was a symbol of change. He succeeded Eisenhower, who represented the old establishment, and here came a bright young fellow. His wife characterized a change of fashion, of youth. So all of it was part of what began in the 1960s as a major change in the social structure of this country.

You believe his death accelerated that?

I think it did. I think it accelerated it in Johnson's programs. The Great Society also magnified it. Poverty program, the Civil Rights program. All the other things that Johnson passed were part of it. Part of the sweeping change that took place in the country.

The shooting was a very traumatic experience for you. Do you dream of it?

Not anymore. I did for many, many months after the assassination, but, fortunately, I don't anymore.

It's something you live with forever. But at least today I can discuss it with a fairly high degree of objectivity. Without too much emotional constraints.

MICHAEL BARONE

LYNDON JOHNSON

The author of Our Country *and senior writer for* U.S. News and World Report. *He believes Johnson faced a very difficult situation in Vietnam when he took office. Our government approved the assassination of President Ngo Dinh Diem, which occurred just weeks before the Kennedy assassination. Therefore, LBJ now had to run Vietnam, as well as the war. He failed at both.*

Mr. Barone points out that Johnson also alienated a large segment of white America with his Great Society because there was little in it for them.

He states that the Great Society afforded the liberals an opportunity to vent their guilt regarding the American system. He believes they took it to extremes, such as the pampering of criminals.

Lyndon Johnson's problems are associated with Vietnam. In your book, Our Country, *you point out that the entitlement programs that he introduced into the Great Society also alienated a great portion of white America.*

I think some of the entitlement programs probably helped. The MediCare Program, for example, was popular on balance, but politically not much of an asset because once it got in there, it was pretty clear nobody was going to take it away. I think the creation of the much ballyhooed anti-poverty programs, the vast increases that started in the welfare programs in the Johnson years and continued into the early Nixon years, were programs that proved to be very politically damaging to Lyndon Johnson and the Democratic Party. They did not go to a voting constituency. They were aimed at the inert poor. They were administered increasingly in a way that did not encourage upward mobility; did not honor upwardly mobile behavior in a way in which earlier programs associated with the Democrats—the G.I. Bill of Rights, FHA housing program did honor upwardly mobile behavior. I think that's an important distinction. The constituencies there were politically kind of inert, non-voters, people whose voting populations were declining. At the same time these programs tended to undercut the historic strength and constituencies of the Democratic Party. The anti-poverty program specifically created what some of the people on the left called "parallel structures to replace the planned substitute for the big city governments," which were a political mainstay of the Democratic Party. I mean, here was the Democratic Party creating counter-machines to undercut the power of Democratic Party machines.

In Chicago Daley controlled the poverty program that didn't work. But in just about every place else it did. I think it accelerated the decline of Democratic Party big city machines, which was declining in any case because of declining population. But this accelerated that and weakened those Democratic constituencies, and it created virtually no positive rallying point for Democratic candidates.

Just to give you anecdotal evidence of my own, in the 1966 campaign I was working for the Oakland County Democratic Party in Oakland County, Michigan, a suburban area outside Detroit. Fairly closely divided between the parties, though tending toward Republican. I remember trying to say, "Well, let me draw up a campaign flyer or a poster or a campaign document that says what are the great things the Democratic Party can do for you based on the record of the last couple of years." The only thing I could think of to talk about was Project Headstart, which people still talk about when they say which programs work 25 years later. Nothing else really seemed to come out of it. Nothing else really seemed to be there that you could actually go to ordinary American voters and say, "Let's do it."

We had a vast increase, particularly in 1967-68, of disorder in America. Visible failure of the society to create an orderly framework in which people could go live their personal, everyday lives. People yearned for that and we didn't have it. We had big city riots constantly threatening the country, closing down the cities. The Los Angeles riot was two days. The typical big cities riots in Detroit and Newark following Martin Luther King's death in 1968 lasted four, five, six days at a time when there were multiples of them. We also had the student rebellions of various sorts, particularly in 1968. That overall picture of disorder, so much greater than the disorder that we see in 1992, was very off-putting to Americans, and I think it worked against the party in power, which was typically the Democrats.

Johnson commits two major errors. He continues a war that's unwinnable, and he can't effectively administer the proper domestic programs.

I think that Lyndon Johnson was clearly a man of great talents and abilities. Sort of awesome intellectual powers. But I think we could also say, to put it in aphoristic terms, that this is a man who knew the South but not the country, and who knew the Senate but not the world. As a southern Democratic, a Texas Democratic, Lyndon Johnson's experience with the kind of electoral politics that prevailed in most American states in the 1960s was minimal. His job was to get himself nominated in a Texas election where he oscillated between left and right, had to deal with oilmen, had to buy votes in south Texas counties, Mexican farmworkers, and so forth. These are not the typical experiences of winning political elections in the northern states that were then, and indeed are now, the main fulcrum point of the closely divided key states in any election. Johnson had relatively little experience with that. He had no experience with running political campaigns from 1948, in Texas, until 1964, and across thc Unitcd States, which is a campaign, as it turned out, nobody could have lost.

So, Johnson was not used at all to the idea of how northerners could win campaigns. I think that he really didn't understand the northern societies very well. I don't think he understood the big cities. I think that he made a leap from the civil rights movement, and the success of the Civil Rights Act of 1964 and 1965, and he made that leap indeed in that speech at Howard University, "We have to eliminate the effects of segregation. We have to make everybody equal in fact and in practice." And that was a promise that the government couldn't keep. I think he just didn't understand northern society very well. Did not understand the ethnic communities. Did not understand middle class suburbs. These were areas that were foreign to him that he'd never spent any time in. He really had no way of knowing or feeling or understanding. So I think that was a problem.

In addition, he was a person who had not had wide experience in foreign policy, and he tended to apply, as it turns out in Vietnam, lessons which he had learned in senatorial vote-trading politics in a context where they did not obtain. When you think about his comments with Ho Chi Minh, "I'll give him a few dams. We're going to dam up the Mekong River. We're going to put public works money into your area." It's almost as if he's trying to use a Senate Appropriations Subcommittee chairmanship to woo over the votes on foreign policy of an obdurate member of another party.

Well, obviously, that didn't work. He had no real feel for how to deal with the person that turned out to be an implacable totalitarian, and a movement that turned out to be an implacable totalitarian movement. They weren't interested in compromise—half a loaf, getting a bunch of things. They weren't interested in economic growth, as we can see what's happened in Vietnam today. Since that war, they've had one of the slowest rates of economic growth—or no economic growth—in the whole world. Johnson didn't seem to understand that. And he did the thing all leaders do to some extent—but he did it in particularly important places, and that is apply the wrong lessons.

Give an example.

The example of Senate horse-trading in dealing with Ho Chi Minh. The whole course of the Vietnam War, he went into it guided by people that said you adapted the game theory strategies that had been developed by the theorists of nuclear war, and applied them to this limited war in Vietnam. They didn't work there. The theories that say, "If you could extract so much pain from the other side, then they rationally wouldn't do this and so forth." Well, it didn't work there because the Vietnamese Communists were going for total victory.

Clark Clifford was a hawk and stayed with Johnson for quite a while, but in March of '68 they had a meeting, and he realized that Johnson didn't have a plan to win the war. That he just wanted to send more troops there. There was no game plan.

Well, the loss of support following the Tet Offensive in February 1968 was astonishing in the polls in America. If you'd looked at the polls, I believe, in December or January, Johnson looked pretty good. He was walloping Eugene McCarthy in the polls and in the primaries. There was a feeling that the war was on its way to being won. Then the Tet Offensive comes along. Some of the hawks told us at the time that the Tet Offensive was militarily a severe defeat for the Communists in Vietnam. The losses they sustained were irreplaceable. They were very large. They made them much weaker militarily.

But what Americans saw on their TV screens was the United States embassy compound in Saigon under attack. They felt that their prospect was for continuing attacks on the very heart of the American presence in Vietnam. That we could not be safe at any place and time. It seemed like there was this stone at the bottom of the hill, and we could only try to roll it up knowing that it would come down again. I think that that attitude permeated the society, and I think that it was the same attitude that Clark Clifford spoke to.

In point of fact, Clifford found out in March of 1968 what Robert McNamara evidently sensed in 1967. This was McNamara's fault because he'd been in there from the beginning, it was not Clifford's fault, that there was no plan to win the war. Clifford asked the generals, "Well, how do we win?" They said, "We want 200,000 more troops." And he said, "Well, how much sooner do we win the thing?" And they said, "Win? Who's talking about winning?"

What were they thinking about?

They were thinking in terms of this game theory. If we escalate to this extent, then the other side will calculate that the cost to them of meeting that escalation and in overcoming it, or prevailing, or holding on will exceed what this war effort is worth to them, and they will therefore sit down and negotiate and make a victory.

A calculated bluff.

A calculated bluff. The fact is, wars aren't won that way. That game theory, nuclear strategy stuff, where if you say you have more missiles to fire than they can destroy the first time, then they won't launch their first missiles because you'll destroy their country. People thought this was the secret. The other factor in Vietnam was that they were terribly afraid of triggering a nuclear war. Johnson, similar to Truman in 1951 when Truman would not attack the communist sanctuaries [in Korea] even though the Chinese were pouring men over the line, because he was afraid it would lead to a nuclear involvement with mainland China...attack by either China or the Soviet Union. So in 1965 and thereafter, Johnson would not attack the Communist areas in a sustained and unpredictable manner. He did it only under the limitations which enabled the Communists to repel the attacks and shoot down our people much more easily. He did that because he was afraid that there would be a nuclear retaliation from China. We know now that China wasn't a great ally of Vietnam and the communist movement. It was the Soviet Union. But there was the fear of nuclear involvement, so consequently they weren't willing to escalate as much.

The Great Society polarized people. Many people were opposed to it. Was this a calculated thing on his part politically? Did he believe in the Great Society?

I think it probably was an idealistic thing to a very substantial extent. With a political leader there's always some element of political calculation in what they do, and I think it can be argued there always should be some element of political calculation in what they do. It shouldn't be totally idealistic and disconnected to the real world. The real world in a democratic society means politics, among other things. I think it was basically a mistake overall because it moved American social policy away from policies that encouraged, subsidized, and honored upwardly mobile behavior and toward the policies that tended to encourage, subsidize, and honor downwardly mobile behavior. Aberrant behavior. I think that we had a society that became very guilty all of a sudden.

I think that in the course of persuading ourselves that we had a major institution in our society that was fundamentally rotten and needed to be changed, that institution being the legally enforced racial segregation in the South— in the process of convincing ourselves that that aspect of society was rotten, we started to cast doubt on all aspects of American society. We became much more skeptical about the legitimacy of every institution in America. You can see in polls this was not just the elite, although it was them especially, it was also very substantial numbers of the voters. You can see declining belief in the confidence of American society in the mid-'60s.

You have this coinciding with the assassination of President Kennedy, which was a severely upsetting blow. This was not a president that people expected to see vanish suddenly from the scene. That cast more of a pall of illegitimacy over the basic institutions of the country. A lot of the impetus for the Great Society movements, a lot of the theories behind them, come from a sort of guilty view that this is a rotten society. That those who are not doing well in this society are the virtuous ones. And those who are doing well are the bad people.

What is left of the Great Society?

Well, there's not much left of the community action, anti-poverty programs for the most part, which is a good thing certainly. The impulse that led in the last year of the Johnson administration for some congressmen to propose guaranteed annual income, and then for that to take great moves forward and nearly become enacted in the Nixon administration, that impulse for guaranteed annual income is gone. The impulse that says the people who play by the rules and obey the law are bad people, and the people who go to jail and are criminals are somehow better people morally, that impulse is pretty much gone from the great mass of people in the society. It is not gone from some substantial number of liberal policymakers and political activists who do believe that. I don't say that they are the preponderant part of the Democratic Party, in fact, I think they are not today. But they are an important part of it and that spirit does live on. You can see it in the operation of our social institutions and the fact that prison populations from about 1964 to '76 were basically stable even though crime was rising very rapidly then. This was a society that somehow did not feel entitled to take people who were violent criminals and hold them in jail for long periods of time. At least it felt less entitled than it had in the past to do that. Remember that prison populations are the result of increments of hundreds of decisions made by wide ranges of decision makers all over the country; prosecutors, police officers, jury members, and so forth. Very decentralized decision making.

Then starting around 1976, we have a change in attitude, and society believes itself again to be entitled to put people in jail, and you have a tripling or more of prison populations. You still have a fringe of the population that is well represented in the liberal media and political elite which doesn't go along with this. Which tries to devise legal means to prevent capital punishment and to spring people from jail. That feels as Michael Dukakis did that it's perfectly okay to give weekend furloughs to people who are sentenced to life without parole; people who are supposed to be held in jail forever can nonetheless go out on the weekends routinely. To speak of the Los Angeles riot as a "rebellion" or an "uprising." So that thought still infects the society, but it's much less strong among ordinary people than it used to be.

Do you think Americans just got sick and tired of it? Of coddling people...

I think so. At some point the attitude was just basically wrong. It transposed from one situation where the guilt belonged, to another situation where the guilt did not belong. This sense of guilt and a sense that the institutions didn't work right. It took our conclusion we reached as a society that legal racial segregation was wrong. And it applied that to a whole other set of institutions, which I think by and large were not wrong things. Every institution makes some mistakes in its operations, and one can argue within limits about how an institution should operate. Reasonable people can disagree, but the idea that you send people who commit violent crimes to jail for long periods of time is, I think, something that really is not arguable. Those people who go to jail are bad. People who work and earn a living and maintain houses in the suburbs and send their kids to school and pay taxes are good. I think a lot of liberals forgot that in the Great Society period and some of them forget that still. They see the suburbanite, middle class people as oppressors and the criminals as the oppressed. I think that as long as you see that, you ain't going to win many votes.

Was Lyndon Johnson in over his head?

Well, I don't know. I think we're all in over our heads. Johnson was given the Vietnam situation as a fait accompli to a very considerable extent. The United States had connived in the assassination of President Diem of South Vietnam, which was done early in November 1963 and with obviously the approval of President Kennedy. Once we had connived in that assassination and had sanctioned the overthrow of the government there, we were basically in a position of responsibility for the conduct of the government of South Vietnam. And once we were in that position of responsibility, I would argue that Lyndon Johnson had a set of choices before him, none of which was very palatable. Like most politicians, he did not really have, as we say, a road to military victory. He did not ever have that set out, but like most politicians he was hoping he might be lucky. You know, he and others were lucky on a lot of things. Some problems solve themselves. Things go better than you expect militarily sometimes. I mean, hey, these things are possible. He hoped for something to come up like that in Vietnam. But the fact is that if you look at the choices that the president faced the beginning of December 1963, you see a series of unpalatable choices. He had really been foisted with the responsibility for which he was not well prepared and which arguably no American was well prepared: to run the government of South Vietnam. Among those urging that result, urging the ousting of the Diem government were people like David Halberstam and Neil Sheehan, who became the great critics of American involvement later. But they urged the step which really got us inevitably involved more.

What was that?

The step of ousting the Diem government and conniving in the assassination of Diem.

You are saying they were responsible for that?

Well, they urged that strongly in their dispatches. They said, "We can win this war if we could just get rid of this corrupt group of thugs running the country," who in fact were unpalatable in some ways.

So Johnson was really star-crossed by the time he took office.

I think he was faced with some very difficult choices. I don't believe, in my judgment, that he made the best choice among those he had, but he did have a difficult choice. On the domestic scene, I think you can also say this about Johnson. It was not that Johnson really put in practice, or tried to put in practice, a bunch of policies that were based on the idea that American society was guilty and evil and undermined basic institutions. He was not acting alone there or entirely outside the spirit of the times. Opinion, and particularly elite opinion, not only among the Democrats, but among some establishment Republicans had moved. Those "liberal" Republicans of the time were really moving in that direction. I think that he was not just a lone person imposing what turned out to be an incorrect vision on a society, but he was part of a large number of persons who had got some wrong ideas, who really drew the wrong lessons from the civil rights revolution, who ended up treating most institutions in American society as if they were as rotten and evil as the institution of legally enforced racial segregation.

I think that was a very strong impulse in the society at the time. I'm not at all sure that President Kennedy would have been immune from it or even some Republicans—Nelson Rockefeller or Richard Nixon or some other Republicans that we can imagine having been elected in some circumstances in 1964. Very important parts of society were leaning in that direction, so that Johnson was, in part, just an instrument as well as an actor.

GEORGE HERRING

THE VIETNAM WAR

The Vietnam War was the longest war in American history. It had a profound effect on the country, its institutions, and its people.

Professor Herring has spent years studying and examining the war and has written a bestselling book on it, America's Longest War.

After all the death, injury, and suffering, he does not believe that the United States benefitted one bit from this war.

When was our first involvement in Vietnam?

The first direct involvement was in February 1950 when the Truman administration commits the United States to provide military and economic assistance to the French, who at that time are waging war with the Communist-led Vietminh revolution in Vietnam.

What effect did Dienbienphu have for us?

It had a major effect. It is often judged one of the decisive battles of the 20th century—the climactic battle in the first Indochina war which leads to the Geneva Settlement, which in turn leads ultimately to the departure of the French from Vietnam, and, more generally, Indochina. Initially, the Eisenhower administration tremendously fears the impact of Dienbienphu, fearing that it's going to result in a communist victory in Vietnam that will have implications for Indochina and perhaps all of Southeast Asia and beyond. Later as the Geneva Conference proceeds in June and July of 1954, the administration ultimately concludes that Dienbienphu is not such a bad thing. It will get the French out, and when it is decided to partition Vietnam at the 17th parallel, Eisenhower and John Foster Dulles, his secretary of state, conclude that this will give the United States an opportunity to construct in the southern half of Vietnam a bulwark against further communist penetration of Vietnam, Indochina, and Southeast Asia.

So, ultimately, the Eisenhower administration may be making a virtue out of necessity, but from more deep seated reasons begins to conclude that here is an opportunity to do something, and the withdrawal of the French will permit us to do it without being tainted by French colonialism as we had been while assisting the French between '50-54.

The Geneva Agreement provides for a partition of Vietnam at the 17th parallel, and ultimately to French withdrawal from Indochina. SEATO comes in September of 1954 and that's the larger mechanism that the Eisenhower administration creates to defend Southeast Asia against any further problems and any further communist threats in that region.

What is our involvement during the remainder of the 1950s?

It's not a military involvement, but the aid program was sizeable, substantial. It was one of the largest aid programs anywhere in the world at the time when we were providing substantial foreign aid in many different parts of the globe. A sizeable private commitment there of agencies like CARE, the Red Cross, Operation Rescue. There were all kinds of organizations involved on a private basis. The military was training the Vietnamese army. So there's a sizeable commitment on the part of the United States. It's just not a military commitment, and there's not a formal shooting war until the end of the decade.

When did it heat up for us?

The Kennedy years really are a major turning point. By 1961 the southern forbearers of the Vietminh felt they had been denied the fruits of their victory by what had happened after Geneva; the refusal to hold national elections— a long and very complicated story. The southern Vietminh conclude that the only way they can achieve their goals is to take arms and they launch an insurgency. By the late '50s, North Vietnam has come to the aid of that insurgency; is infiltrating men and supplies into the south. There is a legitimate shooting war throughout many parts of South Vietnam by 1961, and it begins to appear that the insurgents, who by this time are called the Viet Cong, partly through their own strength, partly through the ineptitude of the government of Ngo Dinh Diem, have a chance of taking over South Vietnam.

So Kennedy, within months of taking office, is confronted, along with the crises in Cuba, Laos, and Berlin, with the issue of whether to make an additional major commitment to try to bolster the Diem government against the insurgents. And Kennedy makes a major commitment in 1961. He continues to build on that commitment between the time he takes office and leaves office; the number of so-called advisors increases from several hundred to more than 16,000.

By the time he is assassinated, these advisors are doing more than advising. They are actually flying airplanes and on the ground shooting. By the time he is assassinated, by virtue of the U. S. complicity in the overthrow of Diem in October-November 1963, the United States has assumed the level of responsibility for the South Vietnamese government that it had not had before that time. Also, I think Kennedy's rhetoric, particularly in 1963, talking repeatedly about how important Vietnam is—you know, the more you say something is important, the more important it becomes. I think Kennedy had, in addition to escalating on the ground, had escalated the level of the American commitment rhetorically as well.

When our government approved the assassination of Diem, did it realize that act would involve us more and more in Vietnam?

I'm not sure that they really did. I think they saw themselves in a very difficult situation. On one side, many felt that we could not succeed without Diem. On another side, many felt we couldn't succeed with him. There was fierce debate. At one point, I think it was Robert Kennedy made the comment, "Well, you know if things are really as bad as people are saying here, maybe the best thing to do would be to get out." And as one participant recorded it, that question sort of floated. Nobody said anything and they went on from there.

I think there was some vague sense of foreboding on the part of people involved in that decision. But I think they really felt they didn't have any choice. Probably in their heart-of-hearts they felt that ultimately the United States would succeed because it was the United States and therefore, although we regret having to do this, we have to do it and we're going to do it.

When did we get in over our heads?

I think the point of no return is probably 1954, 1955. I think 1954 and '55 is probably the last chance when we could have stood by and done nothing without major impact for U. S. foreign policy or domestic politics. I think once the commitment has been made in 1955 to assist Diem in South Vietnam, you're pretty much launched on that course.

The crucial military decision is July 28, 1965, when Johnson, in effect, makes a sort of open-ended commitment to send whatever level of combat troops is needed to achieve U. S. goals in South Vietnam. In the sense of a military commitment, that's without question, in my view, the crucial decision.

That was a year after the Tonkin Gulf incident.

Almost to the day. Just short of a year.

When did the North Vietnamese make an irrevocable commitment to the war?

That's a very good question. I'm not sure I have a very good answer for it. My guess probably is 1963-64, but I don't have a really good solid answer for that one.

We did not formally deploy our combat troops until March 8, 1965. It consisted of 3,500 Marines.

That's right. Formally. Marine or Army units going as units. U.S. troops had been involved in combat, but they were still nominally in an advisory role.

After Diem was assassinated, the South Vietnamese experienced many different governments.

Revolving door. It's what eventually leads to the commitment. First, the beginnings of the air war and the commitment of U.S. ground troops. I think there is a conclusion ultimately that the situation in South Vietnam is hopeless, and that we're going to have to take drastic measures on our own in order to hold on to what we feel is an important commitment.

How did our troop buildup begin?

The first troops are sent in to guard the air bases. The Marines come in March of 1965 to guard the air bases. That's the reason for bringing them there. But the larger increments of troops that follow come because the South Vietnamese government remains very, very unstable, and because the South Vietnamese army is not able to contain the insurgents backed by North Vietnamese regular units at all. It's simply the inadequacy of the South Vietnamese militarily that more than anything else leads to the major commitment of U. S. combat troops.

At this point, was President Johnson lying to the American public regarding the number of troops being called up?

No, I don't think he was lying. He wasn't always telling the whole truth. I would make a distinction. He didn't tell anything he felt he didn't have to, and he wasn't always totally candid. I don't think he outright lied. I think that's an exaggeration.

By 1965, he had more or less taken Goldwater's position regarding Vietnam.

There's that famous Herblock cartoon of Johnson staring into the mirror and Goldwater staring back at him, which sort of summed up the conclusion that many people reached. Maybe not in '65, but certainly early '66. Johnson, while he said in the campaign he didn't want American boys doing what Asian boys should be doing, was in fact doing what Goldwater had recommended with heavy bombing of North Vietnam and major commitments of U. S. troops.

General Vo Nguyen Giap, Ho Chi Minh's commander, was prepared to take those losses. He thought public opinion in the United States would not support the war.

The perception the North Vietnamese, including Giap were operating on, was that a long drawn out war in which the United States suffered extensive casualties would be to the advantage of North Vietnam. Quite clearly, I think their strategy was predicated on wearing down the United States and exacerbating what they would call "the contradictions in American society." So, yes, very much so.

Did we benefit from the bombing of North Vietnam?

It did not stop infiltration. It did not cripple the fighting capabilities of either the insurgents or the North Vietnamese regulars. It imposed a heavy cost on them, and it forced the North Vietnamese to devote a whole lot of resources to repairing the damage from the bombing. To devote a whole lot of resources to air defenses. It forced them into greater dependence on the Soviet Union than they would have probably preferred. So it had an impact, clearly. But it neither forced them to surrender, nor severely crippled their ability to fight.

What was the consequence of the Tet Offensive on January 30, 1968?

It has several consequences. In terms of North Vietnam and the National Liberation Front or Viet Cong, it has a huge impact. In the sense that the Viet Cong, or the NLF is beaten to death, bludgeoned, beaten down to a point from which it never really recovers. The two major military thrusts from this point on are carried out by North Vietnamese regulars in 1972 and again in 1975. So it changes the nature of the war in that sense.

On the side of the United States it leaves the impression that no matter how much the United States commits to this effort it probably cannot succeed at an acceptable cost, and so it forces first Lyndon Johnson and then, subsequently, Richard Nixon, to change American tactics on how they approach the war. So it has major effects in both camps.

What it does is to raise the stalemate that had already developed in Vietnam to a whole new level, which over the longer haul, works very clearly to the advantage of North Vietnam. If they don't lose, they win. That's the essence of their position.

By April of 1968 we had 550,000 troops in Vietnam and nearly 23,000 deaths.

It's not generally recognized, there was very, very heavy combat after March of 1968. There's a general impression that the war was "winding down" in the parlance of the day, but in fact, U. S. casualties the rest of '68 were probably the highest of any comparable period in the war.

When did we go over to fighting defensively?

Well, probably the latter part of 1968 and early part of 1969. That's the point where your fighting becomes a holding action to support your withdrawal.

By 1970 we had 44,000 deaths, so it's a very serious and bloody war at that point.

...remains so. The next three years while the United States is ostensibly getting out, it's still very bloody and very high casualties.

When did we invade Cambodia and why did we?

April of 1970 is the actual time of the so-called incursion into Cambodia. Various reasons have been attributed to it. The reason Nixon gave was to try to do sufficient damage to North Vietnamese units in sanctuaries across the border in Cambodia so that they would not pose a threat to South Vietnam while the United States was implementing

Nixon's Vietnamization policy, which meant turning over ultimate responsibility for the fighting to the South Vietnamese. Other reasons have been ventured; Nixon trying to show the North Vietnamese that he was tough and, even though withdrawing, was prepared to take risks to achieve his policy goals. Some have even said it was a way of showing his domestic critics that he was tough and a factor to be reckoned with.

This was a terrible public relations move.

Yes, it had a huge impact in the sense that the peace movement was rather on the wane during the first year or so of Nixon's presidency. But Cambodia, and particularly the shootings of students at Kent State and Jackson State, had a tremendous impact in reviving the peace movement and increasing general American weariness with the war.

We invaded Laos, February 8, 1971, and that was also a disaster for us.

Yeah...less so in terms of domestic opinion. What happened was that it seemed to prove that Vietnamization wasn't working. That without the sort of support they were accustomed to from the United States, the South Vietnamese simply couldn't hack it on their own.

May 1972 we mined the harbor at Haiphong and other North Vietnamese ports. Did this help our effort?

Yes, for the short term. What Nixon is responding to by renewing the bombing of North Vietnam and mining Haiphong and other harbors is the North Vietnamese Easter offensive of the spring of 1972. At the point he takes these steps the Easter offensive is very close to achieving a dramatic success and very close to perhaps winning a military victory for the North Vietnamese in the south. So the steps that Nixon took had a tremendous impact in the sense that they denied North Vietnamese military units the spare parts, the gasoline, and other things that they needed to complete the offensive. And along with the heavy use of American air power, close air support on the ground, made it possible for the South Vietnamese to turn back the North Vietnamese offensive and avoid what could have been a disastrous defeat in 1972.

So this prolonged the war.

Exactly. And also, it's main impact was to make possible the peace settlement of 1973. Nixon, I think, realized after the Easter offensive that his days were numbered in terms of needing to get out. The North Vietnamese felt that they had taken a beating in the latter stage of the

Easter offensive and shifted to a new strategy, and therefore both were ready to engage in serious negotiations which led to the abortive October agreement, and then ultimately to the January 1973 agreement.

Some people forget that we started to wind down the war in the early '70s. We had gone from 550,000 troops in April '68, to 47,000 troops in June 1972, and 24,000 by December '72.

The high point, according to the figures I have, is April 1969. There is a steady decline from 543,000 in April '69 to 414,000 in June of 1970. 239,000 in June of 1971. Then 47,000 in June 1972.

How did it end?

The agreement that was negotiated in October 1972, and finally signed in January '73, and implemented by March '73, provided for the withdrawal of American military forces, but we still maintained a major commitment. The hope, obviously, on Nixon's part was that the status quo could be maintained for an indefinite period of time, or that the Vietnamese might work out some sort of peaceful settlement for themselves. Of course, this doesn't happen. But it's still two years. Our military forces are out in March of '73, and the final North Vietnamese offensive is in March and April of 1975. So it's a two-year period.

We didn't get very good advice regarding Vietnam.

There were a number who were right. They just weren't listened to. If you're saying that ignorance of Vietnam was a major reason for our intervention, and our ultimate failure there, I couldn't agree more. We went in blindly ignorant of the history of the country. We went in ignorant of the people, of their culture, their customs. We remained ignorant to a considerable degree throughout much of our involvement. We made major miscalculations. We seriously underestimated the staying power, the resiliency, the dedication, the commitment of the Vietminh in the first Indochina War and the North Vietnamese and the National Liberation Front in the second Indochina War.

On the other hand, at every juncture along the way you can find people who predicted with some degree of foresight what was going to happen from 1954 and '55 on.

Who were they?

In 1954-55, the secretary of defense, Charles Wilson, is very opposed to the commitment and warns of disaster. You've got George

Ball in 1964 and '65. These are just two. There are many lower level people who have some insight and express foreboding going all the way back to 1950.

Why were so many Americans bent on saving Vietnam?

That's the crucial question. I think the only way you can understand it is in terms of the cold war mind-set and the containment policy that derived from that mind-set. Any gain for communism is automatically a loss for the United States and which all areas of the world are seen as of equal importance. It takes root in the late 1940s and early 1950s as far as Vietnam is concerned, and really isn't questioned until we have 200,000 or 300,000 troops there. At which point the number of troops there becomes sort of the argument for the importance of it.

Did we accrue any benefit from that war?

No, it would be hard to find any advantage that we gained from it in any way, except that maybe sooner or later a Vietnam was going to happen somewhere. And until it happened, we were an accident waiting to happen. That's putting it very crudely and sort of colloquially. No, I think you'd be hard pressed to find anything really good that came out of it.

DAVID HALBERSTAM

THE 1960s AND VIETNAM

One of America's foremost writers believes Kennedy would have pulled out of Vietnam had he lived and won re-election. He thinks we lost Vietnam by 1963. That LBJ got caught-up in a "macho" situation and also was afraid he would lose his Great Society if he pulled out.

It is his opinion that the country has not yet properly dealt with Vietnam: "In a way, we're afraid to tell the truth to ourselves about why it failed, which was that we were on the wrong side."

1960 began with the presidential campaign of Nixon and Kennedy. Kennedy was to win by the narrowest of margins, two-thirds of one percent, or 112,000 votes.

A couple of things. The coming of technology in the election. The coming of television—not just the Kennedy/Nixon debates, but John Kennedy's use of television, from start to finish in the campaign, as a way of defeating the traditional party leaders, most of whom were Catholic, and therefore were afraid of having a Catholic candidate. They were very nervous about it. Therefore, by dent of television, he used the primary system to go outside the traditional party structure and was the first modern use of television in a campaign.

The '60s marked a speeding-up of the cycle of life. The speeding-up—more technology, faster pace, more movement, more transportation, more communication. The Kennedy election reflected that. That's the doorway to the '60s.

You think about the '60s as being a moment when people, in effect, used television as a means of social protest, whether it's Martin Luther King in Selma, or Montgomery, or a number of other things. Television and social protest are connected in the '60s. The speeding-up of the cycle of life.

The second thing is John Kennedy. The sense of his modernity. He represented a break with previous leaders: Adenauer, De Gaulle, Eisenhower, men who were born in another century. There he was in his '40s. Young. Attractive. Modern. There was a sense that this was the coming of age of a new, powerful America after the war. That phrase "the torch has been passed to a new generation of Americans." America was beginning to become a superpower. Europe, the old order was in decline, and here now was America in the assent. I think those two things are very important.

I think John Kennedy was a good pluralistic politician. I think there's always been too much romance about him, because he was attractive, because he was very skillful with the media, because he was slain. In a tragic way he has always seemed to be a rather romantic figure. I have always regarded him somewhat differently, as a very cool piece of work. A very good pluralistic politician. Sort of a first Irish Brahmin. He wanted to know whether he could win. He wanted to get 51 percent. I think he was a very good working politician, which is by the way, a phrase I admire: working politician.

One of the things that happens in an age of television, particularly if you have someone as attractive as John Kennedy, there is a tendency for the symbolic to become more powerful, or more important, than the substantive. You have an attractive young man and you look at him and he's on television. He's attractive at a press conference and giving good speeches. A sense that the country is going to do things well and do the right things, and you don't at that moment see all the other parts of the power structure that slow down an attractive politician trying to modernize the society. But I think he was a good, professional politician.

How would you rate him as a president?

Well, I think he's a comet. We can't tell. You know, he got a thousand days as a president. He is murdered in Dallas. His presidency becomes part of a joint presidency that ends up in Vietnam. There's the private doubt and the greater public confidence or hawkishness on Vietnam. But I always thought he probably would not go into Vietnam. I've always thought he would paper it over with Goldwater in '64 for a second term and then get out. I thought he was too smart and cool and Irish "Pol" to waste his second term in the rice paddies of Vietnam.

You can't rate him. The best thing about him was his intelligence. His modernity. His almost fatalism. His sense of history. His liking of the political act—in contrast to Nixon. He really liked being a professional politician, and I think he liked being president. He was very good at it. But he was there at the height of the cold war and the McCarthy period still existed. The senator himself had been banished seven years earlier, but looking soft on communism wasn't a powerful thing. He had to contend with that.

But there were things he was doing. For example, the Test Ban Treaty and other things that were a sign of someone trying to get beyond the log jam.

You believe he would have gotten out of Vietnam.

The Kennedy loyalists think of it as an automatic call. They are apt to make their case based on this speech or that speech. You had both the private doubts, which were dovish, and the public sentiment, which often turned out to be more hawkish. My instinct is that he was just too shrewd a professional politician to waste his second term in the rice paddies of Vietnam. That he knew it didn't work, and he didn't want us to get sucked in a neo-colonial war in the footsteps of the French. He was very shrewd about it.

Michael Forrestal was his liaison man in Vietnam, who I got to know very well, and who's probably the first government official to be nice to me when I was a young reporter. Michael always felt that John Kennedy had more doubts about it than anybody else. But he was not about to go out and take too much heat. I said earlier that I thought he would patch it over. Keep it on the back burner in '64. Run against Goldwater. Beat him handily and then figure out some way to negotiate out.

But you have to say that he escalated the number of Americans who were there from roughly 600 to about 18,000. The number of American deaths and some of the public rhetoric was rather heated, and, in addition, he gave the country the "can-do" team that with Lyndon Johnson took us to escalation.

I think the Oliver Stone stuff is just silly. I think it's a silly vision of complicated events.

Many people believe that America changed forever at the time of the Kennedy assassination.

There's been a lot of things suppressed under the surface of this society for 30 years. We hadn't looked at our domestic program in 30 years. We'd been taken up with World War II and then the cold war. So a lot of stuff was there. The society was in dramatic change. The pace of life was accelerating quickly. People were more affluent and therefore more confident. There was a beginning of change of gender. There was the beginning of the change of the definition of public citizen as embodied by Ralph Nader. There was the Berkeley Free Speech movement. There was a sense of all kinds of visceral protests with the spearhead or the shield of that being...the umbrella being Vietnam. All kinds of protest movements were taking place, and they were taking place because of modern technology. Live and increasingly no longer in black and white, but in color, in people's living rooms, and Johnson, who was a less nimble politician than Kennedy, did not make a particularly good adjustment to them.

Johnson was a much more skillful politician than John Kennedy. Working within the Senate, he knew how to bend Frank Church and he knew how to press flesh on Bill Fulbright. But in a kind of intellectual sense, in terms of picking up new and different currents within the society, he was almost like moving back a generation.

John Kennedy was very supple, very astute, and he understood viscerally the change of forces in the society. That's one of the reasons why he used television so well. There it was, and he understood it, and he understood what he could do. He made a nimble adjustment to the civil rights thing, to which he had really not made much of a commitment earlier on. But he understood that it was something that was powerful and happening. He was better on the free-fall of politics. He could better understand viscerally profound social changes than Johnson, and he obviously did not trigger some of the antagonisms that Johnson did.

But you must understand that other than Vietnam, Lyndon Johnson tried very hard to keep up with the Kennedy legacy. What he tried to do in terms of the Civil Rights Act; used John Kennedy's death to pass it, was an extraordinary accomplishment. Then to go on from that to the Great Society. There were just an awful lot of people in the country who were not going to accept progress as it was mandated by a president with a Texas accent.

Why did Johnson change so quickly after the '64 election?

There was a great joke. A voter saying, "They told me that if I voted for Goldwater we'd have American boys fighting in Asia within a year, and I voted for Goldwater and we had American boys fighting in Asia." Why did he turn so quickly? He didn't turn so quickly. It happened. I mean, people like me, back as early as the fall of '63, thought the war was virtually over, despite all the official optimism of the American military in Saigon which kept saying, "We're winning the war, we're winning the war, we're winning the war." In fact, by the time I left Vietnam in late 1963, the VC were almost in absolute control of the countryside. The war was almost over, and therefore you had a dual problem if you're a Democrat.

First, it was going to be sort of all the way in or all the way out. We were no longer going to only use a proxy to keep the Communists from winning the country. You had to send American combat troops.

The second problem was going back to the McCarthy period and the fall of China. The fear loomed much more with Lyndon Johnson than it did with John Kennedy. That if he lost Vietnam, he would lose control of the Congress, and therefore he would lose the Great Society. Bill Moyers and I both think that that is terribly, terribly important. I think, again, Oliver Stone is really wrong on this thing. Johnson really did not like the idea of the war. He didn't want the war. But it was closing in on him, and he was not going to be the president of the United States who let Ho Chi Minh walk into Saigon because (a) it was manhood, but (b) it was also the loss of the Great Society.

Regarding the Tet Offensive, you have stated that "the real casualty was our strategy of attrition and the credibility of General Westmoreland."

Almost every American public official the last couple of years before Tet had his credibility damaged. And the last person that they thought had credibility was this very handsome, attractive general out there, who seemed to be promising again and again that there would not be a long war, that there would be light at the end of the tunnel. It worked pretty well. The idea that Johnson always was selling was that it was going to be a small war. It wasn't small. We went quietly to 500,000. And it wasn't going to be quick. What the Tet Offensive showed was that we hadn't damaged them. We hadn't damaged the dynamic. We were in a stalemate.

The great debate starting in late '66, and into early '67, was on the part of a number of well-informed journalists and some of their colleagues who worked in the CIA, and a few rather shrewd military men who had some history in the place who, in effect, believed that although we were fighting well and bravely, we were not denting their dynamic, that we were fighting the birth rate of the country, that we could kill 100,000 men a year, but they would send 200,000 men down the trails. So it could go on forever. There's that great quote of Harrison Salisbury when he goes to Hanoi in December '66. Pham Van Dong, the North Vietnamese prime minister, says to Mr. Salisbury, "How long do you Americans want to fight? One year? Two years? Three years? Five years? Ten years? Twenty years? We will be glad to accommodate you."

What the Tet Offensive had shown was that the pessimists, primarily the journalists, but some of their sources in the government who could not come public because they would lose their jobs, were accurate in their prophesies. It was not going well. The other side was resilient. That we were not fighting in effect a static army, but we were fighting the birth rate of a nation. You could kill them and then another 100,000 come down the pike. It was their national war of liberation. That's what undercut Westmoreland and undercut his credibility. It showed that the war could go on forever.

Tet is what really started to turn America against the war.

Well, I think it had already begun in the fall of '67. I think by the fall of '67 it had seeped into the bloodstream of the upper middle class, in colleges, all kinds of people. Centrist people. We are not talking about the left, or even the right. We're talking about the American center. Even the Establishment. All kinds of people who normally support their government, support their war, and have traditional definitions of patriotism and loyalty, were beginning to falter by the fall of '67. Beginning to doubt the optimism. We could fight them, fight well, but they would keep coming.

The doubts had been growing in '67. There was a great uneasiness in the government. A large number of people in the White House, in the government had been getting out. There was a constant migration of centrist individuals starting I think in mid '67. This was a man who had said there was not going to be any war at all, and then said that it was going to be a small war. Suddenly, there's 500,000 men there.

There had been a systematic loss of the government's credibility and a general belief that the other side was really very tough and very good. Also, a sort of uneasiness about using that much technology in a peasant nation. Is that what America wants to do? Even if we could win the war, which I didn't think we could do, is it worth the price? And then along comes Tet.

Why were so many people wrong on Vietnam?

Because they took all the stuff that they'd learned from World War II and from containment. They hadn't read their history and they hadn't read about the French-Indochina War. They thought it was the West vs. communism instead of being nationalism vs. feudalism. The other side was the nationalist side and our side was the feudal side. Our Vietnamese generals were former French corporals. Our military had a great deal of respect based upon its extraordinary showing in World War II. Not a lot of people knew how to make the adjustment to the fact that traditional American power, high technology, was not applicable in this particular war. It was a good deal more applicable in Korea than it was here. You come to Dean Rusk if you are a young State Department guy, and say we have this problem. And Rusk would say, "We had those problems in Korea." As if this was Korea done over. But in Korea we had a viable ally. It was a traditional border-crossing war. This was a political war where our power was not applicable.

Nobody had read the history of it. There was an arrogance of power, a belief we were so big and powerful and with all our technology that, when the first American bomber flew over and the first American gunship loaded up with weapons showed up, that the VC would get the word and surrender. There's a story about Otto Ferbinger, the very, very, very hawkish managing editor of *Time* magazine. Probably the single biggest hawk in the country—more so than the military. Going up to Cam Rayn Bay, which is where we built this huge engineering complex so that we could bring in our big ships, and turning to a *Time* magazine guy named Frank McCullough, who had a lot of doubts, and saying, "I know how we can get this war over in a few months." McCullough says, "What's that?" "Bring the top VC generals here and show them this and they'll know that it's over." It was about Western blindness.

Did we learn anything from this war?

We've learned some things. I would not go off the deep end as to how much we've learned. I've never found anything in the rhetoric of Ronald Reagan and George Bush that shows very much that they've learned. But I think a lot of people who were in the national security complex are aware. Of course now, because of the end of the cold war, we don't have to get sucked into one of those things again.

I don't see a lot of benefit. I think it's a great tragic moment for the Vietnamese. For us. I think we damaged the center of our country. We damaged the fabric of it. I think we damaged the kind of confidence in government that you're supposed to have. It's still haunting a generation. We've never really dealt with it. We've never articulated. Ronald

In Our Time

Reagan and Nixon called it our finest hour. Bush is always praising it. We have never really dealt at a high level as to why it didn't work. Certainly people like I have. And there are certain senators who have. In a way, we're afraid to tell the truth to ourselves about why it failed, which was that we were on the wrong side.

Mike Royko

THE 1968 DEMOCRATIC CONVENTION

Jerry Rubin, Abbie Hoffman, Tom Hayden, and a cast of Hippies, Yippies, and dispirited liberals arrived in Chicago, August 3, 1968, to disrupt the Democratic Convention, Mayor Daley, the police, and Chicago—not necessarily in that order.

Mike Royko, one of America's leading journalists, was there and thinks it could have been averted if Daley had listened to Ramsey Clark, the attorney general.

But Daley listened to few men, especially a liberal from the "outside." He cracked down hard on the demonstrators, and on Wednesday evening, August 9, 1968, all hell broke loose.

The trouble first began on Thursday, August 3, 1968. This was before the start of the convention. Preceding that, David Dellinger had been active in putting together the Committee to End the War in Vietnam and said he was going to bring 100,000 people to Chicago. Actually, only about 10,000 came. The police were on 12-hour shifts. The National Guard was on alert. Mayor Daley said he was going to call up the Army if necessary. Chicago was ready. Do you think the problem was blown out of proportion before the start of the convention? Was there a mind set that there was going to be trouble?

Yeah, I thought there was a lot of scare talk. It was not just Dellinger, it was Abbie Hoffman and Jerry Rubin coming up with all their bizarre threats. They were going to put LSD in Lake Michigan and make everyone high. A lot of silly stuff that some elements of the press played up and scared people. But at the same time you had rationale people saying, "Look, there isn't enough LSD in the world to put in Lake Michigan that would have an effect on the drinking water." They were talking about seducing the delegates and all kinds of nonsensical stuff. I didn't take any of that seriously.

My view of the convention, and what happened, has always been that if Daley had listened to Ramsey Clark, who was then attorney general, and his people, the whole nightmare could have been avoided. They knew the demonstrators. They knew their tactics. They knew their methods. They tried to persuade Daley this is not going to be chaos. These things can be handled in a sane way. But it was his town, his convention, and he was going to do it his way. He wasn't going to listen to them. He wouldn't. It was this belligerent position that led to the thing getting out of hand.

The demonstrators were located in Lincoln Park. The police started with them the first night. It escalated every night.

Yeah, see, a lot of people who weren't in Chicago didn't really understand the geography. The convention that Daley was trying to prevent from being disrupted was at the International Amphitheater, which is out near the stockyards. Forty-some hundred south. Lincoln Park, where they were, is 1600 north. So we're talking a distance of about 56 city blocks, which is about seven or eight miles. So you had demonstrators congregating in a park that was bordered on one side by the outer drive and Lake Michigan, and on the other side by part of the city's entertainment district, Wells Street and Rush Street, and about nine miles from the convention hall. So, how in the hell was somebody in Lincoln Park going to disrupt something going on nine miles away?

The cops, when they went in there finally, busting heads...it was the justification you were violating the curfew. The park district rules are that you gotta be outta there by 11:00 P.M. Well, that may be what the ordinance says, but it's never been followed in Chicago. I mean, Christ, people are in the parks sometimes all night. Nobody really pays attention to 11:00 P.M. People sleep in the parks. When I was a kid, hundreds of families used to go out to Humbolt Park, our neighborhood park. We didn't have air conditioning, and during the sweltering weather we'd go and sleep out there. So, it was really unnecessary for them to say you gotta be outta the parks and to go in there and start chasing them.

What they could have probably done and I discussed this with Jerry Rubin years later. If the police had been there and at 11:00 P.M. said, "You are violating the curfew, you have a half hour to get out of here or we'll move you out," and then maybe waited until midnight and then said with their loudspeakers, "You are in violation of the law, we are ordering you to leave, you have one hour to clear the park." Then at 1:00 A.M. they do it again and at 2:00 A.M. Well, by morning, you have a bunch of people who are chilly, tired, exhausted. They've been up all night, afraid the cops are going to come in, and they would have looked around, and the city would have been bustling. People would have been going to work. There would have been this tired and haggard group of people who sat up all night in the park to accomplish nothing. That's all they would have had to do. Just keep them awake and keep them scared. Could they have gone on a rampage? Where were they going to rampage? On Wells Street. I think not. The whole thing was so mishandled.

Do you think this was just paranoia on Daley's part?

Sure. And also on the part of the police. You've gotta remember, we're talking 1968. You've got a bunch of cops, most of them from blue collar families. Many of them grew up in the southwest side of Chicago and the northwest side of Chicago. Most of them with a view of life that was more 1940s and 50s than the view of life that people in the parks had. You had people with very middle class values. They had already been exposed to rioting because of King's death. They were looking at guys with hair down to the middle of their backs. All the things that they found offensive, they had to deal with. You had the sexual revolution, you had racial revolution, you had the drug revolution...all the things that they believed were bad...they had been dealing with for a year or more. There had been all kinds of things going on in Chicago, and they were at a boiling point. This was a very angry police department.

They were harassing the police. They were not shy about that. On Wednesday evening, August 9, the police had had six days of this. Dellinger had a meeting in the bandstand at Grant Park and told them, "We're going to have a nonviolent march to the amphitheater. Any of you who cannot be nonviolent, don't go." They then collected at Balboa and Michigan Avenue. The TV cameras were there. They started to harass the police, and that's when the police charged the group.

Well, yeah, they were looking for confrontation. There's no question about it. They wanted confrontation. They wanted this stuff on television. Abbie wanted it and Jerry wanted it. The whole bunch wanted it. Tom Hayden and everybody. They wanted confrontation.

Do you think the cops could have held back?

Sure they could have held back. As I say, in Lincoln Park where it all started, they could have held back there. All this stuff about the terrible things they were throwing, well, hell, if somebody tosses something, that doesn't mean that the entire police force is supposed to go berserk and start busting whatever head is available. They reached the point that reporters wound up in the hospital with busted heads and delegates. They were out of control.

You think it was a "police riot" as it was later described?
Yeah. Yeah.

How did Daley handle that afterwards? How did he rationalize it?
Well, nobody got killed. That was something he kept emphasizing. They preserved order and protected the city. And these are outsiders. I received during that month about 4,000 pieces of mail, and it was just about 50-50, for Daley—against Daley. So, it didn't hurt him politically because Chicago and Illinois are essentially conservative areas. There was far more support for Daley and the cops around here than for people like Abbie and Jerry. I mean, they represented danger and revolution and all sorts of things to the public. So, Daley wasn't hurt politically.

Daley simply took the position that there was some plot going on, he was going to be assassinated. He spun poor Walter Cronkite all over the ballpark when he was interviewed by him. Cronkite didn't know how to respond. You know, when Daley starts claiming that they had evidence of a plot to assassinate him and assassinate others. It turned out to be a lot of bullshit. But it turned out to be bullshit long after it had gone out on the air. Cronkite was in no position to challenge him, to demand "What evidence do you have? Show us the evidence of this plot."

So Daley did a pretty good job of propagandizing, and he did so with the cooperation of some editors who developed a great concern for Chicago's image. The paper I worked on put out a special section that was pretty well handed to them, giving nothing but Daley's version of what happened. Put together by his press secretary. And then we printed this crap—which is full of lies and distortions—we printed it as something that could be mailed by Chicagoans to people in other parts of the country. We had a staff rebellion over that.

This was at the Daily News*?*
Yeah. I told the editor it was the most disgraceful thing that had ever happened since I'd been on that paper. But from Daley's standpoint it all worked. Sure the delegates went away furious, saying they'd never come back to Chicago, blah, blah, blah, blah. But Daley didn't really

care what some guy from California thought, or some guy from New Jersey. They don't deliver votes for him.

Chicagoans, though, were on Daley's side.

Well, my mail was not just from Chicago. It was from all over the country. The city's bungalow belts, the working class areas, blue collar areas, the suburbs. They were all for Daley. The younger people, anti-war people, they saw it differently.

The political loser was Hubert Humphrey, the Democratic candidate for president.

Sure it was Hubert Humphrey. With a sane convention, Humphrey would have been elected president. I think I wrote at the time that Daley exceeded his reputation as a kingmaker. Everybody always talked about how Daley won the White House for Jack Kennedy by stealing all these votes, which was nonsense. Votes were stolen not for Jack Kennedy, they were stolen for the Democratic candidate for state's attorney, because that was the priority. The precinct captains in Chicago and City Hall didn't give a shit about Jack Kennedy. They wanted to get rid of Ben Adamowski, a Republican state's attorney, who was looking to get indictments against most of the top Democrats. So, a partial recount showed that, yes, there was a great deal of vote fraud, but no, the vote fraud wasn't to benefit Jack Kennedy. The vote fraud was to benefit Dan Ward, the machine's candidate for state's attorney.

Daley had this reputation as being a kingmaker, but the only president he could really claim to have elected was Richard Nixon, because it was the Democratic Convention in '68 that persuaded a large segment of the population that the Democrats weren't even capable of holding a convention without it turning into a riot. Why should we elect one of them, put one of them in the White House?

No question about it, Hubert Humphrey was the big loser in that convention, and it turned out to be a very close election. Had there been an orderly convention, his campaign would have been off and running, rather than staggering. And he would have won.

GEORGE MUELLER

HE PUT US ON THE MOON

He was the man in charge of putting us on the moon. With NASA from 1963 to 1970, he was in command of Apollo, Gemini, Sky Lab, and the Space Shuttle programs. He is known as the father of the Space Shuttle.

He maintains that if we had kept level funding, as with the Apollo program, we would be on Mars today and have a lunar colony since the late '70s. He believes Ted Kennedy's remark, "If we can get a man to the moon and bring him back safely, you ought to be able to solve the problems of New York City," contributed significantly to the budget cut-back NASA subsequently suffered.

I was associate administrator for Manned Space Flight. The three centers associated with the Manned Space Flight reported to me. One was now Kennedy, at that time the manned space craft of the launch complex at Cape Canaveral. Second was the manned space craft center at Houston, which was just being formed at that time and is now the Johnson Space Center, and the Huntsville complex under Werner Von Braun, which has been named the Marshall Space Flight Center.

Where did you stand in the hierarchy?

Essentially, [I] controlled two-thirds of the budget of the NASA Organization and that turns out to be what controls the programs.

To whom did you report?

Jim Webb. I worked directly with Webb.

When did our space program begin in earnest?

Back in about 1954-55, when the ballistic missile program started.

Were the Germans as helpful as advertised... Von Braun and people like that?

Very much so. In fact, the Peenemunde crew were basic in the space activities to both Russia and the U.S. Essentially, they proved you could do it. That is, to fly ballistic missiles. Then it was a matter of development from there on.

I guess that if you look at some of the early programs like Yeager's X-1 program where we had rocket powered planes, you had an alternative route that was developed here in the U.S. almost in parallel with the Germans. The ballistic missile program, although it drew on the German expertise, never really used it; it was working on American expertise. Things like this are run in parallel. You find that the same people are inventing the same thing, at the same time, in various parts of the world, not knowing the other one is working on it.

Did we have "better Germans" than the Russians?

Well, we used them quite differently. We integrated them into our operations, whereas the Russians put them in a separate room and tried to bleed them for their knowledge and [with] quite a different end result. But, I think that we had the cream of the German activities when we brought them over.

We started differently. We wanted smaller space loads, and they wanted bigger loads.

Actually, the difference was not so much in terms of payload capabilities. They didn't have the technology that we had in terms of rocket engines, nor in terms of material, so they went a much more conservative route than we did. And that leads to bigger vehicles and larger payloads.

Were you always convinced that we would ultimately get to the moon before the Russians? That we had a better program?

By no means was I convinced we were going to get there ahead (of the Russians). We were aware that the Russians had an active lunar program and that they were planning to make the next great stride in space activities by landing men on the moon before we could.

Our program started in the Eisenhower administration. What was Eisenhower's approach to the program?

He was a conservative person who didn't believe that there was a great deal to be gained from space activities as far as national security was concerned. And never was convinced that technology really was the basic strength of any nation. So, he had a very low key approach to the problem until Sputnik, which really galvanized the nation. I don't think it changed his view of life particularly, but it certainly changed the view of the nation as a whole.

Did the Kennedy administration get behind the program?

Well, he started out being an enthusiastic space supporter because it was a new technology, and Kennedy had the view that the nation ought to be a leader in everything—from arts to science to whatever. Space was high on his list of things, but it was the time of the Bay of Pigs incident, where he needed something dramatic to change the attitude of the nation and the world with respect to the U.S., that he decided to go forward with the lunar program. As a matter of fact, at that time, they were looking at whether they ought to go for the moon, or would the Russians beat us to the moon. Or, should we go to Mars where we were sure we had an equal playing field.

The Bay of Pigs occurred in April of '61, and Yuri Gagarin went up three months later. JFK had to contend with the Bay of Pigs and Gagarin, which was the first manned space flight. When did the Apollo Program start?

It actually started in about 1960, when NASA was just being formed and we were looking at the possibilities of carrying out a lunar flight. But it wasn't until '61 that Kennedy committed the country to a lunar excursion, if you will.

From that point forward, was it almost a 24-hour-a-day project?

Well, in order to carry out that large a program starting from essentially scratch in 1961, it was a "full-court press" all the way through.

The highlight, of course, in the beginning was simply the commitment to go to the moon and the backing of Congress, as well as the president, towards accomplishing that. I think it's tremendously important to have a consensus in Washington and amongst the people of the nation on a program if you're going to succeed, when it's that large, and that visible a program.

What was the low point in the early years?

Well, about the time that I joined NASA, Congress and the administration were becoming disillusioned with our ability to carry out the lunar program. This was in '63. The Congress had just cut the budget by about 20 percent, and people were really scrambling trying to figure out what you can do to carry out the commitment to land on the moon by the end of the decade.

What did we do?

Well, they did change management at NASA and brought me in. We reorganized the agency at that point.

This is in '63?

1963. And we restructured the program. We had several different approaches that we were studying from '61 to '63. One was an earth orbit rendezvous, followed by a lunar orbit rendezvous, followed by a landing. A second one was an earth orbit rendezvous followed by a direct flight over the lunar surface and return. The third was a lunar orbit rendezvous, which is the one we actually used, with a direct flight to lunar orbit. The trade-offs were really the availability of the technology and the time that was available to carry out the missions. Probably in retrospect, if we had gone to an earth orbit rendezvous and a lunar orbit rendezvous, we would have created a much more viable infrastructure than the one that we did create in terms of being able to continue on, because we would have had a space station. But the time required to carry out, to develop that infrastructure was one that would have made it very difficult to carry out the mission by the end of the decade. So, we had to make some trade-offs in terms of time.

You worked under three administrations: Kennedy, Johnson, and Nixon. Were they all cooperative in this effort?

Oh, for getting to the moon, they were all tremendously cooperative. In terms of getting a viable, long-term space program, Johnson got so involved in the Vietnam War, and Nixon really wasn't interested, so that by the time it became clear that we were going to be able to land on the moon, the emphasis on the follow-on programs diminished—disappeared. Before I left NASA, we had in place a fairly ambitious program that would have built on the technology we had at that time and would have had us with a lunar colony by the end of the '70s and a Mars outpost by now. So, we had in place a plan that would have done this if we had kept the constant funding at the level we were at in the Apollo Program.

We would be ahead of where we are today?

Incredibly better off and more than that, I think the nation itself would be incredibly better off.

You know, the one thing that really killed the follow-on space program was Teddy Kennedy saying, "Well, now, if you can get a man to the moon and bring him back safely, you ought to be able to solve the problems of New York City." That's a nonsequitur of the first order, because you can't solve the problems of New York City by pouring money in. You've got to do something different in the way of the structure.

From that point forward, do you feel it's been a program that's been lagging behind where it should be?

Oh, yes, indeed. In fact, we've had no new technology developed in the space program over the last 20 years. It's only the SDI Program that has begun to create some new technology for the nation.

You were in Houston on July 20, 1969 when we landed on the moon. What was the feeling?

We had been following the launch down at the Cape, to the actual landing, which was roughly midnight on the 20th. We had assembled our science and technology advisory committee for essentially their final meeting down at Houston. We were meeting there, and I went down to the control room during the final minutes of the landing. Probably the most harrying thing was to hear over the intercom that there was a problem with the landing radar, and the question was, "Should we abort?" That was a tense three or four minutes while they evaluated the situation. Found out later that they had been trying out a new landing radar just to see whether it would work or not, and it was creating a set of false data which was feeding in and overloading the computers. They went ahead and landed because it wasn't any problem.

That had to be a tremendous thrill when they walked on the moon for the first time.

Oh, yes indeed, that was a world-shaking event.

What's the most important thing we've learned from our space program?

Probably the most important single thing is that, if you decide that there's something you want to accomplish in the way of putting a man on the moon, or putting a colony on Mars, we could do it. We have the technology available to do it and all we lack is the will to do it. That is, in my view, the most important result of the space program.

We've been living on the technology that we developed during the course of the '60s through the last 30 years. This country is falling behind because we haven't been investing in new technology, and we're becoming uncompetitive in a technologically oriented world.

One of my great concerns is that the space program will flounder because of lack of a challenge. However, what you probably don't recognize is that the European Community is moving out to create their own space program. They have a manned space flight program underway. And surprisingly, Japan has a very active manned lunar program beginning. So that in space activities, we're going to find ourselves either joining these other countries, or groups of countries, or we're going to find ourselves competing with them, or both.

What was the most interesting thing that occurred during your time with NASA?

We made the decision to go to all-up testing. We'll fly the entire spacecraft and launch vehicle as a unit and test it to see whether it will run. After the Apollo fire, we had a hiatus of about almost a year while we were fixing the space craft so that wouldn't happen again. Then we were getting ready to fly the Saturn V. We made the decision somewhere in the middle of '68, that we would try to send a spacecraft around the moon—a circum-lunar flight. And the reason we were doing that is because we knew the Russians were getting close to sending their own circum-lunar flight around, and we didn't want to get left behind at the last moment. This was before their major launch vehicle blew up and wiped out their launch pad.

So we had scheduled a couple of Saturn V flights before we took off for the moon on that circum-lunar flight. The first one went off flawlessly. That was the first Saturn V launch with everything stacked up on it. Worked fine. The second one, however, about halfway through the second stage, burned. Two of the engines shut down and then the third stage ignited successfully and it started up, and then about halfway through its burn, it shut down. That was a real harried experience. I can remember very clearly the amount of instant testing we were forced to do in order to understand just what was happening.

Well, we had, of course, test programs running anyhow, so we went back and found out that really there was just one little line that was flexible. It worked fine at room temperatures or ground temperatures, but when it got out into space, it froze and cracked. So we replaced the line, and we felt fairly confident we could go forward and went ahead. That was the highlight, to make the lunar flight after a failure, and before we had another flight to check it.

What about UFO's? Is there anything to that?

Well, there's been a tremendous amount of interest in UFO's, and people have tried to verify in a scientific manner whether or not there have been any actual sightings. A friend of mine, Allen Heynek, was point man for the Air Force in looking into these sightings. Almost all of those that represent a distance, or where you see something moving in the air, are real images from distant objects reflected in the inversion layers.

There's been no verified evidence of any UFO. There are no unidentified flying objects. There are a few occasions where there isn't enough data to make a decision, but those are very few, and no reason to suspect that there is any such thing as a UFO.

What is the future of our space program?

I think the president (Bush) has provided us with a goal and that's putting men permanently on the moon and on Mars. I think that's going to drive our space program for the next several decades, and I think that's probably one of the best ways we can possibly spend money in terms of supporting our own activities. People don't realize that we spend all of that money here on earth, and in the course of carrying out these programs, we develop the technologies that we need in order to be competitive in the world environment. We haven't spent any money yet in space. It'll be quite a while before we get around to the point where we can spend any money in space. We spend it all on the ground. My view is, it's certainly a better way to spend money than on welfare, because we build an infrastructure that will support a greater population and support them better. Whereas, a welfare program works in exactly the opposite direction, it stultifies people's ability to grow as individuals, as well as stultifies the nation.

VI

Bent and Broken Dreams

JOAN HOFF

RICHARD NIXON

She is a professor of history at Indiana University and a specialist in Domestic and Foreign Policy of the 20th century. She has recently written a book on Nixon entitled, Nixon Without Watergate.

Professor Hoff believes Nixon was one of the best presidents of the 20th century who ruined his political career with his cover-up of Watergate.

Richard Nixon came to national prominence in 1950 in conjunction with the Alger Hiss case. He was instrumental in getting Hiss ultimately convicted. Why did this earn him the enmity of the liberals? They never forgave him. Hiss is recognized by most historians as being guilty of complicity with the Communists. Why do the liberals still hold this against him?

It's not an easy question to answer. I think the enmity that one can find, especially among liberals for Nixon, antedates the Hiss affair. You have to go back to his very first election. He conducted a controversial campaign against a five-term liberal Democratic congressman, Jerry Voorhis, in 1946. He went on in 1950 to also defeat the equally liberal and well-known Democratic Senator Helen Gahagan Douglas. In both of those elections, Nixon received criticism both correctly, and incorrectly, for having Red-baited his two opponents.

On the other hand, when I say correctly and incorrectly, one has to consider that this was the beginning of the cold war era and most candidates, whether they were Republican or Democratic, were Red-baiting. For example, Helen Gahagan Douglas raised the question of communism and implied that Nixon was soft on it before Nixon, of course, nailed her as the "Pink Lady" and went on to defeat her in 1950. So liberals, especially in California, had already decided that Nixon was, if not dirty, at least a devious campaigner as a result of these '46 and '50 campaigns against Voorhis and Douglas.

All that the Hiss affair did was to shore up in the minds of Democratic liberals that Nixon was the symbol of anti-communism and anti-communist tactics in the United States, when, in fact, his record during the McCarthy era was quite a mild one. In other words, he was never the extreme anti-communist warrior that they made him out to be. I think his record during the McCarthy era was indeed a rather moderate one. He, as vice president, was ultimately the person who appointed the committee which criticized McCarthy and finally brought about his demise.

So the Hiss case, as you've said, is a curious one in the sense that historians have long since agreed that Hiss indeed belonged to the Communist Party and probably did, if not give important secrets, communicate to his communist contacts certain information about the American government and its military capabilities. That should have garnered Nixon praise for exposing him. Instead, because he already had encouraged the suspicions of liberal Democrats, his role in the Hiss case was simply blown out of proportion, and they instead made him a kind of evil figure of anti-communism for that time period. That is, the decade of the 1950s.

In '52, he was taken on by Eisenhower as his vice president. One of the reasons was that he had a reputation of being tough on communism.

There's no doubt that his rise in political prominence is almost a phenomenal one for American political history. If you think about it, he was elected for the first time in '46, at the age of 33, to Congress, serving two terms. Then he ran successfully for the Senate in '50, and by the time he was nominated for the vice presidency in 1952, he was 39 years old. So this is a very, very meteoric political career, which is another factor that perhaps has contributed to his negative reputation. It was almost too fast for people even within the Republican Party to accept without assuming that he was doing something—either campaigning in a particularly dirty fashion or in some other way—rising too rapidly within the ranks of even the Republican Party.

The controversy of the "slush fund." It was investigated and Nixon was clean. It was not illegal. People were contributing money towards his campaign. He defended himself on network television and network radio on September 25, 1952 with the famous "Checker's" speech. This was a great success. He thought it was a failure because he had run out of time and wasn't able to tell the audience where to send their comments. But it was a great success. But to this day it is brought up as a negative. Why?

Well, I think again it has to do with the fact that from the very beginning people questioned his tactics as a campaigner, and also because I think from the very beginning he exhibited a combative personality that offended people within the Republican Party, as well as Democrats. You're quite right in noting that the 1952 "slush fund" that he was accused of keeping, it turned out that there was less than $20,000 in that fund, and it had been raised and spent quite legally. But the fact that his opponents would jump on that issue once it was revealed, and the fact that even Eisenhower backed away from Nixon temporarily and let it be known that unless he could convince the American people that he should remain on the ticket, Eisenhower was prepared to remove him over the issue of the "slush fund." And that's why the "Checker's" speech became such an important landmark in his early career.

What it does represent is his very effective use of television in 1952, even though we don't normally think of Nixon as a television president. Nonetheless, his career was really saved by that speech because Eisenhower kept him on the ticket, and he went on to have a very successful career as vice president. The "Checker's" speech—I've shown it to my students a number of times and watched it myself over and over again—when one looks at that, it is for the early '50s, a very effective use of television. You can actually look at his entire political career and show him effectively using television with the possible exception—this is the exception we all remember—of his debates with Kennedy in 1960. So the "Checker's" speech was very personal. He addressed the camera very directly. Looking right into the lens. Not blinking or looking shifty-eyed as he's usually characterized. In fact, the American people responded quite positively to an image of a young politician fighting for his political life and trying to show, in this case successfully, that he really didn't have any money to hide and that the "slush fund" monies had been raised legally and had been expended legally.

He was considered a good vice president.

Yes. One thing that he did that is sometimes overlooked is that he actually institutionalized the office of the vice presidency. He, in essence, made it an office that became more powerful and more significant than it ever had been before. Eisenhower didn't give him many formal responsibilities in those eight years. But Nixon still managed to upgrade the office of the vice presidency and make it more meaningful. In part he did that through several well-publicized trips abroad on behalf of the president in the 1950s. One can cite, for example, the 1953 trip to Asia. But keep in mind that Eisenhower was ill for part of the 1950s having suffered a heart attack in 1955. Another illness in '56 and then a stroke in '57. So consequently, Nixon was able to learn a great deal about international affairs, and then promote his knowledge of international affairs as vice president. So, in essence, he kind of marked out the vice presidency as a foreign policy job for himself. Most vice presidents have followed this kind of tactic or pattern ever since. And the other thing was that in the course of Eisenhower's illnesses in the '50s, Nixon conducted himself with considerable tact and self-effacement, even though he was forced to preside over 19 cabinet sessions and 26 meetings of the National Security Council during Eisenhower's illnesses.

What you find in his vice presidential years is a learning process, largely positive because of his garnering of foreign policy knowledge, but also somewhat negative in the sense that he never felt that Eisenhower really gave him the credit that he deserved for preparing himself for the presidency.

You believe Eisenhower didn't give him proper credit?

No, I don't think so. Not surely in the 1960 election. He was much more supportive of Nixon in 1968, much more committed to supporting Nixon in 1968 than he was in 1960. You might recall that in the course of the 1960 campaign against John Kennedy, Eisenhower was once asked what contributions Nixon had made to the vice presidency, and he told the reporter, somewhat tactlessly, if he gave him a week he might be able to think of something. That kind of ambiguous or tenuous support characterized Eisenhower's attitude and actions during the course of the 1960 campaign. But, by 1968, Eisenhower was fully behind Nixon's candidacy.

In 1960, he lost to JFK by only 112,000 votes.

Yes, you're right. It was the closest election in U.S. history since Grover Cleveland defeated James Blaine in 1884. There's strong evidence to suggest that the Democrats didn't legally win in either Illinois or Texas, where the combined electoral college really tipped the election in favor of the Democrats. They came out of the electoral college 303 to 219 in 1960. So the election was not only close, the difference of 112,000 popular votes, but the electoral college victory was skewed by very, very questionable victories for the Democrats in Illinois and Texas. It's usually held now that if Nixon had chosen to ask for a re-count, or an investigation, neither of those states would have been in the Democratic column. He conducted himself in a very statesmanlike fashion in 1960, saying something like "our country can't afford the agony of a constitutional crisis," which is ironic in retrospect since he gave the country a constitutional crisis over Watergate in 1972. But in 1960, he said that he was not going to contest the election, even though in this case Eisenhower and other prominent Republicans recommended that he do so.

He went on to run for the governorship of California in 1962 and lost. He then stated he would leave politics. He went into law practice, but got back into politics and started helping the Republican Party. In fact, he began to collect many political IOU's. In 1968, he decided to run again for the presidency. What persuaded him to do this?

I think a variety of things. After he was defeated for the governorship of California in 1962, he told the press corps that they wouldn't have Nixon to kick around anymore. What he did first, as you note, was to go into law practice in New York. He moved from California to New York City where he felt not only financial, economic, and political power resided, but where he also felt he could begin to build a better base for himself within the party. Between 1962 and 1968, he not only wrote a very popular book about himself called *Six Crises* and brought positive attention to himself in that fashion, but also he went out of his way, even though he carried with him this stigma of defeat from 1960 and 1962, to campaign vigorously for Republican candidates.

In that decade, the Republican Party became very divided. At least in 1964 between conservatives and more moderate Republicans over the very controversial nomination of Barry Goldwater. Nixon tried prior to '64, and after '64, to court moderates within the Republican Party, but also to campaign very unselfishly for conservative and liberal or moderate Republicans all over the country. He did this in such an unflagging way, never taking any money for any of these activities, that he was able then to call in some chits in 1967 and 1968 when clearly he was going to be considered seriously for the nomination along with

Nelson Rockerfeller and a few of the more liberal candidates that the party had put forward since 1964.

He won the 1968 election.

Again, it was close.

His popular vote was 43.4 percent to Humphrey's 42.7 percent. Only a .7 percent advantage.

But the electoral college, being 301 to 191, skewed by the fact that Wallace received 46 electoral votes. Humphrey received even fewer electoral votes than Nixon had in 1960.

Without Wallace running and absent the fiasco at the Democratic Convention, do you think Humphrey could have won?

It's a good question and it's a hard one to answer definitively. It would have been difficult for any Democratic Party candidate to win in 1968 because, unlike 1960, the Democratic Party was really hopelessly divided over the Indo-Chinese War, and I think somewhat haplessly led by Hubert Humphrey. Whether another candidate could have lead the party to unity and to a victory, one could argue perhaps. But I don't think Humphrey was the man to do it. 1968 was such a disruptive year politically that it's almost impossible to say anything about it that would constitute a generalization that might hold up. You have to consider Robert Kennedy's assassination, but prior to his assassination Reverend King's assassination, and consequently the year was such a disruptive one politically that it is hard to generalize about it. I just don't think that anything could have pulled it out for Humphrey except some kind of peace terms in Vietnam, and the Democratic Party was simply too divided over it. What Humphrey did, unfortunately for his own chances, was to accept the war and actually to appear to be a greater proponent of the war than Nixon. Humphrey was left with this very unpopular and unsavory LBJ record in Vietnam. Nixon actually looked as though he were prepared to negotiate a quick end to the war in the course of the campaign. It would have been difficult for any Democratic candidate to pull that out simply because of the divisions in the party over the war.

Nixon took office in January 1969 and inherited a very surly mood in the country. What effect did this have on his first administration?

He wasn't as thin-skinned with respect to popular opinion as

President Johnson was. Also, keep in mind that even if he were as thin-skinned, it was really under Johnson that the demonstrations reached the height of their vociferousness and their publicity on the media. I think it's probably Johnson, rather than Nixon, who suffered the most from popular opinion in that time period.

The other thing about Nixon was that he'd been so criticized since the beginning of his political career that he seldom really changed his views because of public opinion, whether it was registered through polls, or registered by criticisms of him on television, or in the print media. So, that has to be kept in mind with respect to how he began to act as president. What's always been interesting to me is that very few people, either Republicans or Democrats, thought that he would do much as president when he was elected in '68. They all thought that he would try to calm things down, as in fact he implied he would. That he was going to bring the people together.

But no one expected him to be a terribly activist president. That's what's surprising about his political record. He ended up not only an activist president in foreign policy, but to my way of thinking, a very activist and very positive domestic record as well. This is the most surprising aspect of his presidency and especially of his first administration. Because of Watergate, we tend to think of Nixon's administration first in terms of Watergate, and then in terms of foreign policy, and last of all, in terms of domestic reform. The book that I've just finished writing about him attempts to reverse that order. So that we recognize his very positive domestic achievements, then look to some achievements in foreign policy, and then look last at Watergate, because his achievements in both domestic and foreign policy came about before Watergate. I think it's unfortunate that we have tended since Watergate to look at his entire presidency as though Watergate started it, when in fact Watergate ended his presidency.

He came to office with a number of liberal Republicans advising him. In retrospect, this seems unusual or it seems, again, surprising, but he had around him men like Robert Finch, men even like John Ehrlichman, who at the time was one of the leading environmental land use lawyers in the country. So when you look at his initial advisors, not always the cabinet members like Finch, but look at his close political aides, many of them were much more liberal than we tend now to think because of the Watergate fiasco.

So what he did in the area of domestic policy was to actively pursue five areas of reform. The very first one was welfare. The second was civil rights. He then took on economic and environmental policy, and, finally, he significantly reorganized the structure of the federal government.

All of these things, with the possible exception of the reorganization of the federal government, were in essence in place by the end of his first administration. The one that he was never able to get through Congress, but which stands out as the major attempt since the New Deal to reform a domestic policy, were his activities in the area of welfare reform. If he had succeeded, he would have, I think, put the United States much more in line with European welfare policies and practices, and we wouldn't still be fighting the welfare question as we are now.

What mistakes did he make in this first administration?

Probably the one that he would not agree with, but which most historians would, were his initial attempts to make Supreme Court appointments. Ultimately, he was successful in appointing Blackmun, Renquist, and Powell. But when he started out with his first appointments, they were turned down by Congress and became very controversial. That was in part because at the same time that he was making early recommendations to the Supreme Court, he was also tackling the issue of civil rights enforcement, which had been dodged by the Kennedy and Johnson Administrations. So he was facing in Congress opposition to his approach to civil rights at the same time that he was attempting to make early appointments to the Supreme Court.

Those attempts to appoint early Supreme Court justices were not terribly well thought out. So that was a mistake. He thinks his indexing of the entitlement programs, especially of social security to the cost-of-living increases, the so-called COLA's that are now being criticized, were a mistake.

When you look at his attempts at domestic reform, he failed to get his welfare program through, but it was a very revolutionary program that was killed by an odd combination of conservatives and liberals in Congress—the liberals not believing that he had come up with such a progressive program and conservatives, of course, believing it and not wanting it to go into place.

But it's in the area of civil rights, though we remember him for violating the civil rights of demonstrators and other groups who opposed his policies. Nonetheless, he is the president who desegregated southern schools. Granted, it was a controversial policy that he pursued through the courts rather than through regulations coming out of the Department of Health, Education, and Welfare. But nonetheless, the record is there that when he started as president in his first administration, 80 percent of the schools were segregated, and when he went out of office, only 12 percent of southern schools were segregated. So he did desegregate southern schools, and, contrary to the claims of the Democrats and liberals, his record there is very, very strong.

He also initiated the first national environmental policies for the nation, and under Reagan one could hear liberals nostalgically complaining that they wished they had Nixon's environmental policies to kick around once again. So when you look at his domestic policies, they remain probably more in place and more significant than his much more touted achievements in the area of foreign policy.

If you look at his foreign record, I think very little of it remains today. That is, his diplomatic legacy is weaker than his domestic one, as far as I'm concerned. I think that the pursuit of peace and honor in Vietnam failed flatly. It wasn't simply the secret bombing of Cambodia and the widening of war into Laos which destabilized the entire area that one can criticize, but the fact that the terms of peace that were finally agreed upon and signed in 1973 were no better, in some ways worse, than the ones that Nixon could have obtained in 1969. I think what he did was to allow Henry Kissinger to become egomaniacally involved in personal negotiations with the North Vietnamese which were simply hopeless and futile from the very beginning. The North Vietnamese were determined not to bargain, but simply to exploit their increasing position of power in South Vietnam.

So the war in Vietnam was a disaster for his foreign policy, and, to a degree, it affected his effectiveness in domestic policy. Had he ended that war very quickly in the first year, I think perhaps he could have gotten his welfare policy reform through and had considerably less resistance from the Democratic Congress that he faced for his entire time in office.

Other aspects of his foreign policy, which I don't think really hold up are the Middle Eastern policy with all of Kissinger's shuttling around, ended up really more show than substance in the long run. The administration had no systematic Third World policy outside of Vietnam. They simply ignored, or handled very badly, or exploited for geopolitical reasons, the situations in the Third World. Detente with the

U.S.S.R., which was much touted at the time, soon floundered in the hands of his successors in office. Even though it was a good idea at the time and paved the way for better relations with the U.S.S.R. ultimately even under Reagan.

His proclaimed "Nixon Doctrine," which in essence was first for Southeast Asia, said that the United States was no longer prepared to commit troops to controversial areas of the world, but rather these countries would have to begin to provide their own troops, has not prevented the use of U.S. troops abroad since that time, to say the least. So when you look at the entire record, only rapprochement with China which remains untarnished, basically, because it did lay the foundation for recognition of China under President Carter.

Now there's criticism of that today because of the lack of democracy in China, but, nonetheless, it was a policy whose time had long since come. Nixon was able, as a Republican, to take advantage of the fact that he could open up relations with China because he had a strong anti-communist record behind him and no one could accuse him of being soft on communism, even though he favored better trade, economic, and cultural relations with China.

In 1972, Nixon was overwhelmingly elected. He carried 49 states. He lost only Massachusetts and the District of Columbia. Nixon had 61 percent of the vote. Did this desire to "win big" lead to Watergate? Leave no stone unturned. A form of "overkill."

I think the way in which he and Kissinger conducted their foreign policy, with secrecy, with early wire taps on people who were considered to be security risks probably led more to Watergate than the '72 election itself. Tactics they had used, questionable and in some cases unconstitutional, in conducting foreign policy were then applied to the domestic scene. What helps to explain what you call "overkill" tactics is the fact that since 1960, and that very, very close election which he probably did not legally lose, he fought every campaign in a no-holds-barred fashion. So when he saw these polls in the summer of 1972 showing that the Democrats were in an even greater state of disarray and even less ably led by George McGovern than they had been earlier by Humphrey, he simply didn't believe them. He simply was not going to take any chance of loosing that election, because he'd been ahead of Humphrey in the polls in the summer and then the election became very close by November.

His mental attitude toward elections from 1960 forward was simply that they were no-holds-barred contests and that practically anything was acceptable in terms of tactics. There is still no evidence that Nixon, or even Mitchell, his attorney general and campaign manager as well, knew about the break-in in advance. But once they learned of it, both of them assumed that it had been undertaken for political espionage purposes, and Nixon began to participate in a cover-up of the event. He considered it a normal political espionage activity. That is, normal in terms of what had happened in previous campaigns and tactics he felt that the Democrats had used against him. That in itself makes the event somewhat ironic. That he and Mitchell, at least, were not aware of the break-in before it took place, but then both decided that it should be covered up.

He handled Watergate poorly. It's incredible what he did.

There's just no doubt about it.

It's clear to me, and I think to most people who look at the documents, that in covering up Watergate, he obstructed justice and that was an impeachable offense. And that indeed, had he not resigned, he should have been impeached. Having said that, I think his presidency is one of the most significant of this century and probably the most important since the Second World War. And on the face of it, appears almost to be contradictory, but the man has so many positive achievements both in domestic, I think especially in domestic, and in certain areas of foreign policy, that they cannot be overlooked even though we have tended to overlook them because of Watergate.

Also, a final fact here is that because of the way in which his papers were processed and handled as a result of Watergate, and because of the existence of these secret tapes which he did not destroy, his will be the best documented presidency in American history because the government has control of the tapes and papers and is releasing them in great numbers. Consequently, we're going to know more about the inner workings of the Nixon presidency than we will about the inner workings of most presidencies, simply because these controversial papers and controversial tapes are being released where the controversial aspects of most presidential administrations are the last things to be released by presidential libraries.

STANLEY KUTLER

WATERGATE

Mr. Kutler is the author of The Wars of Watergate. *He believes the Watergate affair was a disgrace and those that participated ranged from stupid to dishonest.*

He states that the "guts" of Watergate is, "a president of the United States resigns his office in the face of overwhelming evidence that he had abused power, that he had obstructed justice, and that he had acted in contempt of Congress."

Whose idea was it to hit the Democratic Headquarters?

This was concocted, as far as we know, in the Committee to Re-elect the President. It was part of Operation Gemstone, which was another hare-brained scheme by Gordon Liddy, aided and abetted by others he was working with—Jeb Magruder and E. Howard Hunt and approved by John Mitchell.

Let me, if I may, borrow a phrase from our former president. Let me be perfectly clear. We have had an excessive emphasis on the "break-in." The "break-in" is to me a very small part of the story we call "Watergate." It is important merely because it parted the veil on what had been a pattern of abuses which John Mitchell himself labeled "The White House Horrors" of the first term. The Watergate "break-in" led Richard Nixon to commit the crime of obstructing justice. What is really important in the Watergate story is what Richard Nixon did and what were the consequences for him and the American constitutional and governmental system. This business about the break-in, frankly, bores me. It is really trivial!

What is the "guts" of Watergate then?

The "guts" of Watergate is what we subsequently learned about Richard Nixon's conduct as president of the United States, conduct that nearly brought him to an impeachment trial. But he fled in the nick of time. What is important is that for the first and only time thus far, a president of the United States resigned his office in the face of overwhelming evidence that he had abused power, that he had obstructed justice, and that he had acted in contempt of Congress.

What brought it to a Senate hearing? The trial of the five Watergate men?

They had plead guilty. But Judge John Sirica made it clear that he would impose excessive sentences unless they revealed their motives or connections. That's when McCord decided to blow the whistle.

Others followed, including John Dean, the ringmaster of the cover-up. Richard Nixon is like the Ancient Mariner, forever tugging at our sleeve, anxious to tell us his story over and over...changing it all the time, by the way. In the meantime, his strange and ghastly crew did not fall on their swords to protect him. They fled for their lives and fortunes, and copped pleas.

Who hurt him the most? Was it Butterfield or Dean during the Senate hearings?

Well, it's hard to say. Dean's testimony was terribly damaging. But without the corroboration of the tapes, Richard Nixon probably would have served out his term. Bloodied and battered, perhaps, but a survivor. People don't understand when Howard Baker asked Dean the question: "What did the President know and when did he know it?" The question was designed to discredit Dean by setting his word against that of the president of the United States.

Meanwhile, other Republicans revealed information to discredit Dean's character. Then Baker asks his question. So, whom, indeed, are you going to believe? Interestingly, however, Howard Baker never again asked the question once we learned about the tapes. Then we could know beyond a doubt what the president knew and when he knew it.

The tape that you always hear about is the one with 18½ minutes missing on June 20, 1972. Is that the most damning tape?

No; the June 23rd tape is really crucial—the so-called "smoking gun" that revealed how Nixon and Haldeman conspired to have the CIA thwart the FBI's investigation.

What was the turning point in the hearing?

I think that the first 37 days of the Ervin Committee hearings was really a model of a congressional investigation. Fair; thorough; well prepared. First, two young men named Sloan and Porter—bright, young, Nixon loyalists—revealed their disillusionment with the Nixon White House. Dean's testimony was a crucial turning point. So, too, Butterfield's revelation about the tapes. My favorite occurs when Ehrlichman testified. At one point when the "Plumbers" were being discussed, Senator Herman Talmadge of Georgia said in his best southern accent: "Well, Mr. Ehrlichman, you remember when we were in law school, we were taught that however high, however low a man may be, the King of England could not cross his threshold without his consent?" Ehrlichman looked at him, eyebrows arched, jaw jutted out, and he said, "Well, Senator, some of us don't believe that anymore." And Talmadge replied, "Mr. Ehrlichman, people in *my* part of the country do." Ehrlichman just froze; he knew he blew it. The scene and the image were devastating.

When did public opinion start to go against Nixon in the hearing?

Dean proved rather credible. The president's own men did him little good. Mitchell, Haldeman, Ehrlichman—did not help him. By the end of the hearing in August, Nixon was in serious trouble. But probably the decisive moment in public opinion came with the "Saturday Night Massacre" in October.

Agnew also resigned in October 1973.

That is a key moment. Agnew wanted an impeachment process; of course, the White House did not want to hear the "I" word. But Nixon made a mistake. First, if he had allowed Agnew to be impeached, my guess is that an impeachment trial would have been a long, drawn-out affair, by which time the country would have been sick to death of the process. Having impeached and tried the vice president, Congress and the public probably would have shunned any other impeachment.

Second, when Nixon cut Spiro Agnew loose, the president lost his best insurance policy. Until then, when people said "We have to do something about Nixon," the response would be: "What, and have Agnew?" But with Agnew out of the picture, we get Jerry Ford. Jerry Ford may not have been Einstein, but he was a "good old boy," liked by all sides. From the moment Ford becomes vice-president, he was a viable alternative to Nixon. Nixon, in fact, did not want Ford; he preferred John Connolly. But Nixon really had no choice; his power was severely diminished by that point. When he named Ford, he sealed his political death warrant.

The release of the first tapes in April 1974 also damaged Nixon severely. Nixon, always so sanctimonious about his behavior, revealed that he used obscenities. Wonderful, I thought, the man has a human side. But the vulgar, spiteful character of the conversation struck a lethal blow to Nixon's image.

Let me go back to October for a moment. When Nixon fired Cox, he still found that public opinion demanded a special prosecutor. What did he do? He named Leon Jaworski, who had been president of the American Bar Association and headed the Democrats for Nixon in 1972 in Texas. Jaworski came to Washington in November. He read the record, and, in December, he went to the White House and told Alexander Haig that the president had serious problems, which included the likelihood of a criminal indictment. Serious business, indeed.

Jaworski also was determined to continue the challenge for the tapes —the reason why Cox was fired. Jaworski, however, was much more than Cox. He had a different constituency out there—something more than Harvard intellectuals and keepers of the Kennedy flame. Jaworski made his Supreme Court arguments in May 1974. They were quite good. In the meantime, the House impeachment inquiry proceeded and then on July 24, 1974, just as the House Judiciary Committee prepared for public hearings, the Supreme Court announced its decision in *U. S. v. Nixon* ordering that he release the subpoenaed tapes to Jaworski. The game was over. Nixon just played out the string for the next few weeks.

He resigned August 8, 1974? Would he have been impeached?

Oh, I have no doubt. The House Judiciary Committee's impeachment recommendation would have gone to the floor and probably passed overwhelmingly. But that is not to say he would have been convicted in a Senate trial. Nixon and his lawyers, I believe, would have delayed and stonewalled the process, and he might well have served out the rest of his presidency. If Nixon had not been pardoned and instead had gone to trial—well, those trials might still be in process! Perhaps the pardon was best for us for it preserved the aura of guilt.

Why did he resign?

He resigned because he had no support left. His supporters told him he had to go—Barry Goldwater, for example. Who was for him at that point? He was a disgrace; he was an embarrassment to the Republican Party. Remember, this is not a partisan thing. Andrew Johnson's impeachment trial was a partisan effort. Then, not one Democrat favored his impeachment or conviction. But Nixon's opposition was bipartisan, reflected in the House Judiciary Committee's so-called "fragile coalition" of conservative southern Democrats and northern Republicans. After the revelation of the "smoking gun" tape, almost all Republicans demanded that Nixon resign.

Nixon said in his farewell address that he had to resign because he had lost his political base in Congress. He made it sound so sinister, like he was a victim of political vengeance. But he lost his political base because he had lied to them...and because he *had* abused power and he *had* obstructed justice. And by resigning, he preserved his perks and benefits—certainly a considerable motive.

Is there a point where he could have turned it around?

I believe he could have gone well into 1974 and admitted his culpability, and still gain forgiveness. He could have looked into the TV cameras, acknowledged his guilt, and then he might have said: "I did it for you—to protect you from radicals, druggies, and abortionists!" Probably the country would have bought it; people just wanted Nixon to say, "I'm sorry."

How has he handled his disgrace?

Since August 1974, Nixon has been engaged in his last campaign —a campaign for history. He has tried to manipulate and spin history. But he cannot win. After he dies, he cannot control history. And what will the history books say of him: "Richard Nixon, the first president of the United States to resign because of scandal." Perhaps some might note his China policy, or the dubious peace he made in Vietnam, or that he blindly supported the Shah of Iran. But we always will remember that he resigned because of scandal.

Nixon writes an endless stream of memoirs and apologies. He entertains young journalists who have no memory of Watergate and then they write about his brilliance and compares favorably to his successors. Well, that to say that the function of every president is to make his predecessors look good. I prefer to evaluate Richard Nixon on his own merits...or lack of them.

What does the country feel about Watergate now?

Nixon is regarded as a curiosity, even a comic figure. Every comeback is accompanied by jokes. Perhaps only vaguely so, but people remember that Nixon disgraced himself, and the presidency, and caused the nation much anguish and embarrassment. After nearly 20 years, the Republican Party never has invited him to a presidential nominating convention. Compare that to the regular invitation to Herbert Hoover for over two decades.

Was there a "Deep Throat"?

Quite simply, there was nothing that is ever revealed in the media that was not known to properly constituted investigative authorities. In other words, everything you read in the media was leaked. By whom? In June 1973, it was the FBI; in early 1973, it was the Senate Select Committee; in 1974, it was the House Judiciary Committee; at other times, leaks came from the special prosecutor, the White House staff, and even Alexander Haig, Nixon's chief of staff. Remember, leakers have a variety of motives. I can safely assure you that Robert Redford and Dustin Hoffman, also known as Woodward and Bernstein, did not save America.

Robert A. Maheu

HOWARD HUGHES IN NEVADA

Chief of Hughes' Nevada operations, Bob Maheu was Howard Hughes' number one man in Nevada. He arranged Hughes' arrival in Las Vegas in November 1966. Hughes bought the Desert Inn Hotel to have a place to live and for the next four years resided on the entire top floor with the curtains continually drawn. By this time Hughes was a total recluse. His withdrawal from the world cost him control of his empire and resulted in a lonely and sad death.

Bob Maheu was there as his alter ego running the entire operation. Hughes was in constant contact with Maheu, 24 hours a day, but Maheu never met him.

I was chief executive officer of Hughes' Nevada operations. It was very exciting and very, very difficult and demanding. The hours never stopped. It made no difference whether you went to bed. If he [Hughes] didn't, he'd call you at all hours of the night. If I went to church, I'd be pulled out of church. If he gave me permission to go to Catalina, en route he'd call and say...in those days you didn't have the communications facilities that you do now, "Ask the skipper if you're closer to Avalon or the Balboa Bay Club." And if I'd make the mistake and say, "Closer to the Balboa Bay Club," then he'd say, "Well, get back there as soon as you can and get to a land phone." If I'd say I'm closer to Catalina, he'd say, "Well as soon as you arrive there, call me on a land phone." To the point that finally the sheriff of Los Angeles made arrangements to have a line dropped in the water that came right up to my buoy.

Never saw him face-to-face. On two occasions I saw him, but just fleetingly.

Was there anything to the story that he wanted to take over Nevada.

That's one of the reasons he wanted to come here [Nevada] because he felt that in California, because of the growth and all, that he was becoming a small fish in a big pond. He felt that if he could come here and make some meaningful moves, that he'd be the big fish in a small pond.

You were dealing with one of the most powerful men in the world and you never met him. Everything was by telephone. Wasn't that terribly difficult?

It was awesome. It was awesome.

When do you think he became reclusive?

That worked out progressively. It started really to manifest itself in the middle-late '50s and became progressively worse. Then the fact that he was surrounded with a bunch of zombies who were trying to steal the empire from him. I mean, they made sure that they kept him in isolation. They made sure that he could not communicate with his top executives, and one by one they were able to break down those communications. And then, of course, they also were able to get him hooked on drugs.

They had tried to get me earlier; they had tried to get me to join the group to wrest the control away from this man, and I could not believe it. But I could, because I knew who the players were. I told them to go to hell in no uncertain words.

They had been successful in breaking off all the pieces, as far as he was concerned, with his top executives. I was the only one left. They had to try to discredit me however they could. What finally happened, I was so busy protecting him, I completely forgot about Bob. I was not protecting myself. Every time that we'd have a problem, we'd straighten it out as long as there were communications. Finally, he became so ill that communications between him and me stopped, and there went his last window to the world.

Thanksgiving of 1970, Hughes left Las Vegas, and you were fired shortly after that. He went to Nassau. He was now heavily into drugs.

I was not aware of the drug problem until way after that time. I knew that there were times when he'd take sleeping pills to rest. He'd take uppers so that he could be awake to watch something he wanted to watch, or work on something he wanted to work on, but I was completely unaware of the dependency that they created on drugs.

Will we ever see anybody like Hughes again?

No, because I can't imagine anyone allowing himself to be so isolated from the rest of the world and putting himself on the altar for slaughter. They took advantage of ever faulty thing that he did.

People that were in contact with him said he was a genius. You never met him face to face, but you had thousands of phone conversations. Do you believe he was a genius?

Oh, yes. There's no doubt about it. No doubt about it. But you know, it's like all geniuses. If you started writing the book of Benjamin Franklin and talk about the things where he failed, you'd run out of paper before you could tell about the good things he did. So, it's not a first in American history.

How is the Hughes empire doing now?

I think fabulously. It's in such good hands, and thank God that Bill Lummis came on the scene when he did and straightened things out. They have done it. There's no doubt about it. They saved the empire.

Do you have any regrets?

It's very difficult. I have mixed emotions. I tell people I would never do it again, and then before that part sinks in, I say, "Well, if I had not done it, I could never have had the experience I've had."

VII

Change

ADAM ULAM

THE FALL OF COMMUNISM

Gurney Professor of History and Political Science and director of the Russian Research Center at Harvard. Author of The Communists.

He feels communism was never the threat to the West that many thought. After Stalin, each succeeding Russian leader wished to make an accommodation with the West, its satellites, and their own people. They feared, though, that if they relaxed things too much the situation would get out of control. They were correct.

China is the last communist state of importance and he believes their time is coming.

Was communist Russia ever strong enough militarily and economically to challenge the West?

No, there has never been a period when that looked likely. I think the most impressive period of Soviet industrial growth was their very quick recovery from the ravages of the war, which was really nothing short of miraculous. They lost something like 27 million people in the war, like 14 percent of the total population. Half of the country was laid in ruins. Within 10 years, they were out-producing what they had been doing in '39-40.

How were they compared to the United States?

Oh, way back. You must remember that the United States at the end of World War II produced more than half the industrial production of the whole world. The Soviets were way behind.

Were the Russians capable of taking all of Western Europe after the war?

They couldn't have. Stalin was smart enough to realize in the modern world, it's industrial power that counts. The United States dwarfed not only Russia, but the whole world. The Russians had bled in the war. They demobilized fast because they needed man and woman on the farms and in industry. They were in absolutely no condition. I know that there were widespread fears in the West that the Russians could move to the English Channel within a matter of days, weeks. But it was ridiculous because the Soviet Union had been bled in the war. We had hardly been touched. Our enormous industrial power had been built up, never mind other Western nations. So those fears were hugely exaggerated, even without the atom bomb.

Communism, to succeed, had to succeed in other Western countries. It did not, and it failed.

Yes. Well, you must remember that right after the war the Communist Parties of Italy and France were fairly close to getting to power through legal means. I think before '48, each party gathered something like 30 percent of the votes. They were the most powerful parties legally in the West, I think. And, of course, that was worrying us enormously.

When did their influence ebb?

Well, their great popularity right after the war was very largely viewed to the prestige of the Soviet Union, which shed so much blood to win the war, and to the fact that, during the war, those parties could act as patriots. After the Soviet Union was attacked, they became strongly anti-Fascist, led the resistance so that their popularity was building up between '45 and '48, but later they started losing this popularity. They were ordered by Moscow to pause and sabotage the Marshall Plan and, of course, that ran so much against the grain, that their popularity largely declined. Still they remained strong, strong parties into the '70s.

After Stalin died in March 1953, the Russian leaders wished to change the system, but did not know how to do it.

Yes, they realized that the power lapsed from a despot to an oligarchy of top dogs. They obviously didn't want another Stalin, of whom they lived in everyday terror. They were struggling for power among themselves, and I think they saw that, without Stalin, you cannot rule with Stalinist methods. Strangely enough, the chief terrorist among them, Beria, the chief of police under Stalin, went furthest in trying to liberalize policies, without of course jettisoning the position of the Communist Party. He wanted more liberal policies of nationalities, better relations with the West. They realized they couldn't rule the old way. They relaxed their rule over the satellite countries somewhat and in '56 Khrushchev tried to reduce Stalin's stature from sort of a deity to a party leader who did many wrong things.

What kept Khrushchev from going forward with this?

Well, several things. I quote in my book several times the statement they wanted "the thaw"—that was the phrase for the relaxation from Stalin. Letting millions of people free from concentration camps. But he said they didn't want the change "to become like a wave which would overflow the walls guarding our system." In other words, he was afraid what would happen might be what actually did happen in 1986-88, when Gorbachev started his reforms and they overflowed the borders of what was permissible in their eyes.

Where was the United States? Did we read those signals correctly?

We didn't read them quite correctly. Right after the war we exaggerated the threat of Russia. In other words, we didn't exaggerate their intentions, they were always bent upon expansion, they had huge military power which could overcome Europe. But, as I said, our industrial power, nuclear bomb, and other things were such that it was very largely bluff on their part. Stalin felt the whole country had been bled during the war, and he had to be ominous and threatening in order not to be pushed by us.

We had the bomb exclusively up to September 1949. Do you think that was a critical period, or do you think it didn't matter that we had the atom bomb, that the Russians were just too devastated to do anything from 1945 to 1949?

Oh, yes, forget the bomb. Our industrial power in '45 was so overwhelming that you could say they might have marched to the Channel. Hitler marched to the Channel and then what defeated Hitler was, of course, our armies, largely the Soviet army, but mainly the American industry which did incredible things during the war.

Khrushchev was ousted from power in the fall of 1964. You had a number of elderly leaders from that point forward, beginning with Brezhnev.

You can say, truthfully, that no communist leader, including Mr. Gorbachev, until he was compelled to do so, ever thought of loosening the monopoly power of the Communist Party over the country. And one should add that the Communist Party didn't mean that almost 19 million or so members of the party shared in ruling the country. It meant that 20-25 people in the Politburo exercised effective rule.

So they wanted to liberalize the system. They were, in their own way, humane men who saw the evil of the survival of certain features of Stalinism. They were, I wouldn't say convinced Marxist-Leninists, so much as people who wanted to hold onto power.

Did Gorbachev realize things had to change or did he wish to keep the old ways?

He felt that he could have his cake and eat it too. In other words, liberalize the system, give it more dynamism. Make it more humane and yet have the Communist Party in the saddle as before and have the economy develop more vigorously. Well, after a year or two, things sort of acquired a momentum of its own. People became horrified of the party. The party lost authority, and by 1988-89 it was clear that the Communist Party was going to be replaced and that the country very likely would fall to pieces.

Did America see this coming?

Certainly, the administration in Washington believed until the last moment, August 1991, that somehow the country could be held together. We did see, of course, that in 1989 the Soviet Union let all its communist vassal regimes in Eastern Europe collapse. We realized that we were witnessing the decline of communism. But how much it would decline and completely fall to pieces is something the majority of the people, certainly the people in Washington, didn't realize until it happened at the end of 1991.

We seemed to be surprised, caught flat-footed with the collapse of Eastern Europe.

We shouldn't have been surprised at all. That was the least surprising development, because what kept communism there in every case, without exception, was the fear of Soviet military intervention, as in Czechoslovakia in '68, in Hungary in '56. I used to tell my class 12 years ago that at any point a Soviet leader would say "under no circumstances would we intervene, no matter what happens in Poland, Hungary," within 24 hours communist regimes would collapse. Well,

I was a little bit premature. It took a couple of weeks, or a couple of months. But there it was, the Berlin Wall collapsed and the regime collapsed.

Did communism need enemies to survive?

Communism needed the mentality of a state of siege. In other words, to contain its citizens, to persuade them that they were better off than people abroad, they had to feed their own people the idea that the West is there. There may be temporary better relations with the United States, but that the capitalists are always there, they're always scheming to overthrow our system.

Also, the whole foreign policy was sort of public relations policy... they may be richer than we are. In this day of communications, you couldn't pretend, as they did before Stalin's death, that they had a higher standard of living than the West. But they said, "We are the wave of the future. Look what's happening in the underdeveloped world where countries choose our side." So they did need that mentality of a state of siege.

Do you think that capitalism reformed itself because of communism? Tried to shore-up its problems to compete and beat them?

To some extent, yes. But we really did it as much because of the growing power of labor. Countries like England and the United States. I don't think FDR introduced all the New Deal and social legislation because he was afraid of communism. Communism was very insignificant in this country. It was insignificant in Europe. So you cannot say that communism gave the benefit of improving capitalism. No, I wouldn't say so.

Did the arms race "break the back" of communism?

I think it played a very considerable role. As I mentioned before, they did a wonderful job in recovery from war in 10 years in the '50s. With the electronic revolution of the '70s, they began to fall behind again, very largely because their resources, their best brains were concentrated on the defense industry. A huge portion of their GNP went to defense. So that certainly contributed to the decision of people like Gorbachev: we must change, liberalize in order to catch up with the West. But I don't think that was the main reason why communism collapsed.

What was the main reason?

The main reason was the complete collapse of idealogy. The Sino-Soviet conflict showed there is no gain in having foreign countries become communist. On the contrary, Soviet security was endangered by having another country communist, which became a threat to the security of the Soviet Union as they saw it. So, ideology declined. For people at large, this idealogy hadn't played much of a role anyway. They didn't believe in it for a long time. They were apathetic about politics. But within the ruling class by Gorbachev's time, the younger people lost their nerve and felt that they had to have reforms or the system could not continue as before.

Do you think communism is dead? Will it ever rise again?

I think what we call Marxism, Leninism is unlikely to rise, just as Hitlerism is unlikely to rise. There may be some other authoritarian version of socialism, but it's unlikely in the near future to prevail. But certain ideas, like planning the direction of economic life from the center, which are currently in great disfavor, may come again to occupy people. But Marxism and Leninism, as exemplified in the communist societies, including China of today, has been so sorely discredited that I don't think it will recur in our lifetime, or the next 50 years.

What do you see for communism in the rest of this century?

China is the remaining big bastion. Countries like North Korea and Cuba are just minor examples. In China, obviously the rulers themselves decided that communism is not for them. They're trying to introduce capitalism. They have the southern zone of China where there is free trade. Private property flourishing. In the second place, they've lost their prophesying zeal. So all those people, those veterans of the movement and the younger colleagues, they hang on to power for power's sake and not out of any conviction. I dare to think what will happen when that collapses because you'll have tremendous chaos again. Perhaps not as bad as what used to be the Soviet Union, because the vast majority of China's population is native Chinese. There are no major groups as in the Soviet Union. But the future of communism is very bleak everywhere.

Soviet leadership was, of course, very expansionist. But it was fairly rational in the realization that the world could not afford a major war.

Right now you have a situation where all those nuclear weapons are still interspersed throughout the old republics. Chances of some tactical weapons falling into undesirable hands, the Iranians or Libyans, are not inconsiderable. The possibility of civil wars within what used to be the Soviet Union is not precluded. Nobody knows what will happen in China when its turn comes to discard communism.

America spent billions of dollars fighting communism. It would have fallen under its own weight sooner or later, but did we hasten its demise?

If we hadn't built up NATO, if we hadn't spent so much on our defense, they could have miscalculated and tried Afghanistan on a larger scale someplace and that might have led to war. Even though we were not in this dire danger of being overcome by the Communists, I think our arming, our alliances served a good purpose and were not a waste of money.

Was Karl Marx simply wrong?

I teach a course in Marxism, and I always point out Marx was a 19th century thinker whose thinking was attuned to the early stage of the industrial revolution. So what he had to say was relevant and illustrative, if not always true, about the condition of the industrial world of the first 70 years of the 19th century. Even by the end of the 19th century his doctrine was not so much wrong as it was irrelevant. Just like saying that scholasticism was wrong. The way people believed Christianity in the 13th and 14th centuries, scholasticism made a lot of sense. So, in that sense, Marx was not so wrong. Marx has become irrelevant.

John Blum

THE COLD WAR AND THE BREAK-UP OF COMMUNISM

Ph.D. of History who has taught at Yale, MIT, Williams, Oxford, and Cambridge. He has written and edited 16 books, the most recent, Years of Discord. He is a specialist in 20th century American political history.

He is not sure we have seen the last of communism as a world force.

Did the cold war begin at Yalta?

That's a tough question. In some respects, the cold war began in 1917 with American hostility toward what became the Soviet Union. But if the cold war is taken to mean, as most people take it, tension between two superpowers, then, of course, we have to push it into the late years of the Second World War and the post-war period. Yalta involved a good deal of tension between Churchill and Stalin, but I think Roosevelt left Yalta with high expectations for being able to work things out with "Uncle Joe" and that those expectations, though diminished, persisted into the early Truman years. There was a lot of division within the Truman cabinet about policy toward the Soviet Union. Henry Wallace, until he left the cabinet in 1946, was probably the most optimistic about finding a rapprochement.

I think the Wallace of '46 is a rather attractive figure. But by '48, Wallace had lost his sense of situation, and the cold war had begun at some point between those two dates. The cold war was sufficiently real so that people could recognize it as such at the time of Winston Churchill's Fulton, Missouri, speech [March 5, 1946]. From there on, it worsened.

At the end of the war, the Russians had an army of 10,000,000 in Eastern Europe and in Russia. We had only two and a half divisions in Europe, at about 50 percent combat efficiency. Why didn't the Russians invade Europe?

I don't think it was their intention to do so because they had lost so much during World War II. One of the things that American policymakers failed sufficiently to take into account was the dreadful trauma that the Russian people had suffered during the Second World War—millions of dead and the extraordinary physical damage to the Soviet Union infrastructure, even its villages, and the morale of the people. I don't think the Soviet Union was capable of aggression at that point, any more than we were prepared in any systematic way to resist it.

The cold war mentality that came to dominate Washington and Moscow emanated, not from the people in the United States or the Soviet Union, at least not initially, but from the military establishments in both countries and the political spokesmen for those establishments. Michael Sherry's book on post-war planning for the Air Force provides a good example.

The enormous growth of the military during World War II, the connections that Eisenhower later meant to point to when he talked about a military industrial complex, the involvement in this military industrial complex of the big academy (the academic institutions of the country) was such that those who had profited from that series of connections were looking for another enemy so as to be able to continue along the line that had marked the years '41-45. The same thing, within limits, was true in the Soviet Union. Entirely apart, of course, from the dangerous state of mind that one recognizes in Stalin. The mutual misunderstandings between the two superpowers created suspicions on both sides.

I think this sort of thing is apt to happen historically when we get into a bipolar situation. The Second World War had eliminated every major power as a real force in world affairs except the United States and, in a lesser measure, the Soviet Union. So there was a kind of bipolarity between these two great continental powers. A bipolarity between the United States and Japan had existed in the Pacific from mid-1940 until Pearl Harbor. I think it's always harder to avoid rising antagonisms between states in such bipolar situations.

March 5, 1946 at Fulton, Missouri, Churchill gave his Iron Curtain speech.

Truman encouraged that speech. He read it before Churchill delivered it. It expressed Truman's views, and actually the response to the speech was pretty favorable to both Churchill and Truman except on the left. I don't mean by that communism, I mean the democratic left, where people like Henry Wallace thought Churchill had been needlessly bellicose.

We needed a foreign policy regarding communism. George Kennan is credited with suggesting a containment policy. He maintained communism was a religion. He stated it was really a theology, and once you embraced it, it was never entirely eliminated.

Kennan stressed in the long telegram, and later in the "X"-Article, the degree to which Soviet behavior replicated the behavior of Russia under the Czars, as indeed it did.

The Russians had long been an imperialistic people and had expanded to gain control over the vast area that ultimately became the Soviet Union. The danger of further expansion is what bothered Kennan and that's why he called for containment, which he considered necessary partly because communist doctrine tended to encourage long-standing Russian proclivities for expansion. Now Kennan did not mean, he later maintained, that containment should be primarily by military means. And, indeed, he broke with the administration over precisely that issue.

So, Kennan was father, if you like, of the expression of containment, contained primarily in the "X"-Article, but earlier in the long telegram. But it is not entirely clear to me that Truman and Acheson and Marshall accurately read what Kennan intended. I think our response was more militaristic than Kennan would have advised.

What was Stalin's agenda during this time?

Nobody knows. The ordinary interpretation of Stalin as a dictator resolved at all costs to maintain his power is 100 percent correct. If he was resolved at all costs to maintain his power, that had a lot to do with his intention to use all of the apparatus of the totalitarian state to still dissent within the Soviet Union. One way, of course, to mollify potential dissenters was to draw their attention to overseas, or foreign issues, and the United States could be used as the "whipping boy." I think Stalin probably misinterpreted us, as we misinterpreted Stalin, and although I don't think negotiating with Stalin was easy or predictable, both nations in a measure overreacted in 1945-46.

That's when it got tough, and it didn't get any better.

That's right. And I don't mean to suggest the Soviet Union was in any philosophic way correct in the pursuit of its objectives at that time. I mean, rather, that on both sides there was a tendency to think the worst of the other.

The United States was dedicated to the defeat of communism. Who in the American government helped contribute to the break-up of the communist empire?

There are several different problems involved in answering your question. I do not think that the hysterical demagogues of the late '40s and early '50s contributed in the least to the decline of communism in the world. They merely contributed to the panic in the American mood. They were counterproductive people, like Jenner and McCarthy.

The question involves different seasons, as well as different individuals. Certainly in moving Kennan's containment doctrine towards its military expression, some of the chief actors apart from Truman were Dean Acheson and Paul Nitze, who wrote "NSC-68" and others who have been called collectively, "The Wise Men," though they didn't all agree with each other.

Harriman was less adamant than Acheson. Bohlen and Kennan were better informed about the Soviet Union than the others. Bohlen was probably somewhat more militaristic than Kennan. McCloy was probably the least interesting of them, but he and Lovett were strong proponents of American military strength. And so, of course, was Dwight David Eisenhower. But Eisenhower reduced the military budget once the war in the Korea was over. He looked instead to find other ways to continue the process of containment.

Now did containment, which of course persisted after Eisenhower and which informed Kennedy's first inaugural address, did it in and of itself lead to the phase in the cold war which we've recently observed, the liquidation of the Soviet Union for the while? Well, I think it helped, but I think there were a lot of other factors at work. It doesn't seem to me that you get very far by saying who won, or who lost, the cold war. What happened was that the Soviet Union had severe economic and political problems, which ultimately led to its demise as a nation-state and at least temporarily to the situation we now observe of a kind of loose confederation of various states.

Politically, and this is the most wonderful part of what's happened, even the long-standing control of what was the Soviet Union by the Communist Party failed to still the human desire for freedom. It was there all the time. There were dissenters all the time. They persisted in spite of the gulag. The freedom they sought and the freedom they properly idealized meant enough to enough of the people, so it worked in the end to get rid of a doctrine which needed totalitarian controls to prevail.

Just as important, though, was the inability of a modern industrial economy to grow and function on the basis of totalitarian planning from the top. The collapse of the economy of the former Soviet Union, its failure to deliver a standard of living comparable to that available in the West, was just as important as the political factors in destroying the state. Marx was simply wrong.

We probably hastened what, I think, could well have happened anyhow. Because of the arms race, because after Truman and Eisenhower, Kennedy called for an enormous military budget. The adventures overseas of the Kennedy, Johnson, and Nixon years provoked the Soviet Union to spend money to support its own client-states, and the Soviet economy actually, much more than our own, was affected by what Paul Kennedy calls "over-reach." In focusing on American problems, he [Kennedy] didn't give enough attention to the Soviets' problems. They're the ones that fell first. We, of course, were strained and the current circumstances of our economy indicate how strained we were. But Russia, which had never had as mature and effective an economy, experienced greater strain, which was more dangerous because of the absence of freedom in the Soviet Union.

So I don't think we should take any quick and misplaced pride or comfort in the collapse of one of many totalitarian states, not wholly unlike others which, in the course of history, have fallen of their own inflexibility.

Were we caught flat-footed? Was our intelligence up-to-date when this occurred?

It seems to me we were slow in the Reagan years in understanding how much Gorbachev was prepared to meet us. I think the time we were slowest to read the right signals from Moscow was in the first months, or years, Khrushchev was in power. He was kind of a pre-Gorbachev, Gorbachev. And Eisenhower and Kennedy misread Khrushchev's intentions, which, at least in his memoirs and in what records we now have, suggest that he was as worried, or more worried, about China than the United States.

Now, to be sure, he tried to exploit what he misinterpreted as Kennedy's weakness. And, of course, with Kennedy, brought us to the brink of what could have been the most disastrous crisis in the post-World War II period. But the Russians got rid of Khrushchev because he and Kennedy were advancing toward detente before Nixon and Brezhnev got there.

You don't think the Russians wanted detente in the early '60s?

I think, after 1962, both Washington and Moscow, as long as Kennedy lived and Khrushchev prevailed, were moving toward detente. I think the Test Ban Treaty was the first of what might have been a whole series of steps. But with Kennedy's assassination and Johnson's ascension and Johnson's embroilment more perhaps than Kennedy intended in Vietnam, the whole matter receded and the Politburo, embarrassed by the Cuban missile crisis, got rid of Khrushchev and embarked on a major arms race which Nixon tried to moderate, but failed to, and which Reagan exacerbated.

Can communism make a comeback?

Well, two questions that you're wrapping up in one. One is "could the doctrines of Karl Marx"—that's what communism is—the doctrines of Marx as modified by Lenin and Stalin—could they make a comeback?

A. To this point, they always have; and

B. There are people who still subscribe to the Marxist faith.

So that in situations of despair and situations of crisis in the future, someone will come forward with Marxist arguments again. Whether under these unpredictable circumstances any substantial number of people will swallow the bait, I cannot say. But the idealogy which is communism isn't dead. It's staggering. It has staggered before without fully going away, and I'm not prepared to say that it's fully going to go away now.

When it isn't wrapped up in the armor of a nation-state, it isn't particularly dangerous. Misleading, yes. But dangerous, not unless it has a militant arm. And the place where it's most apt to be dangerous is the Middle East where it can be wrapped up with nationalism and reproduce the kind of communist state that the Soviet Union represented very early in its national existence.

The second question is, of course, will the vast extraordinary area which was the Soviet Union, will that area enjoy a renaissance of unification and renaissance thereafter as a nation-state? Will some government ultimately once again control the destiny of what was the Soviet Union?

I think right now the evidence seems to militate to the contrary. The area seems to be fragmenting. But I can imagine the situation arising in which it would go the other way. That is, if the ethnic tensions within and between these new states explode in constant belligerency, if concurrently the economy doesn't move to produce better standards of living for the peoples living in the area, then discontent could reach proportions that would provoke the army under some leader—unidentified and unidentifiable—once more to try to impose order on the entire area which was the Soviet Union. And in that event, after further conflict, you might have another nation-state of formidable size and strength. I don't think that's going to happen tomorrow, but when you say, "could it happen," well, it might.

JOAN HOFF

THE WOMEN'S MOVEMENT

The author of Law, Gender and Injustice—A Legal History of U.S. Women, *she discusses the past, present, and future of the women's movement.*

When did the women's movement first take hold in America?

There were two basic movements. One began in the late 1840s before the Civil War, and the second women's movement didn't get off the ground until the late 1960s. From 1848 until the 1920s reflects the first women's movement. A second women's movement began in the late 1960s and continues down to the present day. There have been two women's movements, and they're separated by a 70-year period in which women simply weren't organized on a national or even a regional basis.

What happened in the interim?

The first women's movement ended in a success in that after having called for the right to vote for the first time in 1848, they ended up achieving that right in 1920, a curious success in that it took 72 years to win that one battle. That's a factor that one should always consider in evaluating successes for women in this country. The long time periods involved very often mean that by the time an organized group of women achieves what they set out to achieve, so many years have gone by that that achievement perhaps isn't as important, or isn't as significant, as it would have been had they achieved it when they first advocated for it.

A perfect example of that is the right to vote which would have been very significant for women to have achieved back in the 1830s and '40s when most white men were achieving the right to vote. Instead, women achieved it in 1920 at a time when individual votes and grass roots politics was beginning to show some of the problems we recognize so readily today. That is, grass root votes and individuals don't count as much because of the kind of media packaging that we have now of candidates. So by the time women achieved that right to vote, it wasn't as significant a right as it would have been had they achieved it 70 years earlier.

Are you saying that the male establishment is letting them have something that they don't really care about anymore?

Yes, it's a theory that I have developed largely in terms of women's legal rights. Any time women in this country have achieved what looks like a significant step forward in their legal rights, you almost can bet that those rights are no longer as honored by the establishment—by the male establishment—as they once were. I think this is quite true of voting rights in 1920. I would even argue that it's probably true of some of the individual rights for access to job markets and to education that women have received in the 1970s. One has to always be suspicious of these successes because very often what happens is that what women achieve is out of sync with the direction or the flow of society at the time.

Let's look at the vote again. The right to vote was achieved in 1920 in very large measure because the first women's movement had become by that time quite conservative. The women supporting the right to vote had largely supported the First World War and our effort in that war. Consequently, women received the right to vote with a lot of conservative support in 1920, meaning that it was no longer considered a threat to the male establishment and also meaning that, in some way, an attempt was being made to reward them for having supported basically a conservative cause, the First World War. So, that's the particular circumstances surrounding the right to vote.

Logically then, women should have also been rewarded for having participated in the Second World War. The reward then should have been the Equal Rights Amendment. But for some complicated divisions among women, they weren't able to achieve that after the Second World War and, as you know, we haven't achieved it yet.

The achievement of the vote was a conservative success that isn't usually recognized when people talk about the success of the first women's movement and obtaining suffrage for women. The other thing about the vote was that, because in part it had taken 72 years to achieve, when women did begin to vote, they did not vote as a block and never have really. Unless women choose to follow the admonition of the party of Alice Paul, the National Women's Party which was established in the 1920s, unless they had followed that advice and voted as a block, their votes simply haven't counted as much as many of them had hoped they would following the passage of the 19th Amendment.

You have to look a little more carefully at the '20s. What you find happening to women and to this first women's movement is that it totally fragments in the 1920s, very much like the progressive movement fragmented in that time period. Women broke up into special interest groups. Some supported the peace movement. Some of them went into voluntary two-party work because women were discouraged from running for office after they obtained the right to vote. Most of them who had political aspirations or ambitions satisfied them by doing voluntary work for either the Republican or Democratic Party.

Some supported the Townsend-Shepard Acts of the 1920s, advocating better maternity and child care. Also, in the 1920s contributing to the fragmentation of women generationally was the fact that the sexual revolution of that decade, the Freudian sexual revolution of that decade, diverted a number of younger women into much more narrow heterosexual roles than older women of that same time period adopted. The fragmentation of the 1920s, to a degree, carried on into the '30s, '40s and '50s. The major fragmentation or major division that divided women from 1923 until 1972 was the split between an older generation of women, among whom you find Eleanor Roosevelt and Jane Adams and Florence Kelly, who supported protective legislation in the 1920s, and a younger group of women, largely following Alice Paul and the National Women's Party, who supported the Equal Rights Amendment. That split lasted until the early '70s when finally the Equal Rights Amendment went out to the states in 1972. So that split is dividing women from 1923 until 50 years later and has to always be considered as some of the background for what happened to women during the 1930s and '40s.

The depression actually had a more traumatic impact on men than it did women. Especially at the working class level where men were laid off in huge numbers. Women weren't working when the depression began, by and large, outside the home. And yet many poorer women had to begin to work at part-time jobs in order to stretch what was left of any family money to support themselves and their children. Also, during the depression, even though working class women went to work in greater numbers than did working class men, the New Deal administration of Franklin Roosevelt passed legislation which discriminated against married women working full-time. You have a mixed picture economically with poorer women working at part-time jobs and married women not being able to obtain full-time jobs because of this discriminatory legislation.

What the depression showed women, and historians who later looked at the period, was that it was very easy for economic distress and set-back to turn the "flappers" of the 1920s into very, very traditional housewives quite quickly, and, in the case of poorer women, housewives who then had to go out and work at any part-time job they could possibly find.

Economic changes, that is, dramatic changes in the economy can very, very disastrously affect women as we know from the high tide of the "flapper" era of the 1920s to the much more traditional picture of women that we get in the 1930s. It's that situation in which women are in very traditional positions trying to stretch family income as much as possible —that's the condition you find women in before the outbreak of the Second World War. We all know, of course, what happened with respect to that war. Hundreds of thousands of women went into the war effort, largely by working in factories or other war-related industry. For the first time, married and single women began to work in greater and greater numbers as a result of necessity wrought by the Second World War.

As I said, it would have been logical for women to have obtained the Equal Rights Amendment as a reward for their war effort had it not been for the fact that Eleanor Roosevelt and the Democratic Party opposed the Equal Rights Amendment in the late 1940s. It was only within the Republican Party and largely through the efforts of, again, Alice Paul and her National Women's Party, that you found support for the Equal Rights Amendment in the late 1940s. So women do not get even a delayed reward as they did following the First World War with the vote. They don't even get the delayed reward of the Equal Rights Amendment in the late 1940s. Instead, what they face is a tremendous post-World War II conservative backlash. Keep in mind that following every war it's almost inevitable that you will find this conservative backlash. It came after the First World War. It came after the Second World War. And, of course, it did affect the second women's movement following the war in Vietnam.

What women of the 1950s faced was a conservative backlash to a great degree directed by the government with respect to the way in which it had chosen to fight the cold war, and to shore up the domestic scene by promoting family views and domestic values having to do with the nuclear family and suburban existence. Women in the 1950s then, and again largely middle class women, retreated to a type of isolation in the suburbs. Fully assured or told by government propaganda and commercial ads of all kinds that this indeed was the best of all possible lives.

Working class women continued to work following the Second

World War. Even though they may have been laid off from high-paying, wartime jobs, they had to continue to work at other jobs. So you always have a class of married women working. It's a relatively small percentage of the work force in the 1950s. In the meantime, the middle class woman became better educated in the 1950s and '60s, but increasingly found that there was little for her to do with the education outside of the home, and so you have a growing group of middle class women in the United States following the Second World War who are, what economists call, "under-utilized" with respect to the economy. Consequently, the stage is set then, as a result of the increasing number of women working, progressively since the depression, to respond in a variety of ways to the new events and developments of the 1960s. And that's of course the decade in which the groundwork is laid for the establishment of the second women's movement.

The '50s consisted largely of societal sameness. The rise of the corporate wife. Then the sudden change in the '60s. Was there a main cause? Was there a turning point?

It's something that sort of sneaked up on a number of women, myself included, as we lived through that time. You have four basic trends, or phenomena, coming together in the 1960s. Since the 1920s there had been this split among what could be called women of the New Deal Coalition, Democratic women, who opposed the Equal Rights Amendment and were promoting protective legislation for women. Well, that protective legislation had, since the 1920s, increasingly discriminated against women in the work force. And as a result of the 1964 Civil Rights Act, specifically Title VII of the Civil Rights Act, in the course of the 1960s, state courts and district courts struck down protective legislation discriminating against women. By the end of the 1960s, the old coalition of Democratic women by and large no longer supported protective legislation because it had been declared unconstitutional by the courts in the course of that decade. The time was ripe for Democratic women, instead of simply Republican women, to finally endorse the ERA. And that's what they began to do. That's one group you have to consider is providing the basis for a new women's movement.

You also had in the course of the '50s and '60s more and more middle class women becoming educated, yet with little to do with that education. A number of them had been reading the works of Simon de

Bouvoir...had been reading the books of Doris Lessing and other feminist writers who were writing about feminism long before the second women's movement. They then had an intellectual approach to the status of women in society that they could bring to bear should they choose to join a new women's movement. You have to consider then the under-utilized middle class woman who would have been reading material even before Betty Friedan's book appeared in the early '60s about the frustration of housewives. You've got both an intellectual base and a frustration level among middle class housewives about what their role in society really should be in the '60s.

The critical catalyst that occurred in the '60s was the increasing number of younger women, many of them in college, who began to react against the discrimination they faced in the civil rights movement and in the anti-war movement. And if you combine those groups, that is the old New Deal Coalition women, an older generation of women coming around finally on the ERA, a whole group of middle class women who were educated enough to understand what their position in society was, and was not, and who also were feeling perhaps frustrated with their own roles as housewives, and then a younger generation who were reacting against male discrimination in the civil rights and anti-war activity. You had a volatile situation that led then to the formation of the second women's movement into the 1960s.

Was there a single incident that ignited the movement?

I don't think so. I think for each group it was different. I think for a number of middle class housewives, *The Feminine Mystique* book by Betty Friedan in 1963 had a great impact. Consciousness-raising sessions which many middle class housewives joined, as well as many radical younger women in the civil rights and anti-war movement were important. But there wasn't a single event that would have affected the three or four groups who made up the second women's movement by the end of the decade. It was an accumulative impact and an accumulative process, each of them being affected by different things. Keep in mind from the 1960s down to the present, that 25- or 30-year period, there's been more improvement in the legal status of women than in the last 200 years. You have to look at what was happening in Congress and what was happening with respect to the Supreme Court in the 1960s as also being factors contributing to the formation of the second women's movement.

In 1963, Congress passed the Equal Pay Act and while it didn't end the pay differential between women and men, it at least called attention to the fact that when men and women engaged in the same jobs, or had the same jobs, that they should be paid equally. The problem with that act is that most men and women down to the present time don't do the same jobs, and so the Equal Pay Act could never do away with the pay differential between women and men or end the segregation in the labor force that continues to exist.

But nonetheless, it was better than not having an Equal Pay Act. It was the 1964 Civil Rights Act and Title VII, of course, that set into motion what we are benefiting from today, and that is equal opportunity for women mainly in educational institutions and in practically every area of employment that you'd want to mention.

So with '63 Equal Pay, '64 Civil Rights Act, with the 1972 passage of the Equal Rights Amendment by Congress sending it out to the states, with the 1973 Roe v. Wade abortion decision—pro-abortion decision by the Supreme Court, and with other acts like the 1975 Equal Credit Opportunity Act where women for the first time could take advantage of the use of credit cards and other kinds of credit for obtaining mortgages and a variety of other things, these kinds of improvements in the legal status of women in the 1960s of course encouraged all of those groups of women to go out and to try to assert their rights in a variety of ways. There's a legal base for the formation of the second women's movement at the end of the 1960s that can't be overlooked. But there wasn't any one single thing that coalesced all of these women. They reacted differently to a variety of stimuli in the period.

Is inequality of income still prevalent in the work force?

Yes, it is. What you have with respect to this wage differential is that, as of the end of the 1980s, something like 60 percent of all women over 16 were in the labor force in one way or another. Compared with around 76 percent of all men who were in the labor force. It's estimated that by the year 2000, between 61 percent and 64 percent of all adult women will be working for wages or salaries. Yet when you look at the median annual earnings of women, compared to the median annual earnings of men, you find that by the end of the 1980s, those women who worked full-time earned about 70 cents on the dollar of what men earned. And that figure is holding. It's not really going up much at all. Women continue to earn approximately 70 percent of what men earn, and what's even more surprising is that this earnings gap between women and men even applied to women with college education. So it cuts across educational levels as well. It seems to be holding.

The other thing is you have so many married women, and in particular middle class married women, in the work force as of the 1970s. That's the decade in which middle class women, instead of simply lower class women, entered the work force because inflation forced them into the job market because they could no longer maintain that middle class status without a two-income household. So the most rapid employment increase occurred among married women in the 1970s. The figure is something like a 500 percent increase between 1940 and 1970 in the number of working mothers. So 52 percent of all married women with children under the age of one were in the labor force by the end of the last decade.

Are men and women competing for the same jobs?

The labor market is still very sex segregated. By and large, even though women have the legal right to enter practically any type of profession or job they want to, the work force still remains sex segregated. So, by and large, the answer to that question is no, because the bulk of women who are working are not competing for the same job. They're usually competing with other women. Most women and men continue to work largely in sex segregated situations. So the bulk of the married women who are working are working in jobs that remain largely female dominated.

Is there a "gender gap" in elections?

None that has been significant. There's always a lot of talk about a "gender gap," especially in the 1980s and again in this current election. But it has yet to prove itself in any significant way. Women simply are so divided along class lines, ethnic and racial and educational lines that their ability to this point of voting as a group has been slight. That's one of the problems that has plagued the second women's movement. It started out as a very radical movement with the object, or idea, of changing society in some dramatic way. Although the improvements in the legal status of women have been terribly dramatic, they've been the type of improvement that have simply allowed more women to act like more men in the society. That is, in the sense of obtaining jobs, getting a better education. It hasn't changed the society in any way, it simply made more room for women in the educational institutions and in the job market if they chose to play the game like most men. That's where you reach a point of diminishing returns because women are not men.

There are a number of areas in which women have yet to make significant improvements. For example, they have really made very few improvements in terms of changing the pattern of their private lives in terms of child rearing, in terms of responsibility for child care, and in terms of many of the traditional roles that women play within the family. They've remained by and large pretty much the same. The figures there are very minor in terms of women's private lives and household duties changing much in the last 25 years.

So there are definite limits to these gains for women, and they have to be considered now because one of the problems that the second women's movement faces is the problem that the first women's movement faced in the 1920s. It seems to be fragmenting and to the degree that it continues to fragment, it could disappear by the end of the century just as the first women's movement disappeared by the end of the 1920s as a national force.

Keep in mind that these achievements have been fewer and fewer in the course of the 1980s because of the post-war backlash that set in with the end of the Vietnam War in 1973.

What has been the most significant accomplishment to date in the women's movement?

I think probably the legal status improvement for equal opportunity in the job market and education has been the single greatest improvement across the board. But again, one might ask if these improvements in the legal status of women hasn't been too little, too late. That is, it's taken so long for women to obtain equal rights in the job market and in educational institutions you might suspect, as I do, that this is because equal individual rights that we have so long prided ourselves about in this country are probably becoming less important, not only in this country, but probably in the world as a whole as the economy of the United States and other countries move to a global level and are much more interdependent internationally.

The achievements of the second women's movement have been almost exclusively in the area of equal individual rights. That is, women now have most of the public equal individual rights that men, white men especially, have had since the American Revolution or at the very latest since sometime in the middle of the 19th century. But the American economy, and even American politics seems to be moving in another direction, and I think especially as we try to work ourselves out of this tremendous national debt and the structural problems with our economy, one could anticipate a situation in which perhaps a depression, a major depression such as the Great Depression, could throw women back into a much more traditional role again. Or more likely, as we limp along trying to improve our own economy and enter the global economy you may find simply that the type of work that women have gone into will not be as important and will not be as highly paid as the jobs being required by more highly technological aspects of the global economy.

So these are the down sides of the success we've achieved. One has to be alert to the fact that equal individual rights and opportunities in the traditional job market may not stand women in good stead in the next century.

What is the most significant setback to date?

Some people would say the failure of the ERA, but I don't think so, because the Equal Rights Amendment in many ways would not have dramatically improved the situation for women beyond what it already is. The one thing it would have done over time was to absolutely make sure that all state laws had to treat women uniformly across the country and that would have been a tremendous improvement in the area of abortion, or even in the area of divorce laws and health care and other kinds of social service laws. I think it's a tragedy that women, by the accident of birth or of residence, find very often that because of where they live they don't have the rights they would have if they lived in another state. So the Equal Rights Amendment would have done that gradually over time. The biggest setback for women wasn't the failure of the ERA, because we obtained a number of these equal rights without the ERA. The biggest setback right now probably has been no-fault divorce. It has literally impoverished women because it's been so mishandled by judges who enforce no-fault divorce laws. By the middle of the 1980s, as a result of no-fault divorce in various states in the country, and I don't think there's a state now in which there isn't some no-fault divorce, the averaged divorced woman and minor children who remained with the divorced woman experienced a 73 percent decline in the standard of living in the first year of divorce. Whereas the former husbands of these women, in contrast, experienced a 42 percent rise in their standard of living because of no-fault divorce laws. So no-fault divorce isn't the major cause of what is called the "feminization of poverty," but it is a large contributing factor to the "feminization of poverty," especially among single women with children.

I think at the moment you can find some no-fault in every state. California started it in the late 1960s and has set the model for the rest of the nation. When you are obtaining a divorce in a state you usually have to ask what no-fault rules and regulations apply. I don't think there's any state where there isn't some no-fault divorce procedure. Some, obviously, are stronger than others. Again, it varies because we don't have a uniform treatment of women under state laws in this country.

Where will the women's movement be by the year 2000?

This decade is very crucial because of the fragmentation of the movement into special interest groups where some are supporting child care legislation. Others are supporting anti-violence legislation against women. This decade is very crucial. If that kind of fragmentation continues, if women can't get back together in some more organized way, then the movement I think will dissipate in the course of this decade. This is also a difficult decade for the second women's movement because I personally believe that the resurrection of family values, which of course we heard so much about in the 1950s, is a code term for a variety of things. I think one of the things that family values represent in this country today is an implicit attack on feminism. I think without communism to fight, feminism may have become the Enemy No. 1, and the code term for fighting it is through family values.

One can argue that family values mean a variety of other things, but one of the things it definitely means is that feminists are really being attacked and being told by and large to go home once again. And, that's also connected with the faltering economy. Any time you have a faltering economy, the first people who are told to go home are women. So this is a very trying decade, and if you add to it the increased violence against women, especially inside the home, and if you add to that the AIDS epidemic which is now beginning to affect married women and women in general more and more, you've got conditions in this decade which are not conducive for a continuation of a woman's movement. Women have to regroup and reorganize and re-evaluate where they stand with respect to all of this, or by the end of this century we may end up as women of the 1920s did—without an organized woman's movement around to further aid women in their 200-year attempt to become full citizens of the United States.

Dr. Mervyn Silverman

AIDS

He is the president of the American Foundation for AIDS Research and was on the firing line as the director of health for the city and county of San Francisco from 1977-85 when AIDS first became a problem.

The disease is growing and spreading to the heterosexual community. No one knows the origins of AIDS, but the first evidence of it in America dates back to the late '60s.

He thinks there will be a drug to control the disease before the end of the decade. He doesn't believe it will cure AIDS, but will allow people to live with the disease.

What are the origins of AIDS?

There are a number of theories. Certainly we know the virus is not new, but we also know that cases started popping up in Africa, Europe, the United States, and Australia in '81, and looking back, we're fairly certain that the spread of the virus seemed to have taken place in any significant degree, probably in the mid-'70s. However, we also have detected the virus, or at least the antibodies in blood that had been stored from a patient from St. Louis in 1968, and another one from London, I believe, in '58 or '59. We know that it had affected humans at least that far back. But it really didn't seem to spread until the mid-'70s, at least as far as Africa, Europe, and the United States. The spread was a little bit later in Asia, the Middle East, and Eastern Europe.

Did it start with humans or animals?

There's theories that it may have started from a monkey virus. Mutated. But they're just theories. Nothing more than that. And of course when these theories were initially mentioned in the early '80s, the African countries felt they were being blamed, and sadly their response was to deny everything. So, for three or four years during this denial process, the virus spread incredibly in many sub-Saharan countries.

Do we know how it started?

No real concrete proof of how it started.

How many people are infected in the United States today?

It's estimated there are about a million to a million and a half people who are infected.

What is the estimate of people that will be infected by the year 2000 in the U.S?

It will probably approach close to two million people.

What percent are men and what percent are women who have AIDS at this point?

It's about 8 to 1 men to women. And that number has changed. It used to be about 13 to 1, and now it's down to about 8 to 1. In Africa it is 1 to 1, which is primarily a heterosexual disease.

So it is becoming more heterosexually-oriented in the United States?

It is. Part of that has to do with the increase in the substance abusing community.

What percent of those who have AIDS are homosexuals?

Well, the problem is, do you go back to Kinsey which many people think was fairly flawed. Unfortunately, the federal government is not allowing the funding to try and ascertain sexual behavior. But it has been estimated, at least based on Kinsey, that about 10 percent of the population is homosexual. Now if that's true, right now about 63 percent or so of all cases are in gay men.

How many will die in 1992 from AIDS in America?

It is possible as many as 50,000. I think last year it was well over 30,000.

What is the time span for someone who contracts AIDS to die?

It's a continuum. From the time you're infected, which means you're now infectious to others through sex, or drugs, or what have you, from the time you're infected 'til you have symptoms can be as many as 10 years or more. Once you start demonstrating some of the symptoms of AIDS, then depending on whether you're taking medications, have early intervention, it can be two-three-four-five [years]. I know people alive seven to ten years. But I would say the average probably is somewhere between two to four years.

But once you contract AIDS, you will die.

We can't say that absolutely because there are some people who seem to be surviving, but I think you can safely say that if you have AIDS, your risk of dying from AIDS, rather than something else, is quite significant and will probably take place in that time frame I gave you.

Being HIV positive—is that the same as having AIDS?

No. A person shares a needle and syringe with somebody who's infected. Shoots himself up with the drug, which means he's also shooting up with the other guy's blood. So on May 27, in essence, he's gotten infected. Probably in about two weeks, he may have a flu-like or mononucleosis-type syndrome; dry cough, low grade fever, maybe some fatigue. But then he feels better and most people don't even remember having that, depending on where they are in the curve, but very likely they may feel fine. No problem...nothing...for years. Now during that time the virus is having its impact on the immune system, and you can tell whether you're infected by getting the antibody test. Usually, it shows positive somewhere between six weeks to six months. But then, years out you start having symptoms. And you're immune system starts demonstrating it's been compromised, and, depending on how AIDS is defined, which keeps changing, but for all intents and purposes, you have now arrived at AIDS. It means that you are either having a wasting disease, you're having dementia, trouble with your mentation, or you have a number of what we call opportunistic infections, which are infections by organisms that most people deal with fine, because they have a good immune system. But in those with [AIDS] it multiplies, it overwhelms the body and then ultimately, the person will die from possibly one of those opportunistic infections. That is the AIDS part. So you look at it as a continuum with AIDS being near the terminal event.

What then is HIV positive?

That means that you are antibody positive. The virus gets into the body. The immune systems responds by producing antibodies, which in many cases, when it's not the AIDS virus, people do well. Our bodies are exposed to incredible numbers of foreign invaders, and our immune system does a very good job of taking care of this, quite often without our even knowing we've been infected. But when the immune system responds, it produces antibodies against the foreign bodies. And those are the things that we generally look for. You could also culture for virus, but it's much more difficult, takes much longer, much more expensive. So the screening test we use is sort of, in one sense, a surrogate. It measures the body's response rather than measuring the actual invading organism.

In medicine we rarely say all, or never, or none. There are people who were diagnosed almost 10 years ago as having the symptoms of AIDS and are still alive. Now what we don't know is what is different about them compared to the ones who die much faster. If we know what is different about the person who is surviving with AIDS, we will then be able to possibly figure out what to do for those who don't seem to be surviving.

What is the longest period someone has survived AIDS?

Nine or 10 years. But those numbers are very small, but they do exist.

But usually, death occurs between four to five years?

Yeah. Probably somewhere between two to four, but again, we now have drugs and newer drugs are coming out which, taken early on, may prevent or push that date further back.

What is the cost of AIDS in America today?

It's running anywhere from $30,000-$80,000 per person. And that's from diagnosis to death. We're spending about $8 billion a year now.

What will it be in 2000?

Probably very close to $15 billion.

What percent is sexual and what percent needles?

Well, heterosexual, sexual spread is about six percent. Homosexual, sexual spread is about 56 percent. So you add those two together, you round them off and say that around 60-65 percent is sexually spread, and the remainder is spread through sharing needles and syringes. A few cases are still going to show up from blood transfusions, things like that.

Can AIDS be spread by mosquitos?

No. From an epidemiologic point, and epidemiology is basically how does the organism behave in the world at large, not what happens in the test tube. When you look at that, you find that people from birth to about age five and then from about 15 to 65 seem to be the ones who are infected in sub-Saharan Africa. Obviously, mosquitos and other bugs don't stop biting at five and start again at 15. So that's from an epidemiologic perspective. From looking at the laboratory grinding up these mosquitos and dead bugs and what have you, although they find some of the genetic particles, they don't find the virus. So, obviously, the virus does not survive whatever little bit gets into these insects. We're talking about a minuscule amount. But if that were a way it was spread, we would have people getting it all over the world.

What are the chances for a cure?

Well, that's difficult. Because the virus gets into the cell and turns the cell basically into a viral factory. In order to get rid of the virus, you'd really be getting rid of the cell, and unless you gave some sort of treatment very, very early in terms of infection, the cure in essence would be almost worse than the disease. So, not so much a cure, as we haven't been able to think in terms of a cure for diabetes or high blood pressure. But what we do for diabetes and high blood pressure is provide medications that people can take and live a relatively normal life. And that's what I think will be possible, and of course we're working very hard on a vaccine.

Do you have any idea when that might occur?

Dealing with it like we do diabetes and high blood pressure, I'm hopeful within the next five years or so. Vaccine probably more like 10 years.

Are you optimistic?

Yes. I wasn't that optimistic about a vaccine several years ago, but I am now. But we've still got a ways to go.

Lou Cannon

THE REAGAN PRESIDENCY

The definitive biographer of Ronald Reagan. His latest book, President Reagan—The Role of a Lifetime, *appeared as a dual main selection of the Book-of-the-Month Club.*

He covered the Reagan White House for the Washington Post, *winning many awards.*

Ronald Reagan followed a different path to the presidency than anybody else. He was a guy who grew up, sort of distilled a lot of what America was, or had been to him, and because of his variety of experiences, was able to sort of give back to the American people images of the country. Images that he held in his heart and his head.

I think there were a lot of things key in his childhood, but two in particular. The religious upbringing of his mother. He was very close to his mother. Reagan has sort of a mystical streak in him and a kind of a belief in God that is not to be confused with much respect for organized religion. And that way he's kind of like Lincoln in a certain sense, who didn't go to church all the time when he was in the White House. Reagan used an alibi which wasn't very convincing; he didn't want the presence of the Secret Service to disturb other people. He could have had ceremonies in the White House every week. People would have come in and held services if he wanted. But Reagan, I think, is deeply religious.

Reagan very graphically describes in his book the alcoholism of his father. But, you know, there's a lot of classic ways in which he's the successful child of an alcoholic. We're on the frontier of research on that. Reagan built his own world. He was kinda happy within that world, and he'd obviously been hurt a lot, but he wasn't going to get hurt again. He had this kind of barrier around him.

I was very struck by Nancy Reagan's point, too. The nomadism of Reagan. The nomadism was in part a function of his father's alcoholism, and part a function of his father's work. He was a shoe salesman. And in part a function of the fact that the times aren't as good as Reagan remembers them even before the depression. They moved around a lot.

Reagan would move from one town to another when he was very young. His playmates, his friends were either imaginary or they were happenstance, or they were his brother who he's still quite close to to this day. And then when he got to Dixon, which sort of became his home, they moved a lot in Dixon, too.

Reagan had this winning personality, which is his charm. This sense of optimism which either he has by nature or his mother instilled in him. His mother was one of these people who always said that something will always turn out for the best. There's a purpose for everything. In God's plan, everything will turn out for the best. So people liked Reagan enormously, but they weren't close to him.

He didn't meet Gorbachev until 1985 in Geneva. He said, kiddingly or not, that all the Soviet leaders are dying and that's the reason he hadn't had any meetings. Why hadn't he met with anybody from Russia or Gorbachev before that time?

I think the more interesting question about Reagan is not why he didn't meet with anybody before Gorbachev, but why he saw Gorbachev as he did. Because you had this succession of geriatric leaders. You had Brezhnev, who was dying. Andropov became sick almost as soon as he took office and then you had Chernenko, and Chernenko was a holding action. There was no opportunity for a meeting—a meaningful meeting—between Reagan or any president of the United States. If it hadn't been Reagan, it would have been Carter. If Reagan had died from his wounds, it would have been Bush. There still wouldn't have been a meeting until the Soviets sorted out their own leadership. And I think you'll find the foreign policy community was pretty united on that point.

There was a question, though, of whether Reagan should have done other things to diffuse tensions. The KAL thing had a lot to do with damaging relations. The KAL incident was so barbaric and so offensive, Reagan denounced the Soviets, and relations reached a very bad point between us and the Soviet Union. But we didn't take any of the more drastic measures that were being advocated, and Reagan, it's very clear from my reconstruction of White House meetings, said that we've gotta keep talking. We can't let this incident become a pretext for breaking off relations. Shultz saw that, but so did Reagan.

I think the more interesting question about Reagan and Gorbachev was that Reagan saw, when most of his conservative pals didn't, that Gorbachev was a different kind of Soviet leader. I discuss that in my book. There was a meeting in the White House, and I remember Paul Weyrich, an influential conservative in Washington, and others tried to convince Reagan that, "Ah, this guy's a Bolshevik just like anybody else." *Now* everybody knows that Gorbachev was different, but at the time Reagan, for all the things he didn't know, saw more clearly than a lot of people that Gorbachev was different. The chemistry was good between the two. They sort of had a symbiotic relationship and needed each other. I think Reagan recognized that he didn't have much to brag about in foreign policy. But the bigger thing about Reagan in my view, and I always make this point, I make it in the book: Reagan believed very strongly that the Soviets were too weak economically to really engage us and had said that if we built up militarily, that they would seek negotiated settlements.

During the campaign, sometime in June of '80, Reagan came to the *Washington Post.* I had arranged the meeting for him to come there. We always invite the presidential candidates. There was some reluctance among some of Reagan's advisors to have him go into the lion's den, so to speak, but it was all right with Reagan. But it took a little working out.

Anyway, he came. And in the course of the discussion, he's asked by somebody about his build-up policies and the question was in the form of...this is going to lead to a bigger arms race. Reagan said—I'm paraphrasing: if we have an arms race, the Soviets won't be able to stay in the race, and they'll come to us wanting to negotiate. I remember Lyn Nofziger was with him. Was sitting right next to me when Reagan said that. He stiffened. He was really worried that this was going to hurt Reagan. But it didn't hurt him at all, and I found out afterwards that Reagan had been saying this for some time. My point is, that while there is a question of whether we rearmed wisely and well, that's a separable question. There is no question, it seems to me, that Reagan saw building up America's military prowess as a means toward an end. The end was to get an agreement.

One of the things about Reagan is that he had this background as president of the Screen Actors' Guild, and I remember him telling me once that the purpose of a negotiation is to get an agreement. He had a kind of union bargainer's mentality even though he could also be uninformed and strident. But the pragmatic side of Reagan, the side of wanting to accomplish something was not ingested into him by his pragmatic advisors like James Baker and Mike Deaver. They saw it was there, and they took advantage of it as the people who were more militant took advantage of other tendencies that Reagan had. I think the biggest thing he perceived fairly early on with Gorbachev was that here was a guy that was different and that we were going to be able to get some kind of an agreement with him.

The other thing is Thatcher. Margaret Thatcher was influential with him. He relied upon her. Margaret Thatcher met Gorbachev before he was the leader of the Soviet Union. And Margaret Thatcher said, "This is a person that we can do business with." And while Reagan didn't always listen to Thatcher, I mean, Star Wars, Grenada, you can name it...it's overdone, you know. Reagan didn't always listen to anybody. But he did respect Thatcher, and I think the fact that she saw this too, from her own very different perspective, probably reinforced Reagan's perspective. British historians tend to give Thatcher more of the credit than I think is justified. I think that Reagan would have done the same things if Thatcher hadn't been there. But I think Thatcher helped because she reinforced this perception of his.

Do you believe his ability to get along with Gorbachev and correctly reading Gorbachev was his biggest contribution during his presidency?

I would put it a little more broadly. I would say his biggest contribution was that he saw there was an opportunity to fundamentally change the U.S.-Soviet relationship, and he took advantage of it. I think that's an even bigger achievement than it seems—what's the British historian who says we see history backward, but we experience it forward. Everything that's happened seems inevitable.

But clearly, there were many ways in which the outcome with the Soviet Union could have been different. You could have had a different kind of leadership emerge. You could have had a different kind of outcome. I don't get hung up in this business, how much of the credit does each of them get. I think they both deserve a lot of credit. It really ended the cold war. I think that 10-15-20-50 years down the track, that's going to be seen as his foreign policy achievement. Maybe more important than anything else he did.

When he was elected in 1980, the prime rate was a little over 15 percent, inflation was running at 12.5 percent, unemployment was 7.1 percent, and the Dow-Jones at 950. By 1988, the prime was a little over 9 percent, inflation at 4.4 percent, unemployment at 5.5 percent and the Dow at 2235. But the national debt had increased four-fold, and foreign investment had quadrupled. We had become a debtor nation.

There is a great irony about the Reagan presidency, which in this piece I'm doing now for the *Encyclopedia*, I'm making a great point of. On the one hand, you have a president who has no experience in foreign policy. Zippo. He used to recite during the '80 campaign when you'd asked him a question about what your experience in foreign policy is, he'd recite the names of foreign leaders he'd met. It was very amusing to the travelling press corps. But what worried me wasn't that it was such an inadequate answer but that Reagan thought it was a good one. He didn't really know anything. On the other hand, he'd been governor of California, the nation's most populous state. It's the only state in which you can have a budget problem that even resembles the national problem, and Reagan had been through a lot of it. He'd had Democratic legislatures, and he'd been talking for years about the necessity of government living within its means.

Even some of Reagan's critics thought he might do well in domestic policy, and even some of Reagan's supporters were a little worried about what would happen abroad. Although he had domestic successes and foreign policy failures like Iran-Contra, he did much better in foreign policy than he did domestically.

Reagan's understanding of economics, even though he had majored in it supposedly at Eureka, was really deficient. He talked so much about waste, fraud, and abuse—he used all these various horror stories about government, many of which were true—he didn't really understand the nature of how badly built-in the deficit was. He didn't really understand it. He didn't really accept it when Stockman and others tried to tell him this.

At one point the senators are trying to get him to accept the break on the cost of living increases in social security, and Stockman, who wanted to do it some other time in the budget process, talked him into not doing it. But if Reagan had understood more himself, if Reagan really had realized that he had to act when he was at the peak of his public popularity, particularly right after the assassination attempt, I think he could have made more fundamental reductions.

I'm not sure that it's knowable, because Reagan had this proclivity for doing political things that he didn't proclaim as political and that he didn't maybe even know were political, but he sort of did them intuitively. He realized politically that in order to do what would be necessary to reduce this deficit and the debt, means tackling entitlement programs to the middle class. It means cutting down on increases in social security. There's no magic to it. Unless we're willing to do that, we're not going to get control of the deficit. And Reagan wasn't willing to sacrifice his political popularity to do that. It's neither in the defense of Reagan, or an alibi for him, to say that neither has anybody else been willing to do that. But that was really necessary to do, because the built-in escalators are so great that every year we're going to spend far more than we take in. And those things just happen. They just go. You can't do it by whittling away at some discretionary spending program. You've got to tackle entitlements. Reagan wasn't willing to do it.

If you look at his campaign promises, Reagan essentially promised to do three things. He promised that he would increase military spending. He promised that he would cut taxes. And he promised that he'd balance the budget. John Anderson was absolutely right when he said the only way you can do all three things is with mirrors. He carried out his first two promises at the expense of the third. And we're paying for it today. One always blames the predecessor's policy. The Democrats ran against Herbert Hoover for years. The Republicans are still running against Jimmy Carter. And now the Democrats are going to blame the Reagan policies. But the fact is that there was an opportunity at the beginning of the Bush administration if Bush and the Congress had been willing to tackle this stuff, they could have done it a lot easier. It's really hard now. It's really going to be hard now.

Reagan is wrong in his argument that Congress was the chief culprit. Wrong, because Reagan never once submitted a balanced budget in eight years in office. Now, if he'd submitted a balanced budget in eight years, it still might have turned out that way, but then I think assigning the blame would be different. But it is also true that Congress made it worse. They made it more out of balance. Particularly the '81 tax bill where Reagan introduced this bill that the Democrats made a Christmas tree bill out of. Not just the Democrats. The Democrats and Republicans in Congress made the thing worse.

So, what you really had during the Reagan years was both branches of the government, and to some extent that's still true, behaving irresponsibly, domestically. It's just that since Reagan had promised another course, one probably should judge him a little more harshly because he sure as hell didn't do what he said. And what we've essentially done—you read the figures—but the phrase has been used by many people, and it's been used demagoguely, but it's essentially true —is that when you're borrowing like that, your prosperity is really based upon a credit card. Now that doesn't mean it's not real. This country produced a lot of goods. It created more jobs. It did a lot of things. If it wasn't as glorious as Reagan says it was, it isn't the basket case that his opponents now present. But the fact is we've now got what? Interest on the national debt is the third largest item in the budget and that money is spent. It doesn't do you any good, or me any good, or anybody any good.

Reagan had a capacity for rousing the public that was much greater certainly than his predecessors, maybe since Kennedy. Certainly a much greater capacity than Bush. If he had actually understood and said these are the facts and we're all going to have to take a hit, but we're going to come out of this as a stronger country, I think Reagan might have pulled it off. The deficit has meaning. You're going to have to have a public leader who is willing to ask for those kind of sacrifices and who has the capacity to rouse passion in people, which Reagan did. But he never used it for this purpose.

Reagan was always a lot smarter than his critics portrayed him. This guy who'd been upstaged by the chimpanzee in *Bedtime for Bonzo.* Reagan had smarts and a sense of country. But he didn't have certain knowledge that he needed to be president, and the White House pitifully exposes inadequacies.

Reagan was detached from the presidency so much, from the day-to-day operations, from the work of the presidency, that sometimes he didn't even seem to be related to it. It was a function in part of the point that I based my last book, in part his training as an actor. There was always this quality of Reagan that somebody else would put it together. Somebody else was the director. The movies is where he'd spent most of his life. There was a producer and a director and there were people who wrote the script and he was the performer.

And related to this was a quality that I think stems from his boyhood; children of alcoholics like to please. He never liked to choose when Weinberger and Shultz would have a big dispute. But he could ignore their advice as he did when they agreed on the Iran arms deal, which I think is his greatest single mistake. If Weinberger sat here and Shultz sat there and on arms control they had different positions, he wanted always to fuzz the differences. I think it's Richard Perle who said, "that sometimes we wound up with the worst parts of everybody's policy." Reagan projected an image of decisiveness, but he was not decisive.

Now related to this, and this is sort of a bridge between the minuses and the pluses, is that Reagan did value—I argue he overvalued—what Theodore Roosevelt called the "bully pulpit part of the presidency." Public communication. Reagan didn't buy all this great communicator baloney. He said that if he was a great communicator it was because he had something to communicate. And he understood that. But Reagan did feel that the public performance aspect of the presidency hadn't been handled particularly well by Carter or by Ford. He was right. It hadn't been. He lavished almost all of his attention on the public performance of the president. The bully pulpit part of the presidency. On the whole, he did that very well. And it's very important as we see now when we had a president (Bush) who didn't have that quality, who didn't pay any attention to the public, or performance part of it at all. But it ain't the whole presidency. When the lights go out, when the cameras aren't rolling, you've got to make these decisions, and Reagan wasn't very good at that.

What he always wanted to do was make the American people believe in themselves again. He didn't say believe in him. I think that Reagan did understand that Americans don't live by arms control agreements or deficits alone. That they want someone in that office who radiates confidence in their country, who has optimism, who thinks about the future, who thinks that America's best days are ahead, not behind it.

We have now gone into another era of pessimism, but when Reagan took over, people were really down on their country. And I think he changed that. It's said that Bush's problem was the economy and that's certainly a large part of it. But I think a greater part of George Bush's problems, and I know you're asking me about Reagan, not Bush, but I think you can see more what Reagan contributed by looking at Bush. Bush was simply unable to articulate any reason why Americans should vote for him, nor did he seem to have any clue as to where he wanted to be at the end of the next four years. "The vision thing." His view of government was that you sort of do it day-by-day, which is where Reagan was very weak. But Reagan had "the vision thing" in spades. He really understood that you had to give people a concept of your leadership and what you want to accomplish. I think he demonstrated that having a public leader who can tune into the American people and communicate with them is damned important. I think that and dealing with Gorbachev, the strategy that ultimately led to the end of the cold war, would be his positive achievements.

One thing we really haven't discussed and I've alluded to. It's important. When Iran-Contra broke, a lot of the focus was on the Contras. I don't think we really know, frankly, how that part of it is going to be judged by history because the way in which we helped the Contras seemed to me to be ineffectual. It was stop and start. Part of that was Reagan. The larger part of it was the Congress. You can argue that the Contras may have helped make the political change in Nicaragua. You can argue that it would have come about sooner if it hadn't been for them...I don't have a settled view of that.

But I think it's quite clear that the point at which Reagan himself made the decision, and he made the decision against all these experts, to trade American arms for American hostages even with his kind of silly rationalization that he wasn't talking to the kidnappers, but to the people who were talking to the kidnappers, was a terrible mistake. And a mistake for which we're still paying because we had told the countries of Europe—"Look, don't deal with these guys. Don't sell them weapons. They're terrorists." And here we're doing the opposite of what we say. Now, it's turned out that Bush has done this with Iraq as well. I think we lost a lot of credibility that we need not have lost by that decision.

I do not think the decision was a political decision. I mean, there were plenty of people in the administration who wanted to capitalize on it politically when it looked like it would be a politically good deal, but I think Reagan really did see these poor people there in chains and in prison and wanted to help them and wanted to rescue them and that he was extremely well motivated, which is I think why the American people forgave him. But it's still a disaster. I mean, you're the president of the United States. Every time they released a hostage they took one because we'd given the hostages value, and if you're president of the United States, you're supposed to know that. So that was a disastrous policy. But I don't think it will be as large in history as the other things we've talked about. Either the dealings with the Soviets or domestically the deficit.

How do you rate him as a president?

I think that Reagan will be seen as an important president and one who accomplished a great deal. But I think that greatness is going to elude him and I think that that's largely because of the domestic legacy. I don't know when we're going to get our economic house in order. At some point we're going to have to. But I think that when we do, it's going to cause a heck of a wrench.

People are going to remember, historians are going to remember the deficits he left. In the short term, I think that Reagan's presidency will be seen negatively. But I think that further down the track, particularly if we're able to maintain a nuclear peace, some of his accomplishments will also loom large. But it's going to be a mixed record. It was a mixed record when he was in office. It's a mixed record now. It will be a mixed record 50 years from now.

VIII

Reflections

JONATHAN WINTERS

TELEVISION AND THE TIMES

The funniest man in America. He discusses the early days of television and the state of the medium today. Also, he has a serious side.

You came to New York in the early 1950s when television was a young industry.

I came in January 1953 married and one child with $56.46 to see if I could survive in the big time, and obviously I did. It took a bit of doing, as it did for all of us at that time, or any time you go to New York or L.A. We all think that we're prepared mentally, physically, and we've got enough money that will last us, and we're fooled about every other day by what we've got in our wallets and in our minds.

Things that were happening then were the "Today Show" with Dave Garroway from Chicago. A very popular guy and I think accepted by the public in general. J. Fred Muggs, his chimpanzee-companion who jumped about the set, and Jack Lasculi and a number of other people. It was right there in Rockerfeller Plaza, this man with glasses and a sign that he held up with five fingers that were joined, saying after every broadcast—"Take care of yourselves and peace."

Jackie Gleason, Art Carney, and Audrey Meadows were going strong in those days. That was a big evening on television to see them along with Sid Caesar and Imogene Coca. Of course, Milton Berle was king of comedy.

What were the financial arrangements then?

Well, needless to say, it varied with the personality. All kinds of deals were made in those days. I think in some respects the talent benefitted more then, than they do now. I may be mistaken. I'm not upstairs dealing with the checks to the actors.

I can only go by what I read or what I heard. For instance, Berle made a deal with NBC that, no matter what happened, if the ratings weren't there, he was still protected, and, to this day, some 40 years later, he still gets a salary to my knowledge. How much it is, I don't know. But certainly when he did retire from television, for all intents and purposes stepped out of the arena, he'd signed this magical deal that has benefitted him and NBC, and he's done very well.

Another guy who started out on radio and graduated to television was Arthur Godfrey, who's not with us any longer. He had a tremendous following with the housewives around the country, and he sat there with guys like Tony Marvin and the rest of the people and commented on Analoki and her ukelele and talked about Lipton Soup and people said, "Hey, wow, Godfrey's something else."

I think Garry Moore found himself a very good deal. Gleason, I'm sure, signed something similar, and Red Skelton had at one time an hour that belonged to him in the evening. I say "belonged to him"—he made a deal whereby he owned just that—one hour of CBS in the evening. I know that's not hearsay, because I took over Red's hour. We had to pay Red so much—it was like renting. I never really understood it but it gave me a season and a half with CBS and Red owned this hour. He and CBS. He owns all the films he ever did on television and through his own choosing decided never to come back and show them. So, he's sitting on quite a bit of money.

What were you paid per appearance back in the early '50s?

It always varies with the talent. If it was $5,000, that was a lot of money. Probably more like $1,500 to $2,000. I know that Sullivan was paying $7,500, and Parr was paying like $300. Of course, Carson today still pays the same amount of money because they're still talking about exposure.

Carson pays around $500. And there again, you're told that the nighttime audience is incredible, and for the most part guys are going on there to talk about their movies, talk about what plays they are in on Broadway, or off Broadway. They're talking about a television show coming up, or a series and talking about their books and what they've written. So it is a spot to capture a chunk of the nation's listeners.

What do you think has happened to comedy? There are people performing who are pretty vulgar.

I don't know. I'm not a prude anymore than the next guy. I'm not on a soap box to lecture. I'm certainly not a censor. I censor my own things. I would always hope to be able to. I paint and I write and I perform and I like to be able to censor my stuff even before I'm told what

I'm supposed to do on television or in the movies. I think what's happened in order to get a laugh, he or she has to drop their pants.

I look at two people who have been dead a number of years, and I still think they're two of the funniest guys that ever lived—Laurel and Hardy. They didn't drop their pants. They weren't dirty.

I've said for a long time Halloween is all year round. They're all wearing an incredible amount of costumes. People are wearing furry shoes, pin-on mustaches. Hair that sticks on the head and then you wear it throughout the evening and many times go to bed in full make-up. A lot of people are putting a third eye in their forehead, and this is to draw attention to themselves at a major football game. "Oh, look, pan in on this guy. This is wild. All these faces. Look at this guy with the third eye." I think a lot of people are auditioning.

I can remember a theater of 500-600 people seeing the movie *Gone With the Wind* when Gable turns to Vivien Leigh and she says, "Well, what is to happen to me, Rhett? What am I going to do?" And he says, "Well, personally, my dear, I don't give a damn." And everybody went "Oh, geez." Well, we've gone from that to "Hey, ass hole, go fuck yourself." And, that's interesting.

"What are you telling me?" That's what I say to writers who are writing motion pictures and television. Which tends to water down some of the language hopefully, but what are we offering up to our children? They're hearing this language at home—they're hearing it on television. Is this going to be their dialogue from now on, because how does this help them? And, of course, we're constantly seeing shows, whether it's "Donohue" or "Oprah Winfrey" or whatever, "Sally really-riley," or whatever her name is—who, everybody is a psychiatrist. Usually, once a week they have people telling the public how to react and what to do. This is very sad.

I have feelings on a lot of things. I look at hard metal rock, and I'm concerned about deafness anyway. If I'm to have Alzheimer's Disease, if I'm to be deaf, I don't want it at a concert where I'm sitting in the 30th row and I see the pink and blue and green smoke coming up around these freaks and they're all covered with vaseline on their faces for some kind of an effect...and there are no lyrics that I can understand. Isn't it funny? I can understand Nat King Cole..."Unforgettable...ta, da, da, dee." If it's hard rock—"yea yi yea yea"...(crank, crank). The only thing they're happy about is the money 'cause this adds to their nose problem. The nose candy, arm candy, whatever...ear candy now.

And apparently the earring business has picked up at an all-time high. I think when we see it with miners, I'm not talking about M-I-N-O-R-S, M-I-N-E-R-S going down 800 feet below, and you see the Star of David or a little cross in the guy's ear lobe, I think we're going to have to look at coal, and maybe gas will replace it after all.

I still have a lot of faith in the young people and the old people and people period. The people that have gone down the Amazon and checked the many trees and the woods. Our concern is what's going to happen as we look up through this smog that envelopes us right here in L.A. and you see it in most of our cities around the world. I mean, it's not just here in L.A. or New York, Chicago...it's in Venice, it's in Rome. Much of what is happening with the smoke from trucks and cars—it's helping the Appian Way disintegrate and to see the various walls and sea walls, and buildings in Venice do the same thing. Disappear in front of our eyes. I think that the planet—I want to believe it—the planet's going to turn around and we can save it.

However, there just might be that chance that we can't save it. I think we've got to look at that. Most of the oceans are dead. And people aren't eating the fish that they used to. And if they do, they die of lead poisoning. Or, if they don't die of lead poisoning, then somehow a strange truck overturns on 101 and toxic poisoning kills all of Van Nuys.

I think that we have to think to ourselves, "Are we going to survive or aren't we?" It doesn't mean that you have to become completely paranoid. I'm very close to that. So don't follow me all the way, but just, all I ask is, just think about this.

We have to think about going out into space. We have the equipment. We have the people. We have the astronauts. The space program—it's one of the few programs I'm for.

I do hope and pray that there's a planet out there with all kinds of animals on it. Maybe they were there from the beginning of time. And I like to think that there are rivers and lakes that are crystal clear and that when these guys in the silver suits and the bubbles on their heads get off the space capsule and on to whatever planet it is, that they'll say words other than just, "a giant step for mankind," or whatever. That they'll say, "Look, the lakes are clear here. Hey, you guys at NASA, the lakes are clear. The ocean—several oceans here. And they're clear. We're able to see hundreds and hundreds of feet down. Everything appears on the surface to be pretty good. The sun is about as it is where we are and the moon over here—it looks right, gang. We haven't seen any life yet."

And then from out of nowhere comes a guy. And, he is not a man with a hydrocephalic head. He doesn't have little carrot hands and five teeth and four eyes. He just says, "Hey, how ya doin'?" "What...you speak English?" "I sure do. Speak about 12 languages. You got to. Everybody reads up here. You don't go down to the local grocery and expect it to be your library. Everybody's got books and cassettes. Don't come in here smoking cigarettes, or booze, or drugs. We don't want to screw this one up. Please. We're from all over the universe. From different planets. There's a group of us here, and if you don't like our way of life, then haul ass."

Jack Woods

THE AMERICAN DREAM COME TRUE

Born on the wrong side of the tracks in Gary, Indiana, he rose from dirt poor surroundings to become a millionaire. He is proof that hard work, properly directed, pays off. Jack believes he is "the luckiest guy in the world," but he has more than luck going for him.

Inspirational speakers and a lot of very bright people tell you that luck is when preparedness meets opportunity. That's probably true, but some of that is bullshit, because luck determines how many opportunities you're going to run into. And it's nothing more than chance. Now, obviously you're ready when it comes, but it's luck to get the opportunity.

I'm the luckiest guy in the world. I was born piss-poor in Gary, Indiana. A tough steel town. Separated mother and father. Very poor. On relief. Growing up with absolutely nothing. My mother was not qualified to even work. Had two kids. Finally got a job working for $20 a week in a grocery store, 12 hours a day, and supported us. I made it out of that—just by luck. The kids that I grew up with, half of them are in jail today, the other half are probably dead.

My father used to come to town about once a month and kick the hell out of me for any reason he could think of. And because of that I wasn't very close to my dad. I mean, I really didn't think very much of him and when I was getting out of high school, war broke out in Korea and my dad came to me and said, "They're drafting people so for Christsake join the Navy so that you don't have to go fight." I hated my father so much that I went down the next day and joined the Marine Corps. Just to say "Screw you, Dad, I'm going to do what I have to do."

Well, one of the luckiest things that ever happened to me—I joined the Marine Corps in time of war. You're never supposed to do that. They told me I was a piece of crap, a piece of crap, a piece of crap, a piece of crap, and then I got out of boot camp, and they said, "Hey, guess what? You made it. You're not a piece of crap. You're a super man. You're a marvelous person. Better than everybody else." And I bought it. Everybody that goes through it, buys it.

They turned me into something that I had never been before. They made me feel like a person. They didn't make me feel poor. They didn't make me feel bad. They didn't make me feel inferior. They made me feel like a winner. And to show you how lucky I am, they put me in the infantry. They sent me to Camp Pendleton. I went through infantry training and the war was going on in Korea. I was assigned to the 4th Marine Regiment of the 3rd Marines for a month or two and then the number came up and I had to go to Korea.

They shipped me to Korea in the infantry, which has gotta be the worst concept in the world. The one thing you don't want to do is go into combat in the infantry. Well, I got to Korea and the first night I was there, I had the watch. I dozed off. That's a nice way of saying I fell asleep on watch. I don't know how long I dozed. I don't think it was very long. I was awakened by somebody poking me in the back of the neck with a rifle muzzle. I woke up, looked up, silhouetted against the sky was a 16-foot tall Chinaman with a rifle, and he was motioning me to get up and nudging me with the rifle. I got up. Put my hands behind my head, and he marched me down a hill. I figured he was taking me back to question me. Taking me back to kill me. Taking me back—whatever. So going down this steep incline with this fella in back of me with the rifle and the rifle was poking me in the back all the time—I decided, middle of the night, to hell with it, I'm going to jump over the edge of this ravine that I'm walking along and see if I can get away from him. I jump over the edge of the ravine— the guy shoots at me half a dozen times and misses me. Is this a lucky guy or what? I fall down the ravine. I'm grabbing trees. I'm falling into the dirt, into the rocks. I don't know what's down that ravine. It's pitch black in the middle of the night. But I get away.

I fight my way back, through the trees, up through the bushes and it takes me about an hour and a half, and I make it through my lines to the outpost. I could just as easily been shot by somebody on my side, but I wasn't. I made it through. Got back into the hole. Everything was fine. Nobody even knew I'd been captured. That's my first day in combat in Korea. I'm captured and I get away. Luckiest son of a bitch in the world.

In high school I had taken a welding course and somebody, somewhere in the Marine Corps looked at my record and said, "Why have we got this welder out there being an infantryman when we can pull him back and make him a mechanic?" So they pulled me out of the infantry. They send me to a tank battalion. The 1st Tank Battalion and make me a tank mechanic. No longer in the infantry and then they decide to pull the 3rd Marine Division out of California and send them to Japan. Ain't no war going on in Japan, and they pull me out of Korea and send me to the 3rd Marine Division.

So I go to Japan. I get out of the service eventually and go back to Gary, Indiana. Stinky town. Place I hated to be. I hated to be there. Didn't want to be there and I get a job as an ironworker. I'm working as an ironworker, but I want to get into radio. I swear this is the luckiest break of my life. I'm working on the Chicago Skyway, which is an elevated toll road that went across the south side of Chicago to connect downtown Chicago with the Indiana toll road. One day we're working at a very high point just before we get to the Indiana state line. I'm on the ground working with a crane, and I hook the crane to some great big sheets of steel that we're going to send up. I'm caught in a narrow spot that I can't get out of easily. I signal to the craneman to take the plates up. I'm right under all these steel plates, and I'm looking up watching the craneman, and I notice at about 40-50 feet up there is a beam sticking out of a structural area where we're building. And as I look up, I say, "Gee whiz. If these plates hit that beam they're going to knock that beam down." So I'm screaming and yelling and waving my warms at the craneman to stop. He keeps going up. I watch that beam begin to raise as the plates hit it and the beam is raising and raising and finally it falls. I stand watching—I mean, I can't move. There's no place I can go. I can't do a thing, and I stand and watch that beam come down. Now it takes what— maybe a second, second and a half to come down? You hear about life passing before your eyes. It didn't pass before my eyes. You don't even get frightened. You just look at it and say, "Fuck—I'm going to die."

I covered—it's a natural reaction. I put my hands over my head as this 32-foot I-beam fell about 40-50 feet and hit me. I didn't feel any pain or anything. I could hear things, but I couldn't see anything. The thing hit me in the head. It fractured my skull. Fractured my cheek. Knocked my left eye out of its socket, although I still have good vision. It broke both my forearms, and it came to rest on my left thigh. As it turned out later, it took out all the bone between my knee and my hip. I can't feel any pain. I can't see anything, but I can hear things. And I hear guys saying, "Jesus Christ, look at that!" One of the guys I know, I can recognize his voice. His name was Joe. And I said, "What is it, Joe?" He said, "Jesus Christ, I can't believe it." And I said, "What's the matter, what's the matter?" I didn't know it was me. I thought they were talking about somebody else.

They put me in an ambulance and get me to a hospital and operate on me. The doctor later said to me, "You're the luckiest son of a bitch in the world. We would have taken off your leg, but it was broken up so high that we wouldn't have been able to trim it had there been a problem. So we decided not to take off your leg. Instead we tried this new procedure." Now this is back in the mid-'50s. He said, "We've worked on this at the University of Pittsburgh, and this is a new procedure. It's worked on dogs, and we've had great luck with it. You're a lucky son of a bitch 'cause we would have cut off your leg, but we didn't have enough leg to work with."

They kept me in the hospital for a *long* time. It was about a month before I could see. When the swelling went down, they found a lot of broken bones and things in my face, so they went in and fixed that. About a year later, I'm out of the hospital. I'm walking like "The Mummy" from the old movies. I'm just limping like hell.

I go back to work as an ironworker. The luckiest damn thing of my life. I don't want to be an ironworker. I say, "I'm getting the hell out of here. I don't want to do this." So I go to school. I'm going to school, and I want to get a degree and get into communications. Get into radio and television. I wanted to be in news. I wanted to be a journalist.

Well, the recession comes along in 1958, and they lay everybody off. They put me out of work. Luckiest son of a bitch in the world. One of my instructors says, "You don't want to be a journalist. Go into radio or television. Do whatever you have to do. Get into it."

I went to a little station in Davenport, Iowa. I didn't have any kind of degree. I didn't have anything that it took to do it, I just did it. I'm there about a year—I get fired. Terrible job. So I get a job in Rockford, Illinois.

A brilliant innovator in the radio business from Dallas, Texas —a guy named Gordon McLendon—is flying from Dallas to Chicago. It is a terrible night in the winter, and they close O'Hare Airport. Gordon McLendon flies into Milwaukee. He rents a car in Milwaukee to drive to Chicago, and as he drives past Rockford, Illinois, he hears me. He gets to Chicago. He calls me. Says, "I want to hire you. I want to bring you down to Dallas, Texas." I had heard of Gordon McLendon. I wasn't in awe of him, but I'd heard of him, and I knew that he was a leader in the industry. In retrospect, he was *the* innovator of all radio. He invented Top 40. He was brilliant. And he hired me. He said, "I'll pay you $700 a month." I said, "Jesus Christ, is that real money? Is that American money?: $700 a month?" And I went down and went to work for him.

I hadn't worked there long. Guy got fired—put me on the morning show. I was just lucky. I've truly had a charmed life. Gordon, for some reason, liked me. A lot of people came and went, but he took care of me. He thought I was great.

From there I got a job at NBC in Cleveland. It was the luckiest thing in the world. A guy came into Dallas to cut jingles. Heard me on the air. Hired me for NBC in Cleveland. I worked in Cleveland for about a year; they decided NBC in New York was going to change formats. They were going to go from a talk format to a music format. Didn't have any music jock. They hired me. Took me into New York and I worked in New York for four years for NBC. It was just happenstance. It was just luck.

Every bit of my life—it was just opportunity. It was good things that came, and I took advantage of them. I ran into a guy when I was in Dallas. I opened up a little disc jockey school to teach other people how to be lucky, how to be brilliant, and how to be rich. I ran into a kid who was working for the newspaper. He was distributing newspapers, which means he was a newspaper boy, okay? He took my course. He paid me $295 for it. I loved him. He was funny. He was a terrific guy. When I got back from one of my little assignments with Gordon McLendon, he was there looking for work and I hired him. And he and I became a team show. We spent 20 years together. How did that happen? 'Cause this kid walked into my school. We became "Charlie and Harrigan," and we had 20 years together. We just went from town to town. Bigger and bigger. Somebody said to me once that "you don't know shit about being a disc jockey, but you know how to get jobs."

And I did. I got a few jobs. And then I decided that I wanted to go into ownership. I wanted to take the next step. So I began to look for backers to give me money, to go into ownership, and my wife was working for PBS. She was working for national PBS. I couldn't find anybody with the dough to back me to buy a radio station. The timing was right, everything was good, but I just had to find people with money, and I couldn't find anybody with dough. So my wife said, "You know, they just fired a couple of guys at PBS. The financial officer and the legal officer have been fired, and they're trying to put together a deal to do some TV. Why don't you go talk to them and see if they know anybody." So I met these guys in a hotel in Washington, D.C. Never met them before in my life. Talked to them for five minutes. Told them what I wanted to do, and they said, "You know, honest to God, we just talked to a guy from New York who's got a group, and he wants to invest in radio stations. Let us send him your resume. Send him your business plan." Twenty-four hours later the guy called me. He said, "I'd like to come in and meet with you." He came in the next day. We got together. We met for lunch. We chatted for about 30 minutes, and he said, "I want to do a deal. What do you need?" I said, "I need $3 million." He said, "You've got it."

We put that deal together immediately. It was done. I mean—I didn't know the guy's middle name. I knew nothing about him and he was real. And we wound up putting no money into a deal. We put a total of $70,000 into a deal. We bought it for $3 million, which we borrowed. It was all borrowed. And we sold it in two and a half years and made $4.5 million on it. And it was....oh....it was luck. Not only that, I bought the station when stations were going through the roof. You couldn't lose. It was absolutely right. And when it came time to sell the station, I didn't want to sell it. They forced me to sell it. And the timing was absolutely perfect. It was absolutely perfect. Timing—I'm the luckiest guy in the world.

Roger Kahn

SPORTSWRITING

His book, Boys of Summer, *is a masterpiece. He is one of America's finest writers.*

He believes the "golden age of literate journalism" was from 1947-57. He states, "it was an era illuminated by literacy and very tough reporting." And probably the best baseball ever played in America.

Many believe the "Golden Age" of baseball was from 1947-57. Do you believe this was the "Golden Age" of reporting?

I think it was a golden age for literate journalism. And I don't just think—I've done a lot of research at the New York Historical Society. I've read the *Herald Tribune* coverage of the 1951 World Series or the 1947 World Series. It's illuminated by literacy.

Stanley Woodward was the preeminent sports editor in my experience. A man of ferocious integrity and marvelous prejudices, much of which would come through in his book, *Sports Page.*

I think the best daily columnists I've read were Red Smith and Jimmy Cannon, who were working side-by-side and glaring at each other. The best beat reporter, for a time, was Dick Young. After a while Young got co-opted by the Dodgers, but up to the mid-'50s, Young was the toughest beat reporter.

The point that asserts itself strongly when you look at these old sports pages is a sense of literate people writing for a literate audience. On the *Herald Tribune*, Al Laney had been business secretary to James Joyce in Paris during the '20s.

The '47 World Series was an extraordinary World Series with the famous Cookie Lavagetto hit breaking up Bill Bevans no-hitter, the famous Al Gionfriddo catch, where he retired DiMaggio on an extraordinary play; DiMaggio kicked dirt in a rare show of emotion on the field. It ended with a dull game. The Yankees won. A dull game. Joe Page pitching very well. In the *Herald Tribune*, Al Laney said, "What a relief it was after all these games which kept nerve pressed against nerve to have this series end with a routine ball game." Now, I haven't got his words exact, but it was a beautiful essay saying, "enough with the no-hitters and the spectaculars. Let's just watch an ordinary game." It was a wonderful, wonderful piece of writing.

I don't see that going on anywhere. That kind of author. Sort of an all-star section where you had so many tremendously gifted people.

Young was a tough, dogged reporter. Young seemed to me to enjoy controversy, enjoy provocative stuff. Young's most memorable adventure was when he decided that the Dodger pitching staff, with people like Ralph Branca and Rex Barney, were choking. So he wrote a lead in the *Daily News* that went like this: "The tree that grows in Brooklyn is an apple tree and the apples are in the throats of the Dodgers." Subsequent to that, Burt Shotton, the Dodger manager, said, "I hate you, you son of a bitch. My whole ball club hates you and you're barred from the clubhouse." Pee Wee Reese got up (this is in the dugout)...Young was standing in front of the dugout. Reese got up, put his arm around Young, and said, "I don't hate you, Dick." The barring persisted because Shotton was going to stick to his guns. The other reporters gathered together, and they gave Young the quotes they got in the clubhouse.

So it was an era illuminated by literacy and very tough reporting.

Was that true in other cities like Chicago and Detroit?

No. I think that Arch Ward's column in the *Chicago Tribune* is embarrassing—"In the Wake of the News." It's embarrassing. Bob Broeg was pretty good in St. Louis. Boston had 17 people covering the game, and it was kind of a joke 'cause everybody was trying to get a scoop on everybody else. You had the Williams' Boston writer situation. The word in journalism was if you're any good, you'll be in New York. Red Smith spent years trying to get to New York. Worked in St. Louis. Worked in Philadelphia. He couldn't make it to New York 'til he was past 40.

At the same time that was going on in the papers, there was this extraordinary column in *Newsweek* by John Lardner, which was first called "Sports Week" and then changed to "Lardner's Week." That was a minor category, but a great column. Minor Oscar category, weekly sports column. Wonderful, wonderful stuff. Lardner on Veeck: "Bill Veeck bought the St. Louis Browns under the impression that the Browns were owned." I haven't seen a lead like that lately.

I started in '52. As a backdrop, some of the papers then in New York and around the country were allowing the ball clubs to pay the travel expenses for the writers. So in New York, it was the *Post*, the *Journal*, the *Daily Mirror*, and, I think, the *World Telegram*. The ball club would pay travel, pay hotel, and once a week the writers would line up and get $8.00 a day meal money from the traveling secretary, in the case of the Dodgers, Lee Scott. And I thought, "How demeaning for reporters supposed to cover a ball club to await and get $56 in small bills. What would happen if you displeased management?"

Well, that must have gone on in some of the minds of those people. There was a term then for a reporter who only wrote good things about the ball club. He was called "the house man," and there were plenty of those. But a major difference was the way we, I'd say Young, myself, maybe Bill Roeder, we defined what we were there to do and that was cover baseball and happenings that were directly related to baseball.

Some of the new journalism nonsense suggests that hard reporting of drinking began with people like Jim Bouton and to a lesser extent, Jim Brosnan. It's not true at all. In 1947, this wonderful World Series which included Bill Bevens carrying a no-hitter with two out in the ninth inning. Cookie Lavagetto broke it up. Al Gionfriddo's classic catch against Joe DiMaggio. At the end of that Series, as the Yankees win, Larry MacPhail announced that he was pulling out of baseball. He then did a lot of drinking. There was a victory party at the Biltmore Hotel, and MacPhail took a swing at a few people. Behaved like a mean, rough drunk. Wept. Finally, he and Topping came to blows in the kitchen. Dan Topping was one of his partners on the Yankees. I don't know these things 'cause I was there. I wasn't. I was a college student. I know these things because they appeared in the papers of the time. They were finally summed up in the last place you'd expect a good sum-up story, *The Sporting News*. This was on the front page. It was called "The Battle of the Biltmore." So quite specifically, you could read that Larry MacPhail was a bad drunk in 1947.

So much for "it all began later." It didn't at all.

You had a bitter-sweet relationship with Dick Young. You mentioned that he got co-opted by the Dodgers.

It occurred in different ways. I'm sure it still goes on. Young had a hard time with Branch Rickey (Brooklyn general manager). He and Rickey just didn't get along. One of Young's glaring weaknesses was his inability to accept points of view that were abhorrent to him. To recognize that more than one point of view is possible. So he found Rickey to be a Bible-quoting, sermonizing, cheap SOB. All of which may be true. But there was another part of Rickey which was quite wonderful.

So, he had trouble with Shotton from the time of Shotton's banning him from the clubhouse. He began to write in the *Daily News* "KOBS," an acronym for "Kindly Old Bert Shotton." The Dodgers would win a game despite the bad managing of KOBS, and they would lose a game because of the bad managing of KOBS. Meanwhile, he ghosted some columns for a hack named Jimmy Powers, who was the sports editor of the *Daily News*, and there Rickey was referred to as "El Cheapo." So the *News* with its two million daily circulation, and its four million Sunday circulation was banging the Dodgers over the head pretty hard.

When O'Malley took over the Dodgers, perhaps his first priority was to get the *Daily News* and Dick Young to stop pelting Dodger management. So he assigned Buzzy Bavasi to be vice president in charge of Dick Young. And the co-opting took three forms.

Young wasn't making very much money and he had a lot of kids and they wouldn't, to my knowledge, give him cash but they would take him to a clothing store and they'd get him a suit. Buy him clothes. That was one level.

The next level was giving him information. He'd have a drink with Bavasi, and Bavasi would tell him something that he wasn't telling the rest of the press. Young was a hell of a reporter, make no mistake about that. But if you're getting exclusive leaks, you're going to look even better. They fed Young material. An example: I remember Young being fed a story when they decided to switch Jackie Robinson to third base and play "Junior" Gilliam at second base. That was a huge thing. Robinson was an all-star second baseman. Now this superstar is having his position changed. Young had a clean beat. I said, "How'd you get that." He said, "Oh, it was only logical." It was only logical after Bavasi told him.

The other thing that went on was that there was a lady that Young became enamored of in Vero Beach. After a while, she began to make western trips with the Dodgers, flying up from Vero Beach. She would appear in hotels. The Dodgers made all those arrangements.

In the vulgate, they bought him a suit, they leaked news, and they threw him a broad.

And he came around.

If he knocked the Dodger management between 1950, with Bavasi and O'Malley in there, and the time it was apparent they were going to go to California, I never saw it. He knocked individual players, but they turned Young into "a house man."

Did the press in the '50s mention drinking and sex?

That was a big problem. Of course it went on. We had talks about it. What do you want to do and how far do you want to go? Do you want to mention it at all? The papers were uncomfortable with it. There was no pressure on the *Tribune* or even in the tabloids. There was no pressure to write about booze and sex. There was a question within the minds of some of us as to whether we wanted to do it or not. My point about the literacy of the *Herald-Tribune* of the late '40s and early '50s; it's not distinguished by descriptions of pubic hair. Nobody much wanted that sort of thing.

The one case on the Dodgers was Billy Cox, who had been, I believe, in the siege at Anzio and had taken quite a pounding from the German 88s. Billy was what they called long ago "shellshocked," and he was a drinker. He played 100 games a year, and he didn't play the other 54 because he was hung over or smashed.

Well, I knew that. I didn't want to write it because I felt he plays 100 great games, and he was a tremendous big series player. A tremendous World Series player. He's got a lot of pain. I know he's got a lot of pain. I don't want to add to the pain. Does the reader who pays the nickel for my newspaper have a right to learn everything about Billy Cox's pain? Not from me, he doesn't. So I never did that.

On sex...and this is where I take a good, deep breath... the issue was not ballplayers ending up in the sack with fans, because of course they did. One issue was black and white sex. The Dodger management was terrified that one of the black Dodger players would be caught with a white woman. So that led to some interesting things. I never went near it.

I remember one day Jackie Robinson said to me, "More white women want me than I got time for." I never wrote that. And even when I wrote it in *The Boys of Summer*, Jackie was alive. I changed it to "When I was at UCLA, more women..." But that's not what he said. We were just a couple of guys talking. Talking about le grand l'amours.

That's just personal. It's a generational thing. It may be the result of somebody who's paid too much alimony in his life. I don't want to contribute to the destruction of anybody else's marriage.

What are writers doing now in this regard?

Well, that's a good question because Pete Rose was certainly protected by all of the Cincinnati writers, and all of the newspaper writers as far as I know until his world blew up. The line I got about Rose from George "Sparky" Anderson was, "You never had to worry where Peter was at midnight, because he had found a nice warm place to put his peter." Nobody wrote about it and then when they turned on Rose, it seemed to me they were turning on themselves also, because then there was a story in *Gentleman's Quarterly* that, you know, what a terrible father he was and how he had jumped on a babysitter on a couch while his wife was putting on makeup. And it all came out.

But there are a lot of satyrs in the major leagues and it's not covered that much. When it becomes profitable, then it gets covered. I suppose the bottom line, to use that obnoxious phrase, is that you can make a lot of money selling a story like that. You can make a lot of money if you found a superstar behaving badly with a hooker.

I'm not going to give you any names, but I know of a case of a super Hall of Fame guy who had a hooker and wouldn't pay her. There was a screaming fight and everybody knew about it. Well, now you can go to the *National Enquirer* and probably pick up $25,000. Somebody would be venal enough to do that.

You mentioned Brosnan's book, I think it was The Long Season. *It was written in the late '50s or early '60s. He was a relief pitcher for the Cincinnati Reds. Was that the first inside book on baseball?*

I think it was. Classically, I have *Pitching in a Pinch*, which is pretty damn good—1912 by Christy Mathewson with John Wheeler. If you want to get a portrait of McGraw, he comes through just marvelously in that book. But the kind of book that was common was sort of juvenile.

"Y.A." they called it. A young adult book. Something that would be nice for a 12-year-old boy. I keep thinking of *A Boy's Life of Theodore Roosevelt.* So you do *A Boy's Life of Babe Ruth. Lou Gehrig—A Quiet Hero.* Brosnan came along. A bright fellow. A lover of martinis and a good relief pitcher. And he wrote the thing himself. He wrote a diary. There was a lot of talk about martinis, and he didn't do terribly much with sex, but it was a fine, fine book. And that was a beginning.

What about Cosell?

My sense of Howard Cosell is there's a fellow who wears a toupee, changed his name, and tells it like it is. I think his impact was entirely theatrical and journalistically zero. Young was a hundred times better, tougher interviewer when he wanted to be than Cosell. Cosell would say, "Oh, boy, Steve Garvey and Sutton had a fight. I'm going to ask..." What the hell would I have done if I were covering the team and there was a fistfight? Walk away? Of course not. I asked hard questions. I'll stay with what I said, that his impact was entirely theatrical and zero journalistically.

Bob Costas told you he thought the modern day journalist had an obligation to name names.

You're always going to have to make a field decision. You know the term a pilot uses..."Are we going to land? Well, I'll check the field, the fog and the snowbanks and I'll decide whether to land or not." Every one of these big things is different. Certainly if you were traveling with the Reds and the manager was betting out of the clubhouse, you should have done better than the Cincinnati papers did. And he was betting out of the clubhouse. What...I don't know exactly. I'll try to turn it around a little bit and say, "How would I like it if this were written about me?" It's a good idea to be a human being first and a journalist second.

Take Arthur Ashe. I don't see any justification in the world for forcing that story out. If Ashe wants to come forward, then it's a big story. But I think a human obligation to Ashe is to let him make a decision as to whether to come forward with this.

The casual womanizing—it's a parody. You're going to write a lead, "Joe Zilch, who spent last night with a hooker from East St. Louis, led the Dodgers to a 7-3 victory tonight over the Cardinals." I mean, is that what you want to do? Do you want to get this *National Enquirer* garbage with breakfast every morning? I don't.

I think a big impact on what goes on, goes about like this: The writers don't feel they make enough money. Numbers of writers say, "Well, look, I have a masters degree from Columbia Journalism School. I'm making $60,000. That stupid son of a bitch never heard of Charles Dickens and he's making $3,000,000." Kind of nasty.

When I was working for the *Trib,* I ended up at $10,000. About $10,000 more from magazines. I was making $20,000. Then Erskine was making $25,000. But we were friends. We were also working guys together. We were way above the national poverty line. But we weren't wealthy.

I think the writers see this and two things happen. They resent the players and with often a lot of reason. Then begin to look for the main chance. How could you score. If you kill the king, you win a prize and you make a million bucks on the book rights. I think that's very strong in there.

If you say, as I say, "There's a reasonable doubt about what Rose did with baseball gambling." That's a nuance and that doesn't pay very well. If you were the one to find the person who can prove that Rose did bet baseball, if he did, then you've become the next Woodward and Bernstein, and you get a big house in the country.

I think that's a huge element and writers are constantly having their noses rubbed in it by people like Eddie Murray, not a very attractive guy. Then we've got to a point in journalism where there's this main chance to impeach the president and you become rich.

What about the use of cocaine in baseball?

I think one of the things you get into, as opposed to booze and as opposed to adultery, is the criminal element of cocaine. I don't think most of these sportswriters and media journalists are terribly good at police reporting.

I've heard stories about major, major drug use on the Mets. I haven't been a newspaper man since 1955, but I know people and I know cops. They gave me a place in Brooklyn where some of the Mets were going to buy their coke. I said to this detective, "If you know about it, why don't you do something?" He said, "Do you have any idea how much pressure the New York Mets can bring to bear in New York City?" So that's the end of that.

But if I were a reporter on the *Herald-Tribune*, and there were a *Herald-Tribune*, I would run that down and I'd run it down hard. Because one of the things is that if you start with coke, you're going to end up with hoodlums. If you start with coke, you've got a good chance of ending up broke.

So it's a major story. It's not saying Billy Cox had five too many drinks last night and can't play third.

What you're saying is that it's changed. The dimension has changed. It was drinking back in the '50s. Now it's more drugs and a bad element of people.

You work with criminals.

So there's been a quantum leap.

Yeah. I'm not recommending alcoholism, but I don't think it's really comparable to the use of cocaine or heroin. The cost of drugs is incredibly greater than the cost of whiskey. I can buy a bottle of whiskey anywhere in the United States perfectly legally. I can even use an American Express card. I can't get coke without breaking the law, without dealing with a chronic lawbreaker. So, I think it's very serious, and I would not say I'm sorry about imposing pain on this particular Met player. I would say he's breaking the law, and that's one of the risks when you break the law.

Was there one story while you were with the New York Herald-Tribune, *covering the Dodgers, that you wanted to report but felt an obligation not to?*

I'd say that the continuing story was the ordeal of Jackie Robinson. I had a sports editor, Bob Cook, who really didn't feel that black guys ought to play major league baseball. He had played hockey at Yale in '36. And he talked about the Canadians—couldn't shoot the way he did, but with their speed they dominated the National Hockey League. Well, it's the same thing he would say with the blacks. They're going to run the whites out of the game. I had to write against that prejudice.

In St. Louis, Eddie Stanky said to me, as Robinson banged up his knee, "Was it black and blue?" Then during the game he held up shoes and said, "Shine these," and they called him "porter." I should have gone with that. What really went on. I suppose had more of a confrontation with the paper.

The *Times* at that point was just completely out of it. The sports section said who won, but not much more. They weren't focused on sports. I don't think The *Daily News* had much of an affection for a black like Robinson. They liked Campanella, who they depicted as kind of an "Uncle Tom," shuffling, genial fellow, and it's not an accurate depiction. But that would go down well with *Daily News* readers.

But an arrow of fire, a proud, intelligent, some times arrogant, defiant black, gave the newsreaders fits. So there I was at the *Herald-Tribune*, which a lot of us felt was the best written paper in New York. I wish I could have done more. That's the one I would like to have back.

One day I was traveling on a train in spring training, going through the pine flats in Alabama. There had been a horrible racial ball game at Hartwell Field in Mobile, Alabama. I said to Robinson, "I just want you to know I think this racial thing is disgraceful." And Robinson said, "You think it's disgraceful?" I said, "Yes, I do." And he said, "Then write it."

Well, I did in *The Boys of Summer,* but I wish I had done it earlier.

Why didn't you?

Well, I don't know, I was getting along. I was discouraged actively from doing it by the sports editor. Why didn't I walk into the office of the *Tribune* brass and say, "Look, there's a tremendous, horrendous thing going on in this country and I want to write a piece about it"...I don't know. I probably didn't have enough confidence in myself. I was 25 years old. And the other thing is that when you're in the middle of something, it's a little hard to have any perspective on it.

In all fairness to you, no one else was writing about it either.

No, nobody touched it.

Robinson was the story and that was the only time he ever said to me, "Then write it." I didn't take up the challenge. I was in my second year with the team and I was....God, there were a lot of really bigoted people on the newspaper. I mean anti-black people on the newspaper. Anti-Robinson people. And the perception of Robinson was that he was some kind of dangerous loud mouth.

Baseball was integrated long before the press boxes were. There was a black guy on the field, there was no black guy in the press box. There was no black in the *Tribune* sports section. There was one black on the city desk and he covered Negro news. There was no black on the *Times*. I think somebody had described the press at that time as, "not really anti-Robinson, but belligerently neutral."

So, in this belligerently neutral world, just going as far as I did was tough enough.

We'll never see anything like 1947 again.

No. Quite a year. That was a marvelous year. I think the Robinson experience, developing when the hotel barriers fell in St. Louis and all of these evolutionary things. And finally, I think seeing Earl Warren at a ball game long before there were integrated schools, long before Warren was a Supreme Court justice and noting, as you had to note in this essentially white activity, the dominant black figure wearing No. 42. So, I think there's a direct line from Robinson's 10 years to the integration of American schools.

Carl Erskine said something when I was talking with him. I thought it was very apropos. He told Robinson: "Jackie, you know, you've helped your race tremendously. But you helped my race a lot more." I thought that was very well put.

I feel that way. This was the first focus on a highly intelligent competitor in a team sport. Everybody had to stop and say, "How racist am I really?" Every decent person would say that.

TIM PLETCHER

THE PERSIAN GULF WAR

A lance corporal in the Marines who saw action in the Persian Gulf War. This war proved to him the importance of air superiority, the inferiority of the Iraqi army, the superior personnel and technology of the United States forces, and to keep his gas mask ready—he was gassed twice.

I went to the Marine Corps because I was dissatisfied with what I was getting through the status quo. I chose to go into the service because I wanted to strip away all of the outside trappings and go to a place where it was a question of my personal character and my personal inner strength that would dictate my level of success. I chose the Marine Corps because it far and away is the most difficult, mentally and physically, of the branches of service. I did my 12 weeks of boot camp and my follow-on schools and arrived at my duty station at 29 Palms on the 4th of August 1990. A week later, we got on an airplane and left for Saudi Arabia.

What was the situation when you landed in Saudi Arabia?

Well, I don't think anybody really had a super clear idea. Basically, the whole premise of us getting there as quickly as we did was to put some sort of blocking force on the ground in Saudi Arabia so that Hussein wouldn't continue to move south and take more oil fields. As everybody knows, this was a war about economics. The Saudis had been our allies for a long time, but when you cut to the quick of it, it was a question of maintaining control over the oil fields, which would affect not only the United States, but the rest of the world as well, were he to seize control of Saudi Arabia.

Do you think that deploying our forces there, at that time, stopped Hussein from going into Saudi Arabia?

I think that was a distinct possibility. Strategically that would have been a smart move for him. In retrospect, with the amount of equipment he had in Kuwait at that time, we would have had our hands full if he had come south immediately, say within the August to mid-September time frame.

The way the Marine Corps works in deployment such as that, is we have what is called the MPF ships. The Maritime Prepositioning Force. And these ships float around with equipment on them anywhere in the world and when the balloon goes up, we get in our planes and fly there and meet our equipment as it comes off. But again, the amount of troops you can land and have equipment for is not that large a force. So, again, we would have had our hands full had he headed south.

The air war started on the 15th of January, and we had our first ground engagement on the 29th of January. The actual invasion into Kuwait happened on February 24.

At that point I was a lance corporal and I was part of a mechanized unit called light armored infantry. We are mounted in light armored vehicles. Basically our function is armored reconnaissance. Our purpose in the time leading up to January, when the air war started, was to be a forward screen. We were the forward most units of anybody in the normal ground units. There was always force reconnaissance and battalion reconnaissance from the Marine Corps and then other reconnaissance units from other services that were right up at the border at Kuwait, and we were a little bit behind them. They were regular units though, and they have a totally different mission.

So, basically, our purpose was a screening element for people that were south of us.

We got to the border on the 29th of January, and there was a very large berm line that ran the entire length of the border, with a few openings at what we call OP's—Observation Points—at what was actually a Saudi Border Police Station. This was about 50 miles inland from the Persian Gulf at a place called OP-4. We pulled up there to sit on the border and screen. We got there around noon the afternoon of the 29th. There was a small team from battalion reconnaissance that was actually in the police station, that sat right at the berm line, and we were 3,000 meters behind them, which puts us within range of our gun systems and our total missile systems.

Now, the evening of the 29th around 2000 (8:00 P.M.), the Iraqis sent what we call a mechanized brigade down at the police station. And, as it turned out, the purpose of which was to be a feint for their actual movement into the town of Khafgi, which was over on the coast.

The battalion recon guys are very lightly armed. All they had was a few hum-d's and a five-ton truck and 30-caliber machine guns and some shoulder-fired anti-tank weapons. They became decisively engaged, which means they're either going to shoot their way out of it and win or they're probably going to die in place. They were calling us on the net asking us for assistance, to come up and help them get out of there, which we did.

Our commanding officer took us up and we engaged the tanks. At that point I think our thermal sights were showing 50 or more tanks and armored personnel carriers. Now our vehicles are designed such that we really had no business going up against a main battle tank. Our armor is very light. Basically designed to protect against artillery shrapnel. We engaged—we lost two vehicles that night and 11 Marines, the tragedy of which was that they were both friendly-fire casualties.

The first one was a tow-missile that hit one of our own vehicles. One of our tow-missiles fired and hit another tow vehicle. You're in the heat of battle and it's what they call our "blooding battle." When a unit goes to combat for the first time, no matter how much you train for it, the fog of war and other things come into play and there are mistakes made. We turned the tide—we were way ahead and really doing very well from the combat standpoint. We had all kinds of close air support on station.

What they'll do is hover these jets behind you. We have a forward air controller, and he'll run the air in on the bad guys while we're engaging them. Now, there is such an abundance of air over the target at that point that it becomes difficult to control all of these people and their official reports say one thing and we know what happened otherwise.

But the long and short of it is when we had the air on station, we pulled back about seven kilometers from the border to give a good open space between us and the bad guys, so we would reduce the amount of confusion. Evidently, somebody made a mistake in the air and fired a missile and hit the vehicle which was off to my right about 50 meters. Again, these are all anti-tank weapons and against an LAV, it's going to make them pretty much swiss cheese. We lost seven people out of that LAV that was to the right of me. It was a tragedy. Not much else you can say about it. At that point the battle was pretty much over. The air had destroyed many targets. We had destroyed many targets and we were pulled back about another five to ten kilometers, and another company swept through and cleared the area.

What we did then is lay up for about 12 hours and then go back up where we were and continue to screen on the border. There was no change in mission for us at that point. It was one isolated action. We'd heard they'd gone into Khafgi the following morning and that had been retaken. That was basically where we sat from the 29th of January until the 24th of February, when we entered the country of Kuwait.

Then what happened?

That was probably one of the more spectacular things you're ever going to see. We were part of a unit called Task Force Ripper. The task force was attached with driving from OP-4 almost due north up through Alwafra Oil Field, clearing that and then taking the International Airport at Kuwait City. The task force was comprised of an entire tank battalion and two infantry battalions. We were the forward screening element for the task force.

In order for us to get to the oil fields, we had to go through mine fields and wire. The first obstacle belt was not manned, it was just a mine field. We cleared that and proceeded on. The interesting thing is there were so many vehicles that were part of this task force that it was like being on the 405 Freeway at rush hour. Everybody was just stop and go waiting for their turn to go through the breach sites.

Now the second breach site was manned, and at that point we started to work it over while taking artillery fire all around us. But the resistance was by most standards pretty light. The Iraqis didn't have much fight left in them. They'd been pretty much isolated in their positions for the entire time that we'd been in the country, and, once they dug in, they just kind of got left there. And if they ate, they ate. If they got water, they got water. And if they didn't, they didn't. So, they really weren't into it. Now, add to this the fact that they've been getting bombed both by airplanes and artillery consistently for 30 days, and they just didn't have much in them.

Once we got through the second obstacle belt, we were wide open and covering a lot of ground. These guys were surrendering so quickly and in such large numbers, we'd just point them south to the collection points and keep rolling. We didn't even stop to search them.

There were a few incidents where we would take prisoners. I know everybody's heard about what the Iraqis reportedly did in Kuwait and all of it's true. We took prisoners who were crying and moaning that they were sorry they had to kill women and children. It was really pretty disgusting. The Iraqis raped the country very badly.

We rolled up through the oil fields, which in and of itself was an amazing experience. The smoke was so thick that at noon it was pitch black as night, and you'd have these huge fires coming out of the ground. I suppose if you look at it one way, you could almost say it was like Purgatory.

We had a few engagements along the way. But once we rolled into the airport there was no resistance. They had pretty much left and they were trying to run north out of Kuwait City back to Iraq. We had a couple of small engagements along the way, it was more of a clearing action than anything else. And—boom— we were at the airport and done. It was a 96-hour operation that freed the country.

We rolled into Kuwait at 0100 in the morning on the 24th, and we were at the airport at about 0800 in the morning of the 28th, and back in Saudi Arabia that afternoon on the 28th.

You were gassed.

Yes, there were two incidents when we had positive contacts on our detection kits. Where it came from we really don't know. I heard over the intel net once that a second Marine division up further north along the border of Kuwait and Saudi Arabia, right up almost where Saudi Arabia runs into Iraq, when they went through the breaches, they hit some gas mines and they were dirty. From the breach on, they were at Mop-4, which means that they had their gas masks and suits on and everything. Now we went into the country at Mop-2. So we had all of our chemical protective equipment on except for our masks.

Now, the thing that people don't realize about gas is that even though we were gassed, in order for gas to be an effective weapon, the concentration in the zone that you intend to contaminate has to be extremely high. So, your body isn't going to be necessarily beaten up badly by gas unless they're dropping hundreds of artillery rounds on you, or spraying you directly with aircraft.

We were issued and took two types of medicine to counteract this. One you take 10 days prior to going into a situation where you may be contaminated and it builds resistance to the nerve agent in your body. The other was a drug that would combat anthrax or any bile agents that we would run into along the way.

Why did the government keep this quiet? Did they think the American public would be irate if they knew the troops were being gassed by the Iraqis?

I think so. Unless it was a major gas attack, it really wasn't going to degrade our combat efficiency too much. We were already at Mop-2 and when you go to Mop-4, yes, it slows you down a little but, but it really isn't that big of a deal. The sophistication of the chemicals themselves also has a lot to do with it. And these guys were not going to have anything near what we have in the States, or the Soviets have.

From a political standpoint, if people would have found out that there was any gas at all, they probably would have been screaming for tactical nuclear weapons, which at that point were completely unnecessary. The other thing is we didn't know where the gas came from, it could have very easily been gas from ammunition storage points that were destroyed. Blown in place by the Iraqis before they left.

Now, they pretty much left everything behind. We all had nice trophies that we would have loved to have brought back, but unfortunately, we're not allowed to. The Iraqis basically were like fighting the Boy Scouts. These guys really were bad. It really wasn't that big of a deal.

Who was the most effective Arab army on our side?

That would be difficult to say. I think the Egyptians are pretty good. We didn't really have that much contact with the Arab forces at all. The Marines operated autonomously for the most part. Even away from the other branches of the service. That was the way we wanted it anyway.

I think in one respect, all the Arab countries were caught with their pants down in this whole situation. They sat back for 10 years and watched Hussein build his army. The Kuwaitis were extremely guilty of this and hoped that when the time came they could just buy their way out of it with oil. All of a sudden these guys are saying, "Hey, no way. We're coming in. It's ours." And what are they going to do. The Kuwaitis had absolutely no military to speak of. The same holds true for the Saudis. I think probably the most effective, as far as combat experience goes, would be the Syrians.

You were there in the thick of battle. Did you feel that the caliber of the American fighting person and the technological advantage we had was overwhelming?

Well, after a month of dealing with the air, anytime you're in a combat situation and you have air superiority, you have a huge advantage. It's almost an unsurmountable disadvantage if you don't have it. We never really got to watch CNN and see all the smart weapons working until we got back into the country. To be able to go in and destroy a particular building by dropping an LGB down the vent shaft, or an elevator shaft, really is going to take the fight out of these people. I think for the most part it was the sophistication on our side, from the individual all the way up to the equipment we were using.

A point that I really want to touch on, not that I consider myself to be a huge patriot, but the people who believe in what they're doing 150 percent as we did, will be unstoppable against people who don't really believe in what they're doing, and don't really have a good ideological basis to fight on. The Iraqis had no ideological basis. You can get into the Pan-Arab question of them unifying the Arab countries and all this other trash, but when it comes down to it, the value system that we have here, that we take for granted, these people have no idea about and could never hope to match, makes us head and shoulders above them.

The fact that we have people who go over and die for the sole purpose of liberating a country that wasn't even ours writes to the whole point. I think it falls down to the individual more than anything else and the strategic and tactical planning that we had going on.

Are you proud you were there?

Oh, definitely. It's an experience I wouldn't trade for anything in the world. You hear that the experience of combat is worth a million dollars, but I wouldn't pay 50 cents for it. What it did is really reawakened in me the fact that people take things for granted they shouldn't. I'll never take another thing for granted. Every time I get up in this country and walk around and am a part of this whole situation here. The fact that our country in two hundred and some years has done more than these people have been able to accomplish in centuries says it all right there about America.

Robert Schmuhl

THE CHANGING OF THE GUARD

He believes people came to perceive George Bush as a man without a program for the future. Someone who could not connect with the public and who was reluctant to address our economic and broader domestic problems. He believes we have entered a new political and media age, and George Bush was looked upon as yesterday's leader.

Ironically, the Persian Gulf War, which was the apogee of the Bush administration, helped to elect Bill Clinton. None of the stronger Democratic contenders wished to run against Bush because of his successful direction of the war and the popularity he enjoyed for several months after its conclusion. This gave Clinton his opening. He took it, ran an effective campaign, and won.

Robert Schmuhl is chairperson of the Department of American Studies at the University of Notre Dame. He has written a number of books, including: Statecraft and Stagecraft: American Political Life in the Age of Personality.

Why did George Bush lose the 1992 election, and could he have won?

There are a number of reasons for the loss, both personal and political. I don't think there is any question about George Bush's commitment to public service. He spent the better part of his adult life in either governmental or political positions. But for many people it was never clear where he was taking the country as president and what he actually stood for. He joked about his difficulty with "the vision thing," but after a while people didn't laugh. They wondered about his core beliefs.

In addition, he never took the "bully pulpit" as seriously as he should have, and he had trouble connecting with people through the media. There was a certain tone-deaf quality to George Bush. You also might say he suffered from image blindness. I always thought one of the reasons the "wimp" label kept recurring is because he had trouble asserting himself in a strong way in public—in front of cameras. In the absence of a strong, consistent image, the media offered another perception: "wimp."

It's interesting. He was very effective one-on-one with people. People who met and talked with George Bush liked him very much. But in this media age that is no longer nearly as important as it used to be. You have to "connect" with the public through popular communications.

I think in large part he won in 1988 on the residual coattails of Ronald Reagan, and also on the pledge that became the slogan—"Read my lips: No new taxes." When he reversed that, doubts took root in the minds of a great number of people. They began to wonder again what he actually stood for.

With the end of the cold war and the rapid completion of the Persian Gulf War, Americans looked homeward and inward. They saw more clearly than before a number of festering domestic sores that George Bush didn't seem to want to deal with. His time to act at home would have been right after the war in the Gulf, and yet he didn't use his political capital to do the things that people thought were necessary.

The challenge from Pat Buchanan should have been the large warning flag that there were problems, particularly politically. I think in the mind of George Bush, and also in the mind of the people working for him, there was boundless confidence, almost cockiness, about what was going to happen in the 1992 election. I don't think the Bush people perceived Bill Clinton as a formidable candidate.

And let's face it: The Bush campaign never really got on track. It was almost a night and day comparison between the 1988 Bush campaign, which was almost flawless, and the lackluster 1992 campaign.

Shortly after the Persian Gulf War and then for the next several months, I think the impression crystallized that George Bush was yesterday's leader. He was the representative of another generation with concerns that weren't appropriate to today.

On the other hand, I don't think that Bill Clinton ever really became a truly known figure among the public. I think the people were so anxious for change that he became the repository of their wishes. If you look at the numbers and add up the votes for Bill Clinton and Ross Perot, you wind up with a figure of about 62 percent voting, in effect, against George Bush. Those results are not a landslide for Bill Clinton, but they certainly signify a rejection of George Bush.

With Bill Clinton you saw the intense focus on the economy and domestic concerns, which appealed to the public's mood and inward-looking nature. George Bush kept struggling to establish a message that worked for him. He tried to negatively identify his opponent—as he did so effectively with Michael Dukakis in '88—but '92 was different. People wanted to hear about the issues and problems, and they wanted the candidates to talk about improving conditions at home.

I think George Bush could have won in 1992. But it would have been difficult for him. By that I mean the economic numbers that were improving somewhat in the fall were not as important as the general mood in the country at that time. For so much of 1992 we focused on such things as the level of consumer confidence. But there was something else happening, and that was a lack of citizen confidence in George Bush.

People kept reading and hearing about these large institutional dislocations of plant closings, of job layoffs, of job eliminations, of people who no longer had health care or retirement benefits. They got a sense that there was something critically wrong with the economy beyond just numbers that would flash on a television screen or be printed in a newspaper on a regular basis. They looked around and saw more and more people living on the streets, and they also saw people in their neighborhoods who had been affected. The impact of some of the economic problems went broader than in earlier times. There was the refrain in the media that the hard times hit white collar workers with a severity unlike any economic downturn in our recent history. In addition, people who formerly had more highly paid jobs were forced into taking jobs where they were paid less or they weren't working full-time. There was the perception that something dramatic needed to be done on behalf of the economy, but that George Bush was reluctant to do very much.

You ask: Could George Bush have won? I think the answer is "yes," but he never gave the people a definite reason or a series of specific reasons to vote for him again. A friend of George Bush went in to see him in the summer of 1992 and in casual conversation asked about the president's plans for the next term. According to reports, Bush was halting in his reply and finally said, "I'll handle whatever comes up." That sense of not having a program that was taking the country in a definite direction became the larger perception of the people. We had reached a point where the public wanted someone who would be more active, and with George Bush in the domestic realm there was great hesitation to do that.

By contrast, on the international front, he was tremendously active, which leads to what ultimately will be the conclusion about George Bush. I think history will show that he was someone who wanted to deal with the world at large and made a number of friends, did a number of things that stand out and will stand out. But in terms of at home, he was passive, in part because he thought it would be difficult to deal with the Democratic Congress to get programs through. He could and did act decisively in world affairs, but in domestic matters it was much more difficult. He should have done much more, when he was so popular.

Why did Clinton win?

Again, there are a number of reasons. First, he emerged at the appropriate time. He was new, youthfully energetic, and he talked about change and rekindling optimism. He kept the focus on the economy and on the concerns of people.

He, frankly, also received a number of breaks. He didn't have the toughest Democratic opponents that he could have had. In a certain sense, he was a beneficiary of the Persian Gulf War euphoria. So many Democrats decided that it was impossible to beat George Bush that the field was open for someone like Bill Clinton to go for the nomination.

Having his personal problems aired at the earliest stage of the campaign was also very important. He got the concerns about his marriage and his draft status out of the way to a great degree. People kept hearing about them, but he addressed them early so that by the time of New Hampshire, even though he finished second, he could project himself as "the Comeback Kid" on the strength of his performance.

Ross Perot withdrew at a very critical time for Bill Clinton. He withdrew on the day that Clinton gave his acceptance speech at the Democratic Convention. Shortly after the convention, Bill Clinton and Al Gore began one of their telegenic bus trips across the country. With Perot out of the picture, the media focused on Bill Clinton and started to give him much more attention. You have to remember that through much of the spring Bill Clinton did not receive all that much coverage. At one point, the polling had Ross Perot first and Bill Clinton a distant third. So that becomes a factor.

Another factor, and we talked about this earlier, the Bush campaign never came together as it needed to with the effectiveness of 1988. When

Perot did return in October, he added to Bush's problems by focusing on the federal deficit and some other domestic problems. It's not accurate to say that Perot caused the Bush defeat or that Perot caused the Clinton win. But Perot clearly made it more difficult for people to focus on a two-person race of George Bush vs. Bill Clinton.

There was another phenomenon worth noting. There was something about 1992 that was distinctive, with what I saw as two tracks operating at the same time.

The political community, the professionals in politics and the analysts or pundits, seemed to measure Bill Clinton against previous candidates from the recent past. Over and over again they said there was no way that he could make it through the primaries and caucuses and ultimately win the election. But the people had a different cast of mind and kept seeing in him someone who kept the focus on the economy and what was happening in the country. When he went on "60 Minutes" in the wake of the Gennifer Flowers story, he confessed and said that indeed there had been problems in his marriage and that he and his wife had worked them out. In that particular program and others, you saw the convergence of the values of the media culture and the political culture. By that I mean so many people watch these shows where people come on and talk openly about their personal lives and how they've been able to deal with personal problems. Well, here we had a presidential candidate doing the same thing. The people, by and large, accepted that. I think they wanted to look beyond the personal problems to the larger public ones that he was talking about. There's also another dimension to it. With the previous revelations about Gary Hart and John Tower and other public figures, the public had become tired of the intense focus on scandal and personal conduct. Such stories were by then old news.

Bill Clinton had a number of qualities that people found engaging. He seemed smart, concerned, articulate, self-confident. In short, a new man for this new time. One contrasts those qualities with George Bush who always had difficulty with the projection of his personality. Clinton was direct with people. He had a common touch of going out among them and touching them in a very appealing way. He reduced the distance between a national political figure and the citizens of the country. Or so it seemed anyway. It was the image of someone who was of the people and who was talking with the people. That was magnified by television and other media, so that the closeness to a person or a group of people became a symbol of his closeness to the American people as a whole.

Of course, there's a certain irony in the victory of Bill Clinton at a time when people were so questioning of politicians, indeed hostile to politicians. Here you had a consummate politician of the old school and new school emerging and winning. What we saw of him was so different from what we had with George Bush that ultimately the people were content in making the choice they did.

In your book, Statecraft and Stagecraft: American Political Life in the Age of Personality, *you state the impact of television has led "to an emphasis on appealing images, symbolic gestures, dramatic encounters, audience-gathering opportunities. Such an environment places a premium on personality, with the personality often taking precedence over political beliefs, principles, and policies."*

Bill Clinton understands how important it is to use the media as a public figure. Interestingly, he frequently goes around the traditional, mainstream press to do that. He prefers to conduct his "media business" in town meetings and open forums where he is able to hold forth with as much command as possible. I think that at his core there is a verbal agility and remarkable self-confidence that works to his advantage in creating his image. He is someone who looks people right in the eye and seems to empathize and sympathize. He offers possibilities for change that help to instill hope in them. This is a marked difference from Ronald Reagan, who tended to rely on scripts, or George Bush, who was very good one-on-one but much less successful in his public performances.

As we look to the future, I think the risk that Bill Clinton runs is that he might be perceived as more of a "talker" than a "doer." As someone who seems to emphasize salesmanship at the expense of statesmanship. But, as he begins in office, you see a balance between statecraft and stagecraft. He seems to have the ability to work inside with people in the political world on a very personal level, and also the skill to go outside to the public through the media in the articulation of his programs and his ideas. Doing both—the statecraft and the stagecraft—will be important to whether he's judged a successful president.

Where do we go from here?

The first thing I'd say is that 1992 was a watershed year in redefining the relationship among political figures, people in communications, and the public at large. Back in 1988, what forms of communication received intense attention? Such things as negative ads, ever-briefer sound bites, repeated slogans, and staged photo opportunities. In 1992, there was much more concern about talk shows, town meetings, debates, and info-mercials. These are longer and potentially more substantive formats. Let's hope that we'll continue to see the more extended forms in the future.

We all have to realize we are entering a new age, with a different political and media environment. When America was founded, political leaders operated on the assumption, accurate or otherwise, that a common body of public knowledge was shared by the citizenry at a given time. The relatively small number of sources of information helped make this possible, and in theory at least this idea had validity until quite recently.

Today, though, we talk about "narrowcasting" instead of "broadcasting" and "niche" or specialized publishing rather than general publications. The explosion of media sources, especially in television through cable and satellite technology, opens many doors, but it also can close off people from the wider world of public affairs. By that I mean, some people might be so absorbed in sports programming, or old movies, or the cooking channel that they don't know what's happening politically or governmentally. When there were fewer possible selections, you could count on a greater sharing of common information. There were fewer distractions or alternatives.

In this new environment, all of us need to work harder in order to understand what a Bill Clinton or any political leader might be doing. We need to actively seek out the kind of information that will help us understand the present and also contribute to building a better future.

With all of the possibilities for information, it is no longer very useful to sit back and criticize "the media." Instead of doing that, it would be better to use what the new technology offers and search out on C-SPAN, CNN, and elsewhere the speeches or press conferences or town meetings in their entirety. What's now called "the new news" of talk shows, open forums, and interactive communication of various kinds expand the potential of political information, but there's also a requirement of more active citizen involvement. We have to take the initiative.

In his day, Lincoln talked about the need to "think anew and act anew." Those words ring true today as we deal with this new political and media environment. It's important for all of us in our own way to shoulder these new responsibilities of citizenship as we try to shape the future.